seeking a post as clerk. I
where he was living at the t...
was living at 13, Little Colleg...

...e, it was
...pleasure
...e. All

...n again you must
...r E. Clarke : Was
...for the statement
...ere compelled to
...!—Witness : Per—

...mination.

...cross-examination
...a stated that your
...are over 40. You
...6, 1854? I had no
...oung.—That makes
...—in reply to furti...
...nd Lord Alfre...
...was between 20 and
...t know him Down
...treet Lord Queens-
...I did not receive a
...hich Lord Queens-
...acquaintance with
...ter the interview I
...was Lord Queens-
...thstanding Lord
...ny intimacy with
...res to the present
...ved with him at
...Oxford, Brighton
...Worthing? Yes,—
...for him? No.—
...laces with him?
...in various hotels
...ne in Albemarle-
...t, and at the Savoy.
...rooms yourself in
...e in Tite-street?
...nes's-place. I kept
...h of October, 1893,
...4. Lord Douglas
...chambers, which
...illy. I had been
...l times, and even
...—You read "The
...? Yes.—You have
...was an improper
...y point of view it
...is impossible for
...dge it otherwise,
...eatment, selection
...ee. I thought the
...subject rotten.—
...e is no such thing
...s.

...story.

...he story was not
...in love with a boy
...tar, and who was
...r in the priest's
...I have only read
...and nothing will
...n.—Do you think
...I think it violated
...auty.—That is not
...one I can give.—I
...rou pose as. I do
...that.—I have said
...I wish to know
...tory blasphemous?
...disgust.—Answer
...a or did you not
...nous? I did not
...sphemous.—I am
...know that when
...inisters poison to
...e words of the
...h of England?
...Do you consider
...sk it is horrible;
...ord.—Mr. Carson
...r the administra-
...the Sacrament,
...altar, and asked

(Image labels: TAYLOR, CHARLEY PARKER, OSCAR WILDE, CHARLEY, ATKINS)

1892. Taylor used to come to his house, to
his chambers, and to the Savoy. Oscar
used, too, to go to Taylor's house, some
seven or eight times perhaps. There were a
bedroom, sitting-room, bath-room, and
kitchen in Taylor's house. He could not
say if Taylor did his own cooking; he had
never dined there. The rooms did not strike
the witness as peculiar, except that they
displayed more taste than usual. He
thought them "most pretty rooms."—Did
he ever admit daylight? I do not know
what you mean. — Did you ever see
any light but that of gas or candle,
day or night? Yes, certainly. I usually
went in the evening, but I believe I have
been earlier and have seen the curtains
drawn aside.—Were the rooms strongly
perfumed? I have known him to burn
perfumes; I am in the habit of burning
perfumes myself.—He never saw Woods
there, but met Sidney Maler there. He
was about 25. Witness had not seen him
for a year, and had not the remotest idea
of his whereabouts. Last Sunday witness
asked Mr. Taylor to go and tell Maler he
wanted to see him. He was unaware that
Maler disappeared last week.—Have you
found him since? I do not know what you...

document. "I come to the more serious
part," wrote Lord Queensberry. "Your
intimacy with this man Wilde must cease
or I will disown you and stop all supplies."
In answer to the letter from his father
Lord Alfred wired back: "What a funny

THE HALL PORTER.
little man you are!" Lord Queens-

The Unrecorded Life of Oscar Wilde

The only known portrait of Oscar Wilde
between those of early childhood
and later undergraduate ones in sporting dress.
J. Guggenheim, Oxford, 1874

The Unrecorded Life
of
Oscar Wilde

RUPERT CROFT-COOKE

W H ALLEN
LONDON & NEW YORK
A division of Howard & Wyndham Ltd
1972

© Rupert Croft-Cooke 1972

Printed and bound in Great Britain for the publishers
W H Allen & Co, Essex Street, London WC2R 3JG
by Butler & Tanner Ltd, Frome and London.

ISBN 0 491 00702 7

Contents

Frontispiece: Portrait of Oscar Wilde as a young man.

A section of illustrations appears between pages 150 and 151.

Introductory Note

This book is the result of a lifetime's study of the character of Oscar Wilde and the events of his life. Even so it could not have been written but for the publication in 1962 of *The Letters of Oscar Wilde*, edited by Rupert Hart-Davis. This book not only brought to light many facts but by its reliable text and wide-ranging footnotes disposed of much nonsense that had accumulated about the subject. Other sources of information open to me over the years I have used, sometimes cautiously. These include the occasional spoken recollections of Lord Alfred Douglas, whose friendship I enjoyed for the last twenty-five years of his life. I have known and been able to question Wilde's son, the late Vyvyan Holland, Wilde's bibliographer Christopher Millard ('Stuart Mason') and, by proxy and for what it was worth, Wilde's least reliable biographer Frank Harris, also one or two minor characters in the story who as old gentlemen gave me their sometimes salacious recollections.

To published sources apart from Wilde's own *Works and Letters* and my friend Harford Montgomery Hyde's carefully edited *Trials* and his book *Oscar Wilde the Aftermath*, I owe very little except a few details from Millard's *Bibliography*. I have quoted from a number of authors but it has been chiefly to disagree with their conclusions or dispute their conjectures. Hesketh Pearson's

Life seems to me the best to have been written, though he was unfortunately far too credulous and gave currency to many fables. My obligation to Robert Sherard's books is a curious one which will be explained in my Prefatory Chapter.

For certain short episodes and descriptions I have drawn on my own two books on related subjects, *Bosie: the Story of Lord Alfred Douglas, his Friends and Enemies* and *Feasting with Panthers: A New Consideration of Some Late Victorian Writers.* I have thus avoided writing the same thing twice in different contexts.

The obligations I have to express are not numerous but they are heartfelt. To the late Vyvyan Holland for his generous permission to quote from his father's letters and to Lord David Cecil for quotations from his biography *Max.* To Mr Frank Houlihan for recollections of his father, referred to by Wilde in a letter to a prospective tenant of Illaunroe Lodge—"My servant, an excellent fisherman, and his wife, a good cook, are in charge of it." To Mr Paul Rowan, who has a house near the Wildes' on Lough Corrib and enabled me to see Moytura House, Abbotstown and Wilde's fishing lodge at Illaunroe, Connemara, where I discovered the frescoes painted by Frank Miles nearly a century earlier. To Mrs Jean Gwynn, the present owner of Illaunroe, to the Rev. P. H. Rogers, MBE, the present headmaster of Wilde's old school, Portora Royal at Enniskillen, and to the Rev. David Keene, the present Rector of Bingham. To Mr Brian Reade, for his generous help in finding photographs, and to several friends and writers for helpful suggestions; Mr Harford Montgomery Hyde, Lord Kinross, Sir John Betjeman, Mr Beverley Nichols and Mr Ulick O'Connor. I must pay a debt of special gratitude to the librarians of the British Museum and Trinity College Dublin, and to my secretary Joseph Susei Mari, who has worked with me brilliantly on this book and every other I have written during the last thirty years.

RUPERT CROFT-COOKE

Glenageary House
Dun Laoghaire
Co. Dublin
Eire

ONE

Prefatory Chapter
The Biographers and the Legends

The many—too many—biographers of Oscar Wilde have been content to follow one another in a rigid crocodile, drawing the same conclusions from the same sometimes dubious sources, which have been passed down from writer to writer and in the process have often become the merest fables.

The pioneer was Robert Harborough Sherard, a well-meaning but clumsy individual with the pompous and humourless prose-style of a Victorian journalist. He did not suppress or deliberately invent evidence but he was obsessed with the need to turn his material into 'stories' dished up with clichés in French, so that many of his incidents are exaggerated beyond credibility or recognition. Also his portrait of Wilde is hidden behind Sherard's own protestations of 'normality' and his self-conscious determination to be at all costs a virile bohemian, a fair-minded man of the world. A writer who could carry his defence of Wilde to the point of describing him, as Sherard did, as 'a thorough good sport', a defender of Wilde who talked so loudly that, as his hero said, the reverberations reached 'from the Authors' Club to Naples', who on the way down to Reading with Robert Ross to visit Wilde in prison 'seemed anxious that the third person in the railway carriage should know on what mission we were bent', could have had none of the subtlety and tact needed sixty years ago to make a convincing apology for the fallen star. What Sherard himself contributed as a character in Wilde's story will appear later; as a biographer, in spite of the five books (almost his life's work) which he devoted wholly or for the most part to Wilde, he did not begin to understand the man or the problem. Indeed his view that Oscar was demonstrating his democratic instincts when he picked up a young man or patronized an amusing old invert on the Paris streets, would be comic if it did not argue a kind of blindness in Sherard which incapacitates him as an interpreter. "Oscar Wilde did not at all mind being seen speaking to social outcasts," he writes proudly after quoting Carson's scornful question about talking to street arabs. "I have frequently watched him in amused conversation with . . . Bibi-la-Purée,"[1] a notorious thieving drag queen who is said to have befriended Verlaine.

There were other pick-ups, some with obvious intent, and Sherard who afterwards recalled them to show what a friendly, broad-minded chap Wilde was, and how ridiculous were the suspicions of Carson, scarcely deserves serious attention when he maintains that Wilde's 'aberrations' were the result of a 'cruel and devilish' madness which fell on him suddenly a few years before the trial.

But, as Vyvyan Holland[2] says, Sherard was the first to attempt anything like a life of Wilde, and his biography is the book on which all subsequent lives have been based. "He was trained as a journalist, and a journalist he always remained. A story was a story to him, so long as it was a good story; and if it was a good story what mattered its accuracy or its source? Sherard's *Life of Oscar Wilde* should be considered from that point of view."

2

Sherard was an honest fool; the second biographer, Frank Harris, was a clever rogue. Physically squat, muscular and ugly, he has been described as a monster. He pushed his way with vociferous effrontery into English life and letters.

His writing in 1915 of a book called *Oscar Wilde: His Life and*

1 Sherard, *The Real Oscar Wilde.*
2 Vyvyan Holland, *Son of Oscar Wilde* (1954).

Confessions was an act of desperation and at the same time greed, as he had not enough acquaintance with the dead man to justify his assumption of familiarity.

It came about like this. Harris was sent to prison in England for contempt of court when he published, in a blackmailing scandal-rag he edited called *Modern Society*, details of the private life of a defendant in a divorce case while it was still being heard. He spoke of his four weeks in Brixton as a 'martyrdom', a Calvary and a crucifixion. There was another warrant for his arrest when he escaped to France at the beginning of the 1914–18 war.

Suspected of dangerous pro-German activities, he had to leave France and went into hiding in England till he could sail for America. Lady Warwick[1] lent a house to him and his second wife, a kindness he repaid by stealing from her a number of letters from 'a certain personage' with which he had helped her in her attempt to blackmail the Royal Family.[2] In America, he was made editor of a magazine and ran it in the pro-German interest until the United States declared war. Then, his funds running low, he set about raising money in the only way he could, by writing a racy and dirty-minded piece of fiction about Oscar Wilde. This is one of the curiosities of literature. No one but Harris would have had the impudence to put into a dead man's mouth a complete apologia for his life which is a shoddy and ill-contrived invention of the author's own. In the few years during which Wilde knew Harris, he was scarcely ever alone with him, for Wilde, like Wells, was unenchanted by Harris's bombast. "I do not know what a football scrimmage is," Wilde said, "but I imagine it must be very like a conversation with Frank Harris." Yet Harris produced two volumes of Wilde's supposed confessions to himself, including long passages of controversy in which Wilde is made to defend homosexuality with arguments that would not convince a moron and in words which would have shamed Amanda Ros. "What you call vice, Frank, is not vice; it is as good to me as it was to Caesar, Alexander, Michelangelo and Shakespeare," and so on, bits quoted from Wilde's answers to cross-examination,

[1] H. G. Wells, *Experiment in Autobiography*, vol. II (1934).
[2] Described in *My Darling Daisy* by Theo Lang (1966).

pages of feeble remonstrance, lurid humourless confessions of an affair with a French soldier, utterly unlike the gay and shameless details Wilde gives in his letters to Ross about his promiscuities with boulevard boys. Moreover, Harris takes phrases of Wilde's used in letters to others, in court, even in his published writings, and giving them a twist or a small change of emphasis, prints them as spoken by Wilde to him in one of the interminable conversations between an upright but understanding 'Frank' and a maudlin 'Oscar'. Most pitiful are his attempts to make Wilde profound or epigrammatic. "And so the great romantic passion comes to this tame conclusion?" suggests Harris at the end of a long admission by Wilde of his failure with a 'soldier boy'. "What would you, Frank?" replied Oscar. "*Whatever begins must also end.*" The italics are mine but the platitude, it is scarcely necessary to say, is Harris's.

Such preposterous invention is relatively innocuous, but when Harris elaborates on a carefully written narrative in a letter by Robert Ross describing Wilde's last hours, and fabricates the most grotesque and revolting scenes to titillate the morbid curiosity of his public and pollute what seems to have been a dignified if tragic end, one feels a personal flush of anger with this literary con man.[1] His biography can be discounted as dangerously bad fiction.

At the end of Volume II appears a letter from Bernard Shaw to Harris which Harris prints as 'My Memories of Oscar Wilde'. Shaw's intention was kindly—it was to help Harris, who as an editor had employed Shaw in bad times, but the effect was of considerable disservice to truth, especially when he writes "I understood why Morris, when he was dying slowly, enjoyed a visit from Wilde more than from anyone else." Morris died at Kelmscott, in a house Wilde never visited, eighteen months after Wilde had been sent to prison.

---

[1] Richard Aldington who knew Reggie Turner, an honest man, writes in *Life for Life's Sake*, "I got Reggie Turner to talk about Oscar's death and I am happy to inform the world that Reggie gave me his word of honour that there is no truth in Frank Harris's sensational account—though I don't suppose that anyone who knew Frank Harris ever believed it."

3

The third biography of Wilde is yet another spurious and altogether unreliable book, *Oscar Wilde and Myself*, nominally by Lord Alfred Douglas, in fact signed by him in circumstances described in my biography *Bosie: The Story of Lord Alfred Douglas His Friends and Enemies*. Alfred Douglas never attempted to deny responsibility for this but in time he confessed the shameful truth, that a man named Crosland had been employed to write it and did so with all the malice he could put into it.

Crosland was accustomed to speedy hack-work, and in a couple of months produced one of the most unpleasant books of the last half-century. Bosie, though he later repudiated much of it, never sought to shift the responsibility for it from his own shoulders. "I am, of course, myself responsible for this mistake, because I asked Crosland to write this part of the book, feeling at the time so shaken and unnerved by the experiences I had been through at the Ransome trial that I felt I could not bring myself to write about it. Crosland wrote the story and I read and passed it."[1]

It is evident from the prose of the book, if from nothing else, that it was written by Crosland, as he himself proudly claimed. If anyone troubles to examine the particular kind of journalistic bombast, pseudo-Johnsonian, laden with clichés and laboured jeers, which Crosland had been employing for twenty years, he will see that *Oscar Wilde and Myself* is written in exactly this manner and that the bad taste, the presumptuous folly of the arguments, the snobbishness that apes bluffness, are all pure Crosland. But that in no way exculpates Bosie, and the pharisaical intention with which the book is rank is his. "In Paris," wrote André Gide in his *Journal* a few years later, "I read (in part) Douglas's abominable book, *Oscar Wilde and Myself*. Hypocrisy can go no further, nor falsehood be more impudent. It is a monstrous travesty of the truth, which filled me with disgust. Merely from the tone of his writing it seems to me that I should be aware he is lying, even if I had not been the direct witness of

[1] *The Autobiography of Lord Alfred Douglas* (1929).

the acts of his life against which he protests and which he claims
to whitewash. But even this is not enough for him. He claims that
he was ignorant of Wilde's habits! and that he upheld him at first
only because he thought him innocent! Whom will he convince?"

The book is a disaster, but though it is full of misrepresentations
it is doubtful whether the impression it gives of Wilde is falser
than that of many more well-meaning accounts.

4

What of André Gide himself, who wrote so loftily about the
lies in *Oscar Wilde and Myself*? Another of the early biographers
who had known Wilde, he published in 1910 his *Oscar Wilde and
Some Further Reminiscences* in his *Journals* and in *Si le Grain ne
Meurt*. In these he invented for the joy of invention, not as
Harris and Crosland did for profit, or as poor Sherard did out of
a mistaken concept of loyalty plus a need to keep himself alive,
or as Bosie Douglas did (or permitted to be done) in an attempt
to save his own name, but because the Nobel Prize-winner, like
so many writers whose books vacillate between truth and fiction
and are never wholly novels or autobiography, like Axel Munthe
and George Borrow, was a liar born, whose tributes even to those
he admired were paid with lies, so that his delightful novel *Les
Faux-Monnayeurs* (1925) is more than half truth and his stories of
Wilde are almost wholly fiction.

This is particularly annoying because Gide was the only witness
to the behaviour of Wilde and Bosie Douglas during a visit to
North Africa early in 1895 and the only observer to have watched
the two friends abroad. Beyond saying to me that he had enjoyed this visit immensely, Bosie spoke little of it. He never
brought himself, in conversation with me or with anyone else, to
chuckle over his own past indiscretions or impudicities, though he
admitted them when directly asked about them. So it would be
pleasant to be able to trust some at least of Gide's account, which
one can only read now with amused scepticism. Hesketh Pearson[1]

[1] Hesketh Pearson, *The Life of Oscar Wilde* (1946).

says of this: "In the course of their holiday in North Africa, Wilde and Douglas met André Gide: that 'egotist without an ego', as Wilde called him. Gide's description of what happened in Algiers and Blindah was subjected to a ruthless analysis by Robert Sherard, who proved conclusively that the statements about Wilde and Douglas in Gide's book *Si le Grain ne Meurt* are wholly false.[1] Douglas also called them 'a mass of lies and misrepresentations', while another of Wilde's most intimate friends, Reginald Turner, declared that 'Anything so preposterously untrue has never been written . . . The whole thing is fantastic'. We must therefore regard Gide's account of their visit solely as a problem for the pathologist who is studying the mental condition of Gide." Moreover Gide has been exposed, like other perverters of the truth about Wilde, by the publication of *The Letters of Oscar Wilde*. Of Wilde after his imprisonment, Gide wrote, "Nothing remained in his shattered life but a mouldy ruin, painful to contemplate, of his former self. At times he seemed to wish to show that his brain was still active. Humour there was; but it was far-fetched, forced and threadbare." Wilde's humour was never more spontaneous or his conversation more lively than in his last three years, as his letters show.

One at least of Gide's biographers[2] further confuses confusion by speaking of 'the pleasures into which Wilde initiated him (Gide), a willing convert, in those few days in Algiers.' Gide was twenty-six in that year and had already been in North Africa where he had picked up (among others) the Algerian boy prostitute Athman, who became known to other visiting Europeans including Eugène Rouart and Francis Jammes and was brought to Paris by Henri Ghéon. Gide had enjoyed all the pleasures which Arab boyhood offered to him and to other homosexual tourists, and to speak of Wilde 'initiating' him is absurd. The two of them cruised around together as any sophisticated queers might, and in fact *do* in Algiers to this day.

[1] 'Conclusive proof' is not to be accepted in anything about Wilde, especially from Sherard, but there does seem to be strong evidence of Gide's tendency to indulge his own imagination.

[2] George D. Painter, *André Gide—A Critical Biography* (1968).

5

Another of Wilde's friends from whom it would have been rewarding to have a biography was Robert Ross, who played a large part in his life. Unfortunately Ross left only fragments, but from his letters it can be seen that an interesting biographer was lost in him and one who knew Wilde in his last years in some ways better than anyone else did. But if Ross did not write a book about Wilde he inspired one, Arthur Ransome's *Oscar Wilde: A Critical Study*. Moreover he edited a collected edition and, perhaps more important still, he persuaded that remarkable man Christopher Millard to concoct with his help one of the most entertaining bibliographies devoted to any modern author[1] and to edit anonymously the first and in certain respects the most detailed account of the Trials.[2] As picturesque a character as any of those who have written about Wilde, Christopher Millard served two sentences for offences with boys and worked as a secretary for Robert Ross. He was an able if eccentric man who had got into trouble as a schoolmaster and worked for a time on the *Burlington Magazine*. A. J. A. Symons, who, like the present writer, knew Millard in his last years (he died in 1927), gives a vivid account of him in *The Quest for Corvo*, for it was Millard who first introduced Symons to *Hadrian the Seventh* and set him on the trail which led to one of the most fascinating biographies in the language. Millard was then living 'in a small bungalow hidden behind a Victorian villa in Abercorn Place, reached by descending area steps and walking round the side of the house'. Symons saw him as a burly, self-sufficient, lonely man and seems to have liked and admired him. I thought there was something slightly sinister about him and his stock of 'curious' literature, compromising letters and typescripts, his intense yet sly manner and his scandalous conversation. His love for books was that of a bibliophile and bookseller, but none the less genuine.

---

[1] Stuart Mason, *Bibliography of Oscar Wilde* (1914).
[2] *Oscar Wilde: Three Times Tried* (1911).

6

When a book entitled *Son of Oscar Wilde* was announced in 1954, those interested felt entitled to hope that they would be told something nearer the truth than the stories of Sherard and Harris. We were not disappointed by any lack of truthfulness on the part of Vyvyan Holland, Wilde's second son; on the contrary we were given an account at once recognizable as unexaggerated and reliable. But Vyvyan Holland, unfortunately, had not one of those freak memories which go back to earliest childhood, and, less than nine years old when he was taken abroad by his mother during Wilde's trial, he had almost no personal recollection of his father. His evidence was valuable on other accounts. He remembered something of the house in Tite Street and of Constance Wilde, and as a young man he knew Ross, Max, Reggie Turner, Adela Schuster ('the Lady of Wimbledon') the Sphinx, More Adey, Ricketts and Shannon, William Rothenstein, Herbert Beerbohm Tree—indeed most of the Wilde *galère*. But these he could only portray as he met them in later life, not as Wilde's contemporaries. When I was writing my book about Lord Alfred Douglas, I happened to sit next to him at a public dinner and although well aware that he took the Ross view of Bosie,[1] I found that he wanted to ask questions about my friend. But he had no recollection of ever having seen him. I reminded him that as late as 1894 when he, Vyvyan, was nearly eight years old, Bosie had stayed with the family in Worthing and played with Vyvyan and Cyril, but he said he could scarcely remember Worthing, and though he was amiably enough disposed to tell me anything he could remember about Bosie, or about his father or mother in relation to Bosie, nothing whatever came back to him.

[1] See the chapters 'The Night of Long Knives' I and II in Rupert Croft-Cooke's *Bosie: The Story of Lord Alfred Douglas his Friends and Enemies* (1963).

7

A far from admirable figure in the gallery of eccentrics who have chosen Oscar Wilde as their theme was that of the man who became the lover and later the acolyte of Wilde's friend John 'Dorian' Gray.

Marc-André Raffalovich was the offspring of a Russian Jewish banking family, minor Rothschilds of international finance. Coming of age, he inherited a large fortune and set out to conquer artistic London. He was well-read, had a dilettante attachment to the arts, and paid for the publication of his verses, *Cyril and Lionel and Other Poems: A Volume of Sentimental Studies* in 1884 and *Tuberose and Meadowsweet* in 1885. The second was reviewed by Wilde with other collections of verses by unknown writers in *The Pall Mall Gazette*, Wilde complaining fractiously that he pronounced tuberose as a trisyllable. ("To say of these poems that they are unhealthy and bring with them the heavy odour of the hot-house is to point out neither their defect nor their merit but their quality merely.") Soon after this, the two men met and Oscar threw off that careless epigram which he afterwards adapted, as he did most of his better remarks, to use in a play —'Dear André! He came to London to found a *salon* and only succeeded in opening a *saloon*.' Raffalovich never forgave him for this, and later took his revenge.

This may not have been Wilde's only crack at André's expense. Something about him seems to have brought out a little malice in Wilde, who rarely said anything that could hurt an individual; but André had an ostentatious way of entertaining and there was a suggestion of patronage in the manner in which he treated his guests, who were not usually as prosperous as he. According to one raconteur, Wilde was once asked to lunch with five other men and was kept waiting at André's front door in a rainstorm. When he was at last admitted by the butler Wilde said: 'We want a table for six, please.' It was not very funny and was said—if it *was* said—to amuse his fellow-sufferers rather than to annoy

André, but this was the sort of remark which André could not forgive.

Within three months of Wilde's conviction there was published in Paris the small book on which André had worked furiously since Wilde's arrest, *L'Affaire Oscar Wilde*. Of all Wilde's acquaintances and fellow homosexuals, the only one who had attempted at the time to defend him in print—ineptly and unfortunately certainly, but with the best of intentions—was Bosie Douglas. Not until after his death did other friends begin to cash in on their acquaintance with him. But Raffalovich had nothing to lose, and with an assumption of high-minded disapproval and a pseudo-scientifically inquiring attitude towards what he called Wilde's 'crime', he wrote a filthy-minded little pamphlet in a tone of moral indignation. A couple of quotations will show its tenor:

Quande je l'accuse de criminalité, je ne m'occupe plus des actes sexuels qu'on lui a reprochés, mais du rôle qu'il a joué, de l'influence qu'il a prise et si mal employée, des jeunes vanités qu'il a faussées, des vices qu'il a tant encouragés.

Seulement l'opinion publique m'inspire peu d'estime à ce sujet; elle l'a supporté, soutenu, entretenu, elle l'a subi, ce malheureux prêtre de Priape, malade de la manie des réclames; l'opinion publique lui a passé bien des mauvaises paroles qui étaient de mauvaises actions, et aujourd'hui c'est sa culpabilité qu'elle attaque plus que sa criminalité.

Raffalovich continued, with a bitchiness almost unmatched, to write of Wilde's sensual lips, discoloured teeth and tongue *qui semblait lécher ses paroles*, and to call him a buffoon who vaunted his egotism, idleness, vanity, inconstancy and all imaginable vices —so on for forty-odd vituperative pages. If Wilde, then with shorn head and broad-arrow slops tramping round the silent exercise yard of Wandsworth Prison, could have read it, he would

have been baffled by its malice. It was not in his nature to understand how his off-hand epigram about 'dear André' could have
festered for years in that mean little mind to burst in this current
of pus.

But even this did not satisfy Raffalovich's craving for ven-
geance on the man who had found him ridiculous, and good-
humouredly said so. Thirty years later when Wilde had been
dead for a quarter of a century, he wrote, under the curiously
inappropriate pen-name of Alexander (Sandy) Michaelson, an
article on Wilde for the Dominican review *Blackfriars*, an article
so full of the old venom that one wonders at the good Fathers
publishing it. 'I detested him and his presence and the traces of
his influence,' Raffalovich writes, and goes on to remember Wilde
bullying a waiter and how he, Raffalovich, was told by someone
in the theatre 'That is a man you must not know'. He remembers
Constance Wilde saying 'Oscar likes you so much—that you have
such nice improper talks together.' Raffalovich was 'furious' and
remembers that he refused to speak to Wilde 'except before
witnesses'. Most improbably of all in view of his notoriously
grotesque appearance and, to Wilde, uncongenial character,
Raffalovich remembers that Wilde passed him or sent him a note
of invitation—'Come for me on Sunday at nine o'clock. Constance will be away—Oscar.' Years later, says Raffalovich, he
gave the note to 'Professor Nacke, the German criminologist.' In
his very last years (Raffalovich died in 1934) he would sometimes
bring himself to speak of 'poor Oscar' but even then only with a
sneer.

8

Another man who knew Oscar in his lifetime and wrote
about him with candour was the artist Charles Ricketts, who
produced a few fairly life-like sketches in his *Recollections*.[1] This is

[1] Jean-Paul Raymond and Charles Ricketts (1932). This was produced with
a vellum cover by Ricketts and published by the Nonesuch Press. Raymond
was an imaginary writer invented by Ricketts, and the book takes the form of
imaginary dialogues.

painstaking and honest but not very informative, though it quotes Wilde in one splendid quip calling Tennyson 'The Homer of the Isle of Wight'. It is possible that the brother-in-arms—or should one say bosom-friend?—of Charles Ricketts, also an artist, Charles Shannon, could have told us more of Wilde, but he seems to have been inarticulate, since Ricketts always used the matrimonial 'we' or spoke of 'Shannon and I'.

There are other personal acquaintances of Wilde, some of whom have written about him at length, but none of them I think quite merits a full place in this zoo. Laurence Housman, for instance, the brother of A. E. 'Shropshire Lad' Housman, reported the conversation of Wilde in Paris in his last years in *Echo de Paris* (1923) and Vincent O'Sullivan (1868–1940), an American writer, wrote *Aspects of Wilde* (1936). He gave a somewhat flamboyant portrait but managed to create incidents and witticisms with more conviction than Harris, perhaps because he himself had a some-what Wildean sense of humour. Hart-Davis considers *Aspects of Wilde* one of the most perceptive and reliable books on the subject —it is certainly one of the most lively.

W. B. Yeats might be included here for his *The Trembling of the Veil* (1926) which was the first book to put about, on hearsay, that ridiculous account of Wilde and Ernest Dowson going together to a brothel in Dieppe, a bad smoking-room story he had picked up from someone else. There is finally Ada 'Sphinx' Leverson's *Letters to the Sphinx from Oscar Wilde: With Reminiscences of the Author* (1930), but the Sphinx has a larger part to play in the life story itself than among the biographers, and can be remembered as an intimate friend rather than as a chronicler.

9

There is however one last mountebank in this motley collection who is worth remembering for his effrontery and imposture, a certain John Moray Stuart-Young. The first glimpse of him is caught in Millard's *Bibliography of Oscar Wilde* which was published while Stuart-Young was still alive and therefore is fairly restrained. (Millard had already had to defend himself against a forger called Mrs Chan Toon who tried to put over as Wilde's a 'Burmese Masque' called *For Love of the King*.) Millard lists a book called *Osrac the Self-Sufficient* (1905) with further editions in October of the same year and a variant *An Urning's Love* (Being a Poet's Study of Morbidity), *Osrac the Self-Sufficient and Other Poems* by J. M. Stuart-Young, author of *Merely a Negress* (1905). In each of these, says Millard, there are photographic portraits of Wilde, or Wilde and Douglas, with forged inscriptions, and in the case of the second book, forged facsimile letters from Wilde to the author.

Who was this Stuart-Young and what induced him to publish a memoir imagining himself to have been a friend of Wilde's, addressed by him as 'Johnny'? The search for an answer takes us into a madhouse of fraud and sheer silliness, books of agonizing verse printed to exhibit photographs of the author, or as Millard says 'poems interspersed with portraits of Stuart-Young at different periods of his life', letters to Ross claiming 'the sincere friendship which Oscar extended to me', excessively bad autobiographical novels, and with all this tales of trading in West Africa, and snapshots of an insane-looking strabismic Stuart-Young sitting with a ten-year-old African in a knickerbocker suit known as 'Ibrahim the Unkissed'. The explanation seems to have been that the man, born John Young in a Manchester slum in 1881, an invert from childhood, came to sexual and psychological awareness in 1895, the year of Wilde's trials, and in some lunatic way identified himself with one of the younger witnesses, seeing himself as 'Johnnie' or 'Jackie', a beautiful Giton of fourteen years whom Wilde was supposed to have summoned to London and seduced. These illusions, instead of dying out as he passed adolescence, grew with the years, so that when he was sent to prison for robbing his employers he saw himself as being martyred with Wilde, or as the minion of Wilde he had conceived himself to be. Thereafter the fantasy never left him and his frauds in print were the results, sad evidence of the effect on public imagination of the Wilde tragedy. It is alarming to find Hesketh Pearson, usually a sane if not always an inspired biographer, accepting a portion of this nonsense and actually quoting as authentic one of Stuart-Young's inventions, a speech supposed to have been made by Wilde on an occasion which could not have taken place.

Nor was Wilde the only writer to figure in the hallucinatory reminiscences of Stuart-Young. Once having learnt the trick of inventing interviews in which he figured, there was no end to them and John Walsh, the author of *Strange Harp, Strange Symphony: The Life of Francis Thompson*, quotes another dialogue, this time with Thompson, in an article reproduced in the *Catholic World*.

10

These, then, are the men and women who wrote at length of Wilde from personal acquaintance (or in the last case from pretended acquaintance) and, but for a few references in memoirs, their works give all we have of first-hand knowledge. They were not, as can be seen, a very reliable crowd or one conscientiously seeking to state the whole truth and nothing more, but from the meagre dole of fact which they wordily got together, every subsequent biographer has spun out his yarn.

This has meant that certain bits of fancy, certain extravagant distortions, certain mere opinions of the biographers have been sanctified into legends and passed down by writer after writer, with perhaps small additions or modifications, to the present day. Fragments of mythology have become solid and unquestioned chapters in the life-story, accepted by earnest students even when their only basis has been some imaginary conversation foisted on his readers by Frank Harris, or perhaps a verbose piece of sensationalism by Sherard.

For instance it needs credulity of an abnormal kind to swallow the monstrous exaggerations by Harris and others of some silly rhetoric by Sherard relating to scenes at the Old Bailey after the last trial. Poor Bob had not been present at the first trial, but described its 'Walpurgis night' atmosphere and the 'coarse crowd of English journalists, bookmakers and racing touts' who awaited news of the verdict. He went on: "The lewd faces flushed with alcohol, mouthing imprecations against the unhappy man, suggested a picture such as Goya might have painted of a dream of the corridors of Hell."

When he came to the final verdict he excelled himself in Hogarthian description. He had attended with Ernest Dowson, and the two of them had been greeted, he claimed, by something very like '*A bas, les aristos!*' "We drove there and as we alighted in front of the court house a shout arose from the rabble that thronged the street 'Here are some more aristocrats! Here are some more of them!' " After these attempts, Sherard had to produce something splendidly grandiloquent for the finale, and did so: "When the verdict and sentence on 'the aristocrat' reached the rabble in Old Bailey, men and women joined hands and danced an ungainly farandole, where ragged petticoats and yawning boots flung up the London mud in *feu de joie*, and the hideous faces were distorted with savage triumph. I stood and watched this dance of death for a few minutes, regretting that Veretschagin was not by my side; and whilst I was standing there, I saw The Evidence, still laughing and smoking cigarettes, being driven off in cabs."

When Harris (who did not attend the trial) came to enlarge on this, we find 'troops of the lowest women of the town dancing together and kicking up their legs in hideous abandonment'.[1] From these two come a whole series of descriptions, each one more clearly defined. Even Hesketh Pearson,[2] though he speaks of its exaggeration, reproduces the story, as does Montgomery Hyde.[3]

Scarcely less fatuous is the picture given by various writers of the Grand Exodus after Wilde had been arrested. This came from another of Sherard's too-melodramatic suppositions, written in prose which went out with the journalism of sixty years ago: "A wave of terror swept over the Channel, and the city of Calais witnessed a strange invasion. From the arcana of London a

[1] Frank Harris, *Oscar Wilde his Life and Confessions* (1918).
[2] Hesketh Pearson, *The Life of Oscar Wilde* (1946).
[3] *The Trials of Oscar Wilde*, edited by H. Montgomery Hyde (1948).

thousand guilty consciences, startled into action by the threat of imminent requitals, came fleeing South. Every outgoing steamer numbered amongst its passengers such nightmare faces as in quiet times one cannot fancy to exist outside the regions of disordered dreams." Yet Harris[1] accepted this as literally and factually true, and wrote: "Every train to Dover was crowded; every steamer to Calais thronged with members of the aristocratic and leisured classes, who seemed to prefer Paris, or even Nice out of the season, to a city like London, where the police might act with such unexpected vigour." "Never was Paris so crowded with members of the English governing classes; here was to be seen a famous ex-Minister; there the fine face of the president of a Royal society; at one table in the Café de la Paix, a millionaire recently ennobled, and celebrated for his exquisite taste in art; opposite to him a famous general." This old-fashioned and pretentious rubbish is rendered by Pearson as though it were an historical event. "The railways and steamers that trafficked with the Continent suddenly had to cope with a sort of holiday rush out of season."[2] Philippe Julian adds to this, "Within twenty-four hours, some dozens of gentlemen, young and old, were scattered over the various beaches of northern France. Some felt the urge to visit Florence, others, hoping to be forgotten, went as far as Egypt."[3] So the Dover–Calais boat, laden with queer fugitives, becomes an integral part of the traditional story of Wilde, until it threatens to capsize through overcrowding as book after book appears.

It was not only the fables of Sherard and Harris which set going stories that have persisted through many biographies, two films and a number of plays. Christopher 'Stuart Mason' Millard initiated one of the most regrettable of these. In his *Bibliography of Oscar Wilde* (1914; p. 392) he notes, "Charles Brookfield was largely responsible for collecting the evidence which brought about Wilde's downfall a few weeks later. After Wilde's conviction Brookfield and some friends entertained the Marquis of Queensberry at a banquet in celebration of the event. In revenge

[1] Frank Harris, *Oscar Wilde His Life and Confessions* Vol. 1.
[2] Hesketh Pearson, op. cit.
[3] Philippe Julian, *Oscar Wilde* (1969).

of this, some of Wilde's admirers entered a protest at the Prince of Wales's Theatre on the night of Charles Hawtrey's revival of Charles Brookfield's play, *Dear Old Charlie*, on February 20, 1912, shortly after the latter's appointment as joint-reader of plays."

Millard is usually to be relied upon, but the only source he could quote at the time he wrote his *Bibliography*, or afterwards when he was questioned, was a remark in a book of memoirs, *Jimmy Glover—His Book* by a certain James Glover, described as 'Master of music at Drury Lane Theatre'. Millard's statements, with the supposed support of Glover, have been generally accepted, and it is interesting to find that they have no basis in fact and that Millard was either disingenuous or careless in quoting Glover at all.

In his book, Glover told the story of a clever burlesque on Oscar Wilde's *Lady Windermere's Fan* 'written by Charles Brookfield and myself which was the introductory idea of the musical comedy'. It was called *The Poet and the Puppets* and originally contained the line repeated at the end of several of the introductory verses—'that was what made Oscar Wilde'. Wilde got to hear of this and invited Brookfield, Glover and Hawtrey to his home to read him the libretto. The occasion was friendly and hilarious and Wilde punctuated each page of the reading with pleased comments—'delightful', 'charming' and so on, and at the end said, 'I feel, however, that I have been—well—Brookfield, what is the word? Spoofed!' In the most amicable way Brookfield changed the name Oscar in the opening lines, so that the words became 'to make neighbour O'Flaherty's child' instead of 'to make Oscar Wilde', but, said Glover, referring to the title of the piece, the conspirators knew they *had* 'spoofed' Oscar, and fearing they had temporized with 'the Poet', they publicly exposed him pulling the strings of 'the Puppets'. All this heavy-handed humour amounted to was that Glover, Brookfield and Hawtrey were proud of their clumsy gags, but Millard seems to have noticed the words 'publicly exposed', and either by mis-reading the sense of them, or from some malice towards Brookfield, made them refer to the events of the trial and started the hare which has run through so many biographies of Wilde. None of the three men wished Oscar ill, and none of them, of course, had any hand in 'exposing' him. The dinner to Queensberry was sheer invention, as was the revenge by 'some of Wilde's admirers' at the first night of Brookfield's play. The evidence Queensberry needed and paid for was collected by two ex-police detectives Littlechild and Kearley, one of whom gained access to Alfred Taylor's rooms and stole papers involving most of the other young blackguards. The two detectives needed no help from amateurs even if it had been forthcoming.

Yet this story of Brookfield's part in the prosecution of Wilde has become a standard feature in almost every account of the trials. Harris, of course, seized on it: "It was Mr. Charles Brookfield, I believe, who constituted himself private prosecutor in this case and raked Piccadilly to find witnesses against Oscar Wilde."[1] Hesketh Pearson[2] enlarged on it considerably: "It is of interest to record that Charles Brookfield and Charles Hawtrey, both of whom had been acting for over a hundred nights in Wilde's play *An Ideal Husband*, gave a dinner to Queensberry to celebrate his victory. As sportsmen they were naturally delighted with the success of their hunt through the West End stews, and over-joyed at the thought that they had brought their quarry to earth. Although Wilde's own folly had enabled them to do it, Queensberry and Brookfield could congratulate themselves unreservedly on having wrecked the career of a genius. Few people in history could boast as much, and their dinner party must have been most gratifying to both of them." Winwar[3] swallows it—'Evidence which, with detective Littlechild, Wilde's former friend Brookfield had helped to unearth.' Philippe Julian[4] elaborates it. Lewis Broad[5] falls into line—"The task of the investigator was lightened by the intervention of a small-part actor, Charles Brookfield, who had been appearing as the valet in *An Ideal*

[1] Frank Harris, *Oscar Wilde his Life and Confession.*
[2] Hesketh Pearson, *The Life of Oscar Wilde* (1946).
[3] Frances Winwar, *Oscar Wilde* (1940).
[4] Philippe Julian, *Oscar Wilde* (1969).
[5] Lewis Broad, *The Friendship and Follies of Oscar Wilde.*

Husband. He came forward to supply the names of the men with whom Wilde had been associating. Envy was the motive that made Brookfield play the informer." Queensberry and Colson[1] become almost hysterical. They do not overstate the case, for there was none, but they use language which would in any event make their story suspect. "Brookfield—who hated him fanatically, insanely—had devoted himself to collecting and putting into the hands of the prosecution every scrap of evidence against him he could discover." H. Montgomery Hyde accepts it:[2] "It is a curious fact, which does not seem to be generally known, that the most damning clues were provided by an entirely voluntary agent who received no fee for his services. This was the actor Charles Brookfield, who had conceived a violent hatred of Wilde, although at this time he actually had a part in Wilde's play, *An Ideal Husband*, at the Haymarket Theatre." Even Hart-Davis[3] refers to this nonsense, though with the saving phrase 'believed to be'. The whole thing has no basis in fact or even in probability. The idea of these hard-working and good-natured actors, who had collaborated in sending up Wilde in an unfunny sketch, chasing round the 'Dilly looking for Wilde's boys is too silly to contemplate and should not have deceived a child.

There is one reference to Brookfield's supposed part in Wilde's exposure which, although it did not appear before 1927, has been supposed to come from some knowledge of the circumstances. A certain John Boon, who had accepted the legend of Brookfield being a sort of Judas Iscariot, tried to make it credible in his book *Victorians, Edwardians and Georgians* by telling an involved story of a 'young Scot' who had mentioned the name of a politician in fan letters to Wilde and an Irish commissionaire or doorkeeper at the theatre in which one of Wilde's plays was produced, and a supposed bargain struck with Littlechild, the detective employed by Queensberry. There is no truth in it and the only origin of this favourite part of the Wilde myth remains Glover's incautious

---

[1] Marquess of Queensberry and Percy Colson, *Oscar Wilde and the Black Douglas.*
[2] H. Montgomery Hyde, *Trials of Oscar Wilde.*
[3] *The Letters of Oscar Wilde*, edited by Rupert Hart-Davis.

use of the words 'publicly exposed' in relation to a gag in a musical comedy staged three years before the trials.

Of the stories which are unadulterated Harris, rising like bad smells from that dirty mind of which he gave evidence in his own autobiography[1]—and it is fair to say that he was no more respectful of truth in that than in his book about Wilde—perhaps the two most worth recalling for their sheer fatuity are those of Wilde's boyhood and adolescence, incidents which Harris claims were confided to him by Wilde himself, though Oscar was never known to speak of his boyhood and would certainly not have done so to such an insensitive listener as Frank Harris. They are marked by those frequent interpolations of Harris's first name which throughout the whole of Wilde's 'confessions' indicate a lie: 'You see, Frank . . .', 'Oh no, Frank . . .' and so on. The first concerns a leave-taking when Wilde was at the end of his time at Portora. He is at the station with one boy, a great friend, who looked up 'with yearning, sad, regretful eyes'. " 'You must go now,' I said to him. 'Yes,' he replied, in a queer muffled voice, while standing with his hand on the door of the carriage. Suddenly he turned to me and cried: 'Oh, Oscar,' and before I knew what he was doing he had caught my face in his hot hands, and kissed me on the lips. The next moment he had slipped out of the door and was gone. . . . I sat there all shaken. Suddenly I became aware of cold, sticky drops trickling down my face—his tears. They affected me strangely. As I wiped them off I said to myself in amaze: 'This is love: this is what he meant—love.' . . . I was trembling all over. For a long while I sat, unable to think, all shaken with wonder and remorse." Not many of the biographers fall for this one, but surprisingly enough Philippe Julian[2] does so, while admitting that Frank Harris is often unreliable.

The other story drags in poor old Walter Pater, a spinsterish don whose love-affairs were cerebral and devoted to handsome athletes, very different from Wilde's friends. The story has been quoted from Harris too often to bear repetition here and I reproduced it in Feasting with Panthers, adding: "This is a more

[1] Frank Harris, My Life and Loves. Complete in one volume (1964).
[2] Phillipe Julian, Oscar Wilde, trans. Violet Wyndham (1969).

obvious fake, not because it is impossible in relation to Pater but as coming from Wilde. If the story were true and Wilde had told it at all—and he certainly would not have done so to Harris during Pater's lifetime, that is until a year before his imprisonment—he could only have made it something grotesquely funny without being unkind to Pater for whom he had a lifelong respect. He might have recalled it to Ross or Bosie with good-natured burlesque, but never with all that hu-ha and mixed metaphor about the enchanting perfume of romance wedded to the severe beauty of classic form, and he would never, Oscar Wilde would *never* have said seriously that he himself 'talked as if inspired'."

There are other persistent legends which continue to crop up— that of Wilde's mother wanting a girl, for instance, and dressing Oscar in girl's clothes. This would seem to have come from Sherard who was misled by a photograph showing Oscar in the old-fashioned dress in which doting parents garbed their young sons even in the early part of this century. Then there is that load of claptrap about living up to his blue china at Oxford, which is nothing but the misapplication to Wilde of a *Punch* joke of 1880 about aesthetes. This again is exploded by the *Letters*, which show Wilde at Oxford in his true character, and incidentally in a sporty check suit and bowler hat. No less absurd is a story at the other extreme which varies in degrees of exaggeration with the teller but at its richest describes how Wilde took on almost the whole college who had come to raid the blue china which he never had. Some were kicked out, others pushed out, some thrown out and one carried out in Oscar's arms. The story seems to have come first from Sir Max Pemberton, but another version, applying to Trinity College, Dublin, was given by an American student and repeated by Hesketh Pearson. Wilde in fact was neither a milksop nor a pugilist, and attempts to see him as either belong to the myths.

Nor was he, as several writers imply, a millionaire. The story of his great riches, like so many stories with the same theme told in other circumstances, is without any factual basis, though it is always understandable that writers, themselves so disgracefully deprived, should goggle at faery gold. Before the production of

Lady Windermere's Fan, Wilde had difficulty in maintaining his modest home in Tite Street and his wife and children, even with the help of Constance's income. This first play was produced on 20 February 1892 and ran till 29 July, just over five months. It then toured the provinces. It was very successful and Hesketh Pearson may not exaggerate when he says it made Wilde £7,000. Supposing that *A Woman of No Importance* did as well in the following year, there remain *An Ideal Husband* and *The Importance of Being Earnest*, the first of which was taken off after 111 performances, the second after three weeks. What then were the sources of Wilde's supposed riches? In 1894, before his third play was produced, he was exceedingly hard up, as his circumstances at Worthing and his letters show clearly. In prison he was made bankrupt. The truth would seem to be that until 1887 he lived on his small patrimony and his wife's income, from 1888 till 1892 he made a little income from writing and editing, from 1892 to 1895 he received sums erratically from his plays, and thereafter, he made virtually no money at all. He appeared to the people of the '90s to be at times almost vulgarly prosperous, but he never enjoyed a substantial steady income, or anything like it.

There is also—a favourite among a good many writers—the fallacy which supposes that the Gilbert and Sullivan operetta *Patience* was written about Wilde, and that the mythical person who would 'walk down Piccadilly with a poppy or a lily' in his mediaeval hand was in fact Oscar. Apart from the fact that *Patience*, which was produced with Sullivan's music in 1881, had been planned and written by Gilbert much earlier, while Wilde was still an unknown undergraduate at Oxford, the whole thing was a satire on all that *Punch* depicted as pre-Raphaelite, Rossetti-ish, Swinburnian and farcical. Admittedly Wilde himself is partly to blame for this confusion, for he quickly realized the publicity value of identifying himself with the so-called aesthetic movement. Did he not say of the walk down Piccadilly, 'Anyone could have done that. The great and difficult thing was what I achieved —to make the world believe I had done it.' And not only the world, but most of those writers who over the years have set out to interpret Wilde.

B

As a matter of fact not only did Wilde fail to walk down Piccadilly, etc., but there is not the smallest evidence that he ever wore eccentric clothes until he was booked for a lecture tour in America in 1881. For this, partly a publicity stunt to advertise *Patience*—which had opened in New York on 22 September— and partly a genuine lecture tour which Col. W. F. Morse, D'Oyly Carte's American representative, thought would be profitable, Oscar admittedly garbed himself in knee-breeches, black silk stockings, a soft silk shirt with wide turned-down collar and a flowing pale green tie. But he never wore this get-up in England. This will, I'm afraid, be a disappointment for some who have accepted the portrait of Wilde in drag as a home production, but they may be compensated by the splendid fur coat which Wilde bought in the States or Canada during his tour and wore 'with a difference', as he said, until the winter before he went to prison.

Another story about Wilde which has become popular among the more knowing of his biographers was first told publicly by Arthur Ransome in his *Oscar Wilde: A Critical Study* (1912), a book almost entirely inspired by Robert Ross, who gave the author his data, supplied the frontispiece and accepted the dedication. In this Wilde's death was said with an air of authority quite unsupported by fact to be 'directly due to meningitis, a legacy of an attack of tertiary syphilis'. It is hard to know why Ross started this unpleasant suggestion unless it was to draw attention to his own self-sacrificing care of Wilde in his last illness. In its most generally accepted form, this story relates that Wilde contracted syphilis at Oxford and 'turned towards homosexuality' after his marriage, when he was alarmed to find that the disease, which he had believed cured, was persisting. The most elementary knowledge of venereal disease, or of Wilde's physiology, or even of his character should have shown any inquirer that there was no positive support for this sensational theory, the only supposed evidence for which is that Wilde, like the majority of Victorians, had bad teeth, said to be due to the mercury used in the contemporary treatment of syphilis. But the usual string of follow-my-leader biographers repeat it.

There are some minor legends. One of them is the story familiar
to most readers that Ross 'introduced' Wilde to homosexuality
when they met in 1886. Since Wilde had been enjoying the life
of a homosexual at least since his time at Oxford and possibly
before, this romantic supposition (Ross was eighteen at the time)
can be dismissed at once, though the two almost certainly went to
bed together then, and again at intervals thereafter, the last
occasion being on Wilde's arrival in Dieppe after coming out of
prison.

A very small fallacy is that of supposing that because Wilde
used for his characters the names of places he had visited, Lord
Goring, Ernest Worthing, Lord Henry Wotton[1] and so on,
therefore all his characters were named after a place Wilde knew.
From this a wholly fictitious visit to the Lake District is imagined
in 1891 to explain the name of Lady Windermere. This does not
greatly matter but it is a pity that serious writers like Hesketh
Pearson and Philippe Julian adopt it.

They and others cannot be blamed, perhaps, for giving credit
to one of Oscar's own stories, though it was told in the witness-
box in answer to his counsel and was designed for his defence. It
concerned Queensberry's call on him in Tite Street when Wilde
claims to have behaved with masterly defiance.[2] This has been
accepted by some writers on Wilde, who have added—on what
authority they do not state—that the 'gentleman with whom I
was not acquainted', who accompanied Queensberry, was a prize-
fighter. They do not seem to find anything strange, not to say
incredible, in the notion of Queensberry, who had been an amateur boxing champion and was described by Harris as 'five foot
nine or ten in height, combative and courageous', standing quietly
to hear that he was the most infamous brute in London and meekly
leaving the house at Wilde's bidding. Sherard says that Wilde
did not 'show the white feather', 'and even if he had shown some
nervousness it would have been very unfair to charge him with
cowardice'. Even Harris says flatly that 'the idea of Oscar "standing up" to Queensberry or "shooting at sight" was too absurd'.

[1] More Adey's home was at Wotton-under-Edge.
[2] See pages 168-9.

Hesketh Pearson was father to another fable, this time with no discoverable basis of fact, and no suggestion of how he came to include it in his *Life of Oscar Wilde*. "The main idea [of *The Picture of Dorian Gray*] came from an actual episode," he wrote, and proceeded: "In the year 1884 Wilde used often to drop in at the studio of a painter, Basil Ward, one of whose sitters was a young man of exceptional beauty . . . When the portrait was done and the youth had gone, Wilde happened to say 'What a pity that such a glorious creature should ever grow old!' The artist agreed, adding 'How delightful it would be if he could remain exactly as he is, while the portrait aged and withered in his stead!' Wilde expressed his obligation by naming the painter in his story 'Basil Hallward'."

There was no such artist as Basil Ward, and if there had been Wilde would not carelessly have given such a similar name to one of his characters who appears as a homosexual and a suicide. Everyone in artistic London at the time knew that 'Basil Hallward' was based, by his own consent, on the artist Charles Shannon, and Ernest Dowson, who was most interested in the matter, wrote to Arthur Moore (9 October 1890) a letter in which he speaks of Shannon as 'the prototype of the artist in *Dorian*'.[1]

Moreover if Pearson had searched more diligently in Stuart Mason's *Art and Morality* (1912) he would have found that the story of a remark by Wilde supplying 'the main idea' of *The Picture of Dorian Gray* had already been bagged by Oscar himself some fifty-six years before Pearson rather irresponsibly created his 'Basil Ward'. Stuart Mason quotes from the *St James's Gazette*, a newspaper at that time waging controversial war with Wilde about *The Picture of Dorian Gray*. The issue was dated 24 Septemper 1890:

Mr. Oscar Wilde has explained. We know now how 'Dorian Gray' came to be written. In 1887, about the genial season of Christmas, a Canadian lady artist (Frances Richards) yearned to

[1] *The Letters of Ernest Dowson*, edited by Desmond Flower and Henry Maas.

transfer to the glowing canvas the classic features of Mr. Oscar Wilde. Mr. Wilde gave her a sitting. When the sitting was over and Mr. Wilde had looked at the portrait, it occurred to him that a thing of beauty, when it takes the form of a middle-aged gentleman, is unhappily not a joy forever. 'What a tragic thing it is,' he exclaimed. 'This portrait will never grow old, and I shall.' Then the passion of his soul sought refuge in prose composition, and the result was 'Dorian Gray'.

The most outrageous and utterly unfounded suggestion made in the whole Wilde mythology is that he was a pornographer and (according to Maurice Girodias) actually wrote a feeble piece of homosexual fiction called *Teleny*. This thing was published by Leonard Smithers in 1893, which date alone would prove to the student of Wilde that he had nothing to do with it. The attribution to Wilde by Girodias is based only on some old lies told by a shady bookseller named Charles Hirsch who sold French newspapers and books in Coventry Street in the '90s, but since H. Montgomery Hyde and Philippe Julian both refer to the canard, it can be answered with a few facts. Wilde abhorred all pornography in writing or conversation and, as Sherard was never tired of saying, and as all Wilde's friends agreed, would not permit even quite ordinary swear-words. His special 'manner' in touching on subjects of homosexual interest was a sort of literary badinage, which was neither solemn nor Rabelaisian. The style of *Teleny*, if 'style' can be used of the book, is totally foreign to Wilde's way of thinking or writing. Nothing in the whole novel has, or could have, the slightest suggestion of Wilde's talent in it. Surely Wilde gave offence enough to the puritan conscience without saddling his reputation with this silly piece of filth?

It would be both unnecessary and unkind to pick out from modern pieces of writing about Wilde all that illustrate the folly of accepting second-hand sources, but scarcely less absurd are the inventions of those who attempt to write about Wilde with present-day mannerisms and terminology. In a recent issue of the monthly magazine *Encounter* (September 1970) appears an article of some 9,000 words called 'The Impossible Culture: Oscar Wilde and the Charisma of the Artist'. Its intention appears to be to show by the use of fashionable word-play that what we had always supposed were the fun and frivolity in Wilde's writings were in fact a prophecy of 'the anti-credal character of an impossible culture'. It can only be answered by a plural monosyllable which Wilde would never have used.

So it can be seen that through one or another writer, the story of Wilde which is in fact a fairly straightforward one, has been cluttered up with odds and ends of fiction till the figure of the Irishman has been quite submerged. To extricate him and brush him down, and set him on his large (size twelve) feet, is my task here. There was nothing enigmatic about him. He was a charming and promiscuous, witty and imaginative queer whose seemingly pre-destined fate it was to bring down the whole temple of Victorian propriety on his shoulders. Even today I do not find totally untenable the estimate of Wilde as a writer which was held by a great many Englishmen for the best part of half a century, that before the production of his plays, he had little more than the talent of a highly educated man who chose literature as his means of winning acclaim. His poetry was derivative, his miscellaneous prose undistinguished, his short stories—the best of his earlier prose work—were written with self-conscious bravura, his *Picture of Dorian Gray* was novelettish, class-conscious and vulgar, primed with stagey melodrama; *The Importance of Being Earnest* is the only play which is something better than a cleverly constructed but old-fashioned 'society' drama, salted with aphorisms; his *Ballad of Reading Gaol* is a mixture of Coleridge, Poe and self-pity. But even those who uncharitably accept this must find, in Wilde's last letters, that the full enchantment of a great individualist and wit emerges and will respond to his freedom from jealousy and bitterness, the diffident philosophy, the indomitable optimism. But if all the *Collected Works* had perished and nothing remained but his letters, a modern reader would still be made eager to go back and search for the truth about one of the most beguiling characters in the history of English—or any other—literature, would still have his curiosity aroused by the grotesque life-story of a man who was a master of comedy even in a prison cell, who saw his own life as the expression of his genius, and his Work, that majuscule Work to which he was fond of referring, to be of momentous significance to the age in which he lived. For he could laugh at everything except himself, and even that, in his last years, he learned to do with whole-hearted geniality.

The most recent books on Wilde, however much documented, do not avoid inaccuracy and flighty, unbelievable narrative. The old stories are quite deliberately reproduced with no attempt to check them or find their origins—usually Harris or Sherard—and are sometimes more or less deftly supplemented with newly invented detail. It is, perhaps, too late in the day to attempt to dam the flood, and readers will go on believing to the end of time that Wilde was a fancy-dress figure, forever firing epigrams like a boy with a pea-shooter, a blubbering confidant in the manly 'Frank' of the *Confessions*, a dealer in blue china and pederastic pornography, a man of extraordinary if not unique sexual predilections, a favourite of the 'highest society', and the only man who ever went to prison under Section Eleven of the Criminal Law Amendment Act, a monster unique in both his vices and his genius. To erase this caricature will not be easy and I am aware that my qualifications for the task are limited. I can only try.

TWO

Oxford

We have not much information about the childhood and boyhood of Oscar Wilde before he reached Oxford, and the little we have is so unfactual and has been repeated in so many wearisome forms that there is no point in returning to it here. The parents are caricatured in most biographies. The father, Sir William Wilde, a brilliant eye and ear specialist who had come down in the world through a scandal over a female patient, has been credited with so many illegitimate children and so much indiscreet philandering that one wonders how he had time either for his profession or for the archaeological studies which were his hobby. The mother, known as Speranza, was a sufferer from giantism, according to Bernard Shaw,[1] with enormous hands, the gigantic splaying of her palm being reproduced in the lumbar region. She had been in her youth a revolutionary poetess who wrote, among other exhortations, "Oh! for a hundred thousand muskets glittering brightly in the light of heaven and the monumental barricades stretching across each of our noble streets made desolate by England—circling round that doomed Castle, where the foreign tyrant has held his council of treason and iniquity against our people and our country for seven hundred years . . . One bold, one decisive move. One instant to take breath, and then a rising; a rush, a charge from north, south, east and west upon the English garrison, and *the land is ours.*" But with time and her husband's knighthood she ceased spellbinding and created a somewhat raffish Dublin *salon*, where she dressed eccen-

---

[1] *Memories of Oscar Wilde* by Bernard Shaw. Appendix to *Oscar Wilde* by Frank Harris (1918).

trically and gave recitations in a deep voice, while crowned with a laurel wreath. The brother, Willie Wilde, older than Oscar and given to athletics, plays little part in the Dublin scene, and the small sister Isola died and inspired Oscar to write an elegiac parody of Hood's *Bridge of Sighs* which appeared in Wilde's *Poems* years later.

Both parents of Oscar Wilde were thus notable but eccentric people. Sir William was a man of considerable achievement, not only in his profession but also as an archaeologist who created a second life of his own in the solitudes of Galway. He built a house there, Moytura, not far from the shore of Lough Corrib, and purchased and restored a fishing lodge fifty miles away on Lough Fee. After being almost ruined by a libel action, he retired from Dublin life, in which he had cut a figure with his large house in Merrion Square, and spent the last years of his life chiefly at Moytura.

Lady Wilde, Speranza, also retired from life in another sense. When, after her husband's death, her two sons settled in London, she gave up both the Dublin mansion and Moytura and took a house first in South Kensington and later in Chelsea. At first she was invited by Oscar to his parties but she became an alcoholic whose darkened rooms, crazy attire and blundering speech betrayed her weakness, and towards the end of her life—she died while Oscar was in prison—she could no longer leave the house.

It would be profitable to learn something of Oscar's relationship with his parents, to know whether Sir William Wilde ever confided in the boy or received his confidences, to be able to judge whether Speranza fired young Oscar with the revolutionary zeal she had once felt. It would even be rewarding to be able to see Oscar running in and out of the large Dublin house or fishing in Lough Corrib during holidays in Galway. The impressions made by childhood must have been deep, and whatever Oscar's racial origins, much of his talent was owed to his Irish birth and upbringing—though in after life his accomplishments seemed peculiarly urban. There is no evidence of this in any account of his boyhood.

2

Oscar and his brother were sent to Portora Royal School, Enniskillen, and again nothing reliable can be learnt of their life there.[1] Harris has some stories which he claims were written for him by a certain Sir Edward Sullivan, who was 'a contemporary of Oscar both at school and college', but if this person really provided Harris with material, one can only say that his literary style was an exact reproduction of Harris's and his reminiscences include remarkably apt foreshadowings of the future—"He told us there was nothing he would like better in after-life than to be the hero of such a *cause célèbre* and to go down to posterity as the defendant in such a case as 'Regina versus Wilde'!" Oscar certainly won a scholarship at Trinity College, Dublin and spent three years there equally unchronicled except for the fact that he came under the influence of a man named John Pentland Mahaffy, a Protestant clergyman, Greek scholar and notorious snob.

What Oscar was 'really like' at Portora and T.C.D., nothing survives to tell us. Did he have affairs with the other boys at school or with fellow students at Trinity College? It seems likely because he 'knew about himself', as queers say, as soon as he got up to Oxford, but it is useless to speculate and Wilde had a strong distaste, unusual among men of his disposition, for talking about his boyhood. Was he on intimate terms with his mother? His attitude during their first years in London suggests that he felt some pride in her and he seems not to have lacked affection. But can one imagine him as a youth of sixteen, say, sitting beside the funny old girl with her whisky-laden breath, telling her about his ambitions? Can one, for that matter, imagine Wilde at all as a boy, or until he reached Oxford? We know he was a good

[1] The present headmaster of the school, the Rev. P. H. Rogers, M.B.E., writes: "Alas, we have little enough that is of interest to a biographer: no printed sources, no school photographs or correspondence." He adds: "In the spate of hysteria about Wilde his name was expunged from the Trinity scholarship honours boards, but I am glad to say it was reinstated in slightly bolder and more effulgent lettering than the other names, I think in 1923."

examinee, winning a gold medal and scholarships, as later he was to achieve an Honours First degree. But that is really all we do know, and the boyhood of no nineteenth-century figure who afterwards reached eminence or notoriety has been so sparsely chronicled.

The Librarians of Trinity College Library have been good enough to make a thorough investigation and all that they can find is this bare account of Wilde's college career.

10 Oct. 1871   Entered (not 19 Oct. as in Harris). Second place in entrance examination.

1871   *Michaelmas term.* Attended 21 out of 28 science lectures (Mr Abbott) and 30/34 classics (Mahaffy).

1872   *Hilary term.* Attended 5/39 hons lectures in Classics (Palmer) and 2/17 lectures in English literature (Dowden). Sat for hons exam in classics, gaining 3rd place in 1st rank.

Trinity term. Sat for hons exam in classics, gaining 1st place in 1st rank. Passed ordinary term exam.

Michaelmas term. Sat for hons exam in classics, gaining 1st place in 1st rank.

1873   *Hilary term.* Passed term exam.

Trinity term. Sat for classical scholarship, gaining 6th place (not 5th as in Harris) and scholarship.

Michaelmas term. Passed term exam. Sat for examination for prizes in classics, gaining 5th place in 1st rank.

1874   *Hilary term.* Passed term exam. Awarded Berkeley medal for classics.

No subsequent entries relating to terms or exams.

19 Nov. 1873   Elected member of College Historical Society (College's main debating society). Did not stand for any office in the society and is not recorded as having spoken in any debate.

The chapel communion book does not record his having taken the sacrament there at any time during his membership of College.

As for letters, there is only one, of dubious authenticity, from school, thanking Lady Wilde for a hamper, and letters to both parents from Italy in 1875 which are impersonal travelogues, though one notes that in writing to his mother, Oscar refers to his father as 'Sir William'.

Since nothing is known, and now almost a century later nothing is likely to come to light, there is no point in inventing, as Harris has done, and we may as well follow Wilde to Oxford and observe his life as revealed in the letters he wrote to his friends.

3

Two of these, William 'Bouncer' Ward and Reginald 'Kitten' Harding, were at Magdalen College with Wilde. The third, George Francis 'Frank' Miles, was two years older than Wilde and no longer a member of the university, though he spent much time in Oxford, sometimes accompanied by his friend Lord Ronald Sutherland-Gower.

William Ward, who was nicknamed Bouncer from the novel *Little Mr Bouncer and his Friend Verdant Green* by Cuthbert Bede (Edward Bradley), perhaps came nearer than anyone else in Wilde's life to forming a sincere and spontaneous friendship with him, uncomplicated by passion. If there was a sexual side to this it was so much taken for granted as part of the lightly sentimental relationship cultivated by two undergraduates, so much less significant than conversations about religion, literature and sport, that it must have seemed (to Ward anyway) something which arose naturally from sharing a bed for convenience sake, or finding themselves obliged to shelter all night from a storm. There may, even, have been no physical expression to the strong attraction between them. Wilde's letters were preserved by Ward and are now in Magdalen College Library. They are in no way explicit on this point but show signs of careful selection by the recipient. We know from a letter dated 6 August 1876 that the two young men discussed what John Addington Symonds called 'the Subject', but even that tells us nothing about Ward himself in this respect.

I want to ask your opinion on this psychological question. In our friend Todd's[1] ethical barometer, at what height is his moral quicksilver? Last night I strolled into the theatre about ten o'clock and to my surprise saw Todd and young Ward the quire boy in a private box together, Todd very much in the background. He saw me so I went round to speak to him for a few minutes. He told me that he and Foster Harter had been fishing in Donegal and that he was going to fish South now. I wonder what young Ward is doing with him. Myself I believe Todd is extremely moral and only mentally spoons the boy, but I think he is foolish to go about with one, if he *is* bringing this boy about with him. You are the only one I would tell about it, as you have a philosophical mind *but don't tell anyone about it like a good boy—it would do neither us nor Todd any good.* He (Todd) looked awfully nervous and uncomfortable.

Ward, although he was of the same age as Oscar, had been at the university two years when Oscar arrived from Trinity College, Dublin, but this does not seem to have made it difficult for them to become firm and affectionate friends during Ward's last and Oscar's first year at Oxford. They wrote to each other frequently during the vacations, discussing philosophy, High Church religion, sports and vacation-time doings. Oscar occasionally broke out into affectionate terms, though only such as might be in any undergraduate's letter, 'those dear rides through the greenwood', 'dear old boy, I wish I could see you again'. Sometimes he gushed:

Our Varsity Sports have just been on and were much as usual with the exception of Bullock-Webster's running which is the most

[1] In one of his invaluable footnotes Rupert Hart-Davis discovers that Charles John Todd (1854–1939), Magdalen undergraduate, afterwards became a Chaplain to the Royal Navy.

beautiful thing I ever saw. Usually running men are so ungraceful and stiff-legged and pigeon-breasted, but he is lithe and
exquisitely graceful and strides about *nine feet*: he is like a beautiful horse trotting, as regards his action. I never saw anything like
it: he and Stevenson ran a three mile race, he keeping behind
Stevenson about a yard the whole time till the last quarter when
he rushed in before him amid awful cheers and shouting: you
will see in Naples two bronze statues of two Greek boys running
quite like Webster.

Ward, who was a short, attractive-looking youth, smooth-
faced and snub-nosed with a merry, appealing expression, wrote
many years later when he was an ageing man, *Oscar Wilde: An
Oxford Reminiscence*, which is preserved in MS in Magdalen
Library and appears in Vyvyan Holland's *Son of Oscar Wilde*. "One
of my greatest friends at Oxford—certainly the most intimate
during my last year—was Oscar Wilde. I should like those who
come after me to know something of the charm of his companionship and conversation, to see him for a moment as he was in those
far-off College days, a laughing but always an interesting personality. How brilliant and radiant he could be! How playful and
charming! How his moods varied and how he revelled in in-
consistency!"

That the friendship slowly died is explained by Ward. After
they had come down from Oxford they met less frequently. "I
dined with him sometimes at Romano's or at his mother's house,
when he told me of his doings, how he had introduced Ruskin to
Mrs Langtry and so on. He came to stay with me at Frenchay
and at Coombe, the last time was for a lecture which he gave at
the Victoria Rooms, shortly before his American tour. And I
remember looking in at his rooms off the Strand one morning
on my way to Lincoln's Inn, when I found him still in bed and his
sitting-room in great disorder. He explained that he had given
a supper party the night before, at which Sarah Bernhardt had
been present and that she had tried to see how high she could jump
and write her name with a charcoal on the wall. From the scrawl

on the side of the room and not much below the ceiling it seemed that she had attained considerable success in the attempt. His was, to use the current phrase, the artistic temperament *in excelsis et profundis*. Money he wanted, no man more, for lack of it was an impediment but to get it only after long and forced labour and at the price of lost liberty; this he thought was a sacrifice of ends to means. What is the use of the open door to the bird so long caged that its power of flight is gone? The drudgery of business, according to his view, made men not themselves, wearers of masks of which their faces by natural mimicry took the dull shape and lifeless likeness. Life itself in his hands was to be a work of art, he and the free and happy artist to give it shape and colour according to his idea and technique." "Later I saw him only fitfully for a few years, when I happened to be in London, and then, as our ways were more and more parted, all intimacy died out, and at length we never met and never corresponded." It was a cheerful undergraduate relationship without intensely emotional undertones.

With Reginald Harding the case was rather different. One has only to study the photographs of that beautiful young man with his thick curly carefully adjusted hair, his deep-set eyes and his warm and smooth complexion, to recognize in him an early example of Wilde's 'type'. It is permissible to ask—supposing that there was no sexual element in Wilde's interest in Kitten[1]—what other quality the young man had that was so attractive to Wilde? The son of a Barnstaple solicitor, a thoroughly nice, rather brainless boy who enjoyed team games and playing the church organ, he was affectionate and cheerful, with no very strong character or outstanding ability. He found it hard to write letters or live up to Wilde's demands on him, though he responded to Wilde's flattering attention and did his best to hold the place that Wilde assigned to him, of his 'best friend'. His conventional good looks and good-natured charm doubtless made him no less attractive to some pretty girl to whom he probably became engaged when that

[1] Not too much notice must be taken of the affectionate nickname of Kitten, for it was an age of nicknames. 'Kitten' came from a music-hall song of the time. "*Beg your parding, Mrs Harding, Is my kitting in your garding?*"

extraordinary fellow Wilde, with his delightful gifts of companionship, was long forgotten as part of the Oxford scene, but in the meantime Kitten was carried away by Oscar and responded willingly, in a schoolboyish, gentlemanly and somewhat supine way, to his interest. That part of it was easy enough to one of Kitten's lazy, sun-loving temperament; it was when Oscar demanded letters and other industrious or articulate responses that Kitten found it hard to oblige. "I wrote to Kitten for your address," wrote Wilde to Ward during the summer vacation of 1876, "and his letter and yours arrived simultaneously. His thoughts and ink rarely last beyond one sheet." "My greatest chum," he wrote later," except of course the Kitten, is Gussy. . . . I am quite as fond of the dear Kitten as ever but he has not enough power of character to be more than a pleasant affectionate boy. He never exerts my intellect or brain *in any way*. Between his mind and mine there is *no intellectual friction to rouse me up to talk or think*, as I used when with you."

In Wilde's letters to Kitten himself (such as have been preserved) he sometimes comes close to more revealing sentences, and this suggests that the frankest of them have been destroyed. When Wilde is lying ill he writes: "Many thanks for your kind note. I have a childish longing for some flowers—I don't care what—only *not* wallflowers. If you have any spare moments and can get me a few you will be doing as benevolent an action as giving groundsel to a starving canary would be! I am very wretched and ill and as soon as possible I am to be sent away somewhere out of Oxford. Could you steal a branch of that lovely red blossoming tree outside the new building for me? I am sick at heart for want of some freshness and beauty in life." And a few hours or days later, "If there is anything that could console me for being ill it is your charming basket of flowers and delightful letter. The roses have quite given me a sense of the swift beauty and light of the spring: they are most exquisite. And I heard your light quick step down the passage this morning and am awfully obliged for your theft of the pink and white blossoms. I can bury my face in them and dream how nice it would be to be out again. You are the nicest of kittens."

4

As one of a trio with Bouncer and Kitten, Oscar was determined not to be anomalous, and contrary to many accounts of him at Oxford, there were only the mildest oddities of behaviour, such as all undergraduates cultivated, to distinguish him from the rest. We see him in photographs of groups, noticeable for his tallness and the rather horsy clothes he wore—check suits might have seemed ostentatious if all the other young men pictured with him were not wearing similar suits—and a curly-brimmed bowler accentuated his height. His thick lips looked only good-natured and ready to stretch into a smile, and were not, as in later years, noticeably loose and sensual. If, as most biographers tell us, he gave evidence at Oxford of his gift for repartee and epigram, one would scarcely think so from this example, of which he seemed particularly proud when he related it in a letter to Bouncer: "Now of course Jupp and I are not on speaking terms, but when we were I gave him a great-jar; the Caliban came into Hall beaming and sniggering and said 'I'm very glad they've given the £15 Exhibition to Jones' (put in all the beastly pronunciation for yourself) so I maliciously said 'What! the old Jugger got an Exhibition! very hot indeed.' He was *too sick* and said 'Not likely, I mean Wansbrough Jones,' to which I replied 'I never knew there was such a fellow up here.' Which confined Jupp to his gummy bed for a day and prevented him dining in hall for two days."

It was a very happy, quite conventional trio. Bouncer and Kitten thought Oscar a clever fellow but in no way outlandish, and he was conscious, as he probably had been at Portora and T.C.D., of the admiration he aroused. He worked extremely hard, and though like other undergraduates he pretended to be very casual about reading for his degree, no one ever got a First in Greats without studying for it. From Wilde's letters to the other two one can see that (outwardly at least) he followed all the normal pursuits and described them normally, including a sympathy with the Tractarian Movement, or more vulgarly the

High Churchery which was common enough among undergraduates of his years. From odd remarks in his letters it may be
gathered that both Bouncer and Kitten were at one with him in
this, though they, like Wilde, stopped short before the gates of
Rome. Wilde did go occasionally to St. Aloysius, the Catholic
Church in Oxford, but his attitude to Roman Catholicism is
summed up all too frankly in a letter to Bouncer—"If I *could hope*
that the Church would wake in me some earnestness and purity
I would go over *as a luxury*, if for no better reasons. But I can
hardly hope it would, and to go over to Rome would be to
sacrifice and give up my two great gods 'Money and Ambition'."
Perhaps he laid emphasis on his addiction to shooting and fishing,
but these were real enough as his letters from his fishing lodge in
Connemara plainly show. He never missed a chance to maintain
that he shared his friends' enthusiasm for pretty girls, but he had
none of the affectations of later years, and his letters to Ward are
typical of those sent by undergraduates for half a century after
his time, since the Oxonian's life scarcely changed from the time
of Wilde to that of Compton Mackenzie, or from then to the
Second World War.

The only occasions on which one detects an alien note in his
letters both to Bouncer and Kitten is when he mentions Frank
Miles, and this brings us to the first of Wilde's passionate friendships with another man; one which lasted five years and survived
the two men's living together in two London homes.

5

George Francis Miles was one of those sophisticated queers who
tell women what they should wear, have rather exaggerated good
manners and camp outrageously, preferably among titled people.
He was frivolous and amusing and inherited from his mother
some rather facile artistic gifts which he (at the time he met Wilde)
was already devoting to pastel portraiture, chiefly of famous
beauties and well-known actresses. He was the son of a Church of
England clergyman, the Rev. R. H. W. Miles, Rector of Bingham

in Nottinghamshire, to whom Wilde refers as Dean Miles. He had an assertive mother with whom he painted the windows and frescoed the walls with angels in his father's church. He was the only son among four sisters, 'all very pretty indeed', Wilde said. With that mother and family, Frank could scarcely help being a queer, and very gaily and humorously so he was, a little beam of sunlight in any company.

When he met Wilde in Oxford, Frank was enjoying the friendship and patronage of a certain Lord Ronald Sutherland-Gower, the younger son of the Duke of Sutherland, seven years older than Frank, a mundane and talented man who followed the life of a promiscuous homosexual and shocked more discreet friends by openly whoring after guardsmen and other male prostitutes in the underpaid Services.

It is only in recent years that students of the period have become aware of this. Phyllis Grosskurth,[1] for instance, learned much about Gower from the papers of John Addington Symonds which she had been allowed to examine, and says that Symonds "unlike Wilde and Lord Ronald Gower, the sculptor who served as the original of Lord Henry in The Picture of Dorian Gray, did not seem to find any perverse pleasure in slumming." "Sexual intimacies must always be romanticized or idealized into 'comradeship' or 'adhesiveness', and he was shocked to the core by the defiantly unsentimental approach of Roden Noel and Lord Ronald Gower." 'Gower,' Symonds wrote in his diary, 'saturated the spirit' by his form of promiscuity. "During the last two years of his life," further writes Phyllis Grosskurth of Symonds, "he grew very intimate with Lord Ronald Gower, of whose abandoned sensuality he had never quite approved." Philippe Julian adds in relation to Gower, "Lord Ronald divided his time between visits to country houses, where he searched for archaeological curiosities and ghost stories, and Paris where he had a studio in the Boulevard de Montparnasse. He was a friend of Sarah Bernhardt; the Empress Eugenie and the Prince Imperial were devoted to him. His circle of friends included such distinguished people as Ruskin and Carlyle. To be within easy reach of Oxford, Lord Ronald had rented

[1] Phyllis Grosskurth, John Addington Symonds: A Biography (1964).

a house at Windsor." M. Julian further states that when Wilde was found guilty 'Lord Ronald Gower installed himself with a friend in the South of France", and finally: "The elegant Lord Ronald Gower also came near to public scandal, as he was one of the admirers of the handsome Captain Shackleton (brother of the explorer) who was involved in the theft of jewels of the Order of St Patrick."

Gower was without question one of the most notorious queers in the London society of that period, along with Roden Noel (a son of the Earl of Gainsborough) and Lord Arthur Somerset, who was already exiled by scandal. (The three were, after a fashion, creative. Roden Noel was a poet, Arthur Somerset a composer and Ronald Gower a sculptor, all second-rate.)

Frank Miles had recently been up at Oxford, as his father had been, and brought his friend and patron to the town to pick up undergraduates as a change from the rougher characters of Lord Ronald's usual choice. He met Oscar, who amused him, and thereafter Oscar hitched his wagon to Frank's star, supported as Frank was by Lord Ronald, and Oscar and Frank 'became friends' with no ambiguity at all about the relationship. In later years Oscar seemed to dislike referring to it, and it was only during a sentimental visit of return to Oxford with Bosie Douglas in 1892 that Douglas learned the bare fact that Frank Miles had been his predecessor in Oscar's affections, and thereafter Wilde could not be induced to speak of Miles, perhaps because of his tragic end,[1] from which Wilde would naturally have averted his memory.

Wilde did not desert Bouncer and Kitten. His letters to them made frequent reference to his new friends, and it was only human in Oscar, who was ambitious both professionally and socially, to recognize what Miles, and through him Lord Ronald, and through him his powerful family, could mean to his future. Perhaps a faintly patronizing touch came into his letters to Kitten —"write me a line like a good boy", "I shall not forget you in Rome", "I heard from little Bouncer from Constantinople lately." So Wilde tactlessly rubbed it in, and Bouncer and Kitten, in their

[1] Miles died in an asylum in 1891, nine years after he and Wilde had separated.

nice professional-class provincial homes, must have grown rather sick of hearing about Frank and Ronald. "I found him (Frank Miles) sketching the most lovely and dangerous woman in London —Lady Desart," Wilde wrote to Kitten; and later to Bouncer, "Had afternoon tea with Frank Miles to meet Lord Ronald Gower and his sister the Duchess of Westminster, who is the most fascinating, Circe-like, brilliant woman I have ever met in England."

This sort of talk would eventually break up Oscar's friendship with Kitten, as we shall see, but for the moment the blond boy remained devoted to his fascinating Irish friend. Bouncer quietly ignored all this chatter of duchesses.

We can see from Wilde's letters how great an influence Frank Miles and his patron acquired over him before he eventually decided (after Oxford) to share rooms with Frank in London and to some extent pool ambitions with him. Already during the summer vacation of 1876 he told Kitten that he was going to stay with 'the Mileses' for a week, and did so, remarking in his next letter (from Bingham Rectory, Notts), "We are having a large garden party here today, and tomorrow one at the Duke of Rutland's who is quite close. I make myself as charming as ever and am much admired. Have had some good arguments with Dean Miles who was a great friend of Newman, Pusey and Manning at Oxford and a very advanced Anglican."[1] To Bouncer he repeated his news about the Miles family and added, "As regards worldly matters, we have had some very pleasant garden parties and any amount of lawn tennis. The neighbourhood also boasts of a giant in the shape of the Honourable Lascelles who is sixteen years old and six foot eight in height! He is reading with a Mr Seymour near here, a clergyman (father of young Seymour of Balliol), to go up for *Magdalen*. What an excitement he will cause, but he is not going up for two years, so we won't see him there." A month later Wilde told Kitten that he was waiting in

[1] The present Rector of Bingham, the Rev. David Keene, writes that Frank's frescoes on the walls of Bingham Church do not remain, and adds: "Rumours of the gay life at the Rectory in Canon Miles' day still persist—that Oscar Wilde, Lillie Langtry and even the then Prince of Wales stayed there."

Dublin for Frank Miles and that they would go down to Galway together. After ten days he wrote from Moytura House, Cong, County Mayo:

Frank Miles and I came down here last week, and have had a very royal time of it sailing. We are at the top of Lough Corrib, which if you refer to your geography you will find to be a lake thirty miles long, ten broad and situated in the most romantic scenery in Ireland. Frank has done some wonderful sunsets since he came down; he has given me some more of his drawings . . . Frank has never fired off a gun in his life (and says he doesn't want to) but as our proper sporting season here does not begin till September I have not taught him anything. But on Friday we go into Connemara to make him land a salmon and kill a brace of grouse.

This visit with Frank to Moytura House and later to Illaunroe, the fishing lodge on Lough Fee which Sir William Wilde had purchased and restored, must have been memorable to the two young men. Moytura was, as it is today, a fairly large house of nondescript architecture set amid spectacular views of mountains and the lake which is less than half a mile away. Sir William had completed it ten years earlier as an inscription, 'W.W. 1865', shows, and it stood—status symbol of so many country houses in Ireland—at the end of an avenue of three-quarters of a mile which divides it from the Cong road.

The journey from Dublin was not a swift or easy one and Oscar and Frank must have gone by train to Galway and then by pony trap (two-and-a-half hours) to Moytura or caught the little steamer which made its way in four hours to Derry Quay on Lough Corrib. When it was time for them to go on to Illaunroe Lodge, another pony trap must have taken them through Cong and Cornamona to the little isthmus on Lough Fee on which the house was built. They certainly passed through what Oscar called some of 'the most romantic scenery in Ireland' with the Maamturk mountains and the Twelve Pins ahead of them as they drove on that August day nearly a century ago, and their stay at Illaunroe must have been an affectionate adventure, alone as they were in the house with the lake behind it and before, and their youth and mutual attraction to make the hours pass.

In Frank's protestation that he had never fired a gun in his life and did not want to, there may have been a touch of girlishness or camp, but Oscar in his letters spoke with manly pride of his exploits. "I have been too much occupied with rod and gun for the handling of the quill (neat and Pope-like?). I have only got one salmon as yet but have had heaps of sea-trout which give great play. I have not had a blank day yet. Grouse are few but I have got a lot of hares so have had a capital time of it."

Wilde also wrote from Illaunroe Lodge: "I hope next year that you and Kitten will come and stay a (lunar) month with me. I am sure you will like this wild and mountainous country, close to the Atlantic and teeming with sport of all kinds. It is in every way magnificent." "Frank", added Wilde, "is delighted with it all."

This is attested by a mural with which Frank adorned the wall of the entrance hall of Illaunroe Lodge. As he had adorned the walls of Bingham church with frescoed angels, he now painted two naked cherubs in the same style, one on each side of the archway facing the front door, and wrote the title under them— TIGHT LINES. They are angling; one is cheerfully rejoicing in his catch, the other is in despair. And there I found them ninety-five years later, their authorship unknown to the many succeeding occupants of the lodge which is now hidden in thick growths of ponticum rhododendrons so that its name, Illaunroe, 'the red island', seems pointless today when the autumn tints no longer make it a russet patch on the lake's surface. So little has been recorded of Frank Miles that this relic of his occupation of the house with Oscar, so characteristic of his facile pretty work, of his pale crayon portraits of Lily Langtry and others (few of which survive), seems an almost defiant assertion of his existence and the chattering love that was between Oscar and him.

Oscar returned to Galway only once during the rest of his life; that was in the August of the following year when he stayed at Illaunroe with two undergraduates whom he found at a nearby fishing lodge which they had rented for July. He took no interest in Moytura House for the next twenty years and only seems to have remembered it when Willie Wilde, on whom it was entailed, died two years after Wilde's discharge from prison. "I don't know what position I hold about this absurd Irish property," he wrote to Robert Ross and asked whether, as a bankrupt, he could obtain any benefit from it. As for Illaunroe, Sir William Wilde's illegitimate son had inherited it, and it should have reverted to Oscar after his death, but Dr Henry Wilson had struck Oscar out of his will for fear that Oscar was becoming a Catholic.

6

After his stay with Frank in Galway, Oscar continued to write of him to his other friends. To Bouncer: "I may be down in Bristol with Frank Miles as I want to see S. Raphael's and the picture at Clevedon . . . I have given up my pilgrimage to Rome for the present: Ronald Gower and Frank Miles were coming: (we would have been a great Trinity) but at the last hour Ronald couldn't get time, so I am staying in Dublin till the 20th."

During the following May Wilde wrote to Kitten: "I had a delightful time in town with Frank Miles and a lot of friends." In July of that year (1878) he planned, as how many under-graduates have planned before and since, to row 'up the river to town', needless to say with Frank Miles. Bouncer can scarcely have taken seriously the afterthought invitation, 'Will you come?' The trip so far as it went was apparently a success. He told Bouncer, "I rowed to Pangbourne with Frank Miles in a birch-bark canoe! and shot rapids and did wonders everywhere—it was delightful."

But before this, in December 1876, was another episode which suggests that Oscar had already begun to show off his attractive young friends to older, possibly jealous ones, a weakness which was to cause him much trouble in future years. "I have taken a great fancy to May, he is quite charming in every way and a beautiful artist. He dined with me last night and we went to see

Henry Irving in *Macbeth*. I enjoyed it of course immensely."
Earlier in the same letter to Kitten he says, "I have been having a
delightful time here; any amount of theatres and dining out. On
Thursday I brought young May down to Windsor and we had a
delightful day with Ronald Gower who has got a new house there
(one of the most beautiful houses I ever saw). He brought us to
St George's Chapel for afternoon service and I did not like the
singing so well as our own." Bouncer is told much the same: "I
had a charming day at Windsor with Ronald Gower. I brought
Arthur May with me and have not enjoyed myself so much for
years. We went to St George's Chapel for evening service after
lunch, and just got up in time to hear the *Creation* at the Albert
Hall. I saw a great deal of Arthur May; he is quite charming in
every way and we have rushed into friendship."

Nothing more is heard of Arthur May. Wilde may not have
seen him again or there may have been further meetings but no
letters preserved. Or perhaps—who knows?—Ronald Gower, with
more skill and experience than Wilde, may have appropriated
him. The interesting fact is that Wilde, so soon after making the
acquaintance of the attractive Arthur May, made a point of
exhibiting him to the far more adept Gower, either to rouse his
jealousy or to pander to him. This was very homosexual of Wilde.
Such introductions with such motives are frequently being made
to this day.

As evidence of the part played by Gower in Wilde's undergraduate life, something of his later days can be gathered from
Phyllis Grosskurth's remarks already quoted and from a book
called *Vicious Circle* by Francis Bamford and Viola Bankes, also
from his own *Old Diaries 1881–1901* (1902). From the first of these
we learn that at sixty-two years of age in the year 1907 he suffered
from an attack of epilepsy and retired to a house called Hammer-
field near Penshurst with his young friend Frank Hird, whom he
had found in Rome and legally adopted. From *Old Diaries*,
written with a great deal of snobbish deference to his relations and
friends and of exaggerated discretion in other matters, we learn
that Symonds, in Venice, was always with his faithful gondolier
Angelo, 'a fine rough rather hulky-looking Venetian who follows

him like a shadow'. But throughout Gower's book there is no mention of the young undergraduate whom he had met through Frank Miles, the (by then) notorious Oscar Wilde, and Gower joins a number of men and women who, when they came to write their memoirs after Wilde's downfall, discovered that they had never had more than a slight acquaintance with him, not really worth mentioning, or had always disliked and distrusted him, or had completely forgotten him. They far out-number those many autobiographers who 'happened to be present' when Wilde spoke one of his epigrams, or who had been told by some distinguished third party of an occasion when Wilde displayed his brilliance. Authentic stories about Wilde, told without sniggering or self-importance, are extremely rare. Hesketh Pearson, although we owe him much for preserving so many of them from such widely different sources, was far too credulous and accepted any anecdote that he found amusing.

So we begin to get a picture of Oscar Wilde the Oxonian, a far more many-sided young man than we might have supposed from popular portraits. When the whole blue-china myth has been swept away, we see his 'aestheticism' as no more than one of the modish labels of the day, like 'advanced Anglicanism', both of which he cultivated. He was much more of a scholar than his biographers allowed, perhaps because few of them could claim to be anything of the sort, and certainly much more of a sportsman. His pleasure in life in Galway and Connemara, his boasting about his catch whenever he stayed there, have nothing artificial or cultivated about them, and the fact that, so far as we know, he never shot a hare or landed a salmon during the rest of his life does nothing to blur the picture of Oscar as an undergraduate in sporty tweeds travelling all day to reach Galway and driving a pony trap for hours under the mountains to find Illaunroe Lodge on its isthmus in the lake.

Only one letter from Oscar Wilde to his father has been preserved, a long impersonal travelogue posted from Florence on 15 June 1875. It seems to have been written for publication and addressed to Sir William Wilde as an afterthought. But at its end there are a few words of personal interest. "Hope Abbotstown will turn out well. It certainly spoiled the look of the place, and that terrible large ditch between us and it will, I suppose, be bridged over. Yours ever truly affectionately."

The Abbotstown which Wilde refers to was an overgrown ruin which stood in the very large grounds of Moytura House. Its history must have been known to Oscar. After the suppression of the Abbey of Cong in 1542, the Cross of Cong, a famous and beautiful piece of work which was made for Turlach O'Connor, the last king of Ireland, and contained a portion of the True Cross, was kept in the possession of the Lord Abbot, who lived at Abbotstown and ministered as parish priest. His successors in this office continued till the death of the last of them, Father Patrick Prendergast, at Abbotstown in 1829. Thereafter the house fell into decay and the famous processional cross was transferred to Dublin Museum, where it remains.

Wilde's reference may have indicated that Sir William intended to restore Abbotstown, (as an archaeologist he would have wished to do so); it also suggests that Wilde took an interest in his father's country home in Galway, which we know he was to visit more than once in the next years, though his father died less than a year later.

Oscar was not a graceful figure, rather gauche in fact, even clumsy in his movements. He had then and thereafter a somewhat muddy complexion. But he had charm, and it seemed to his friends to compensate fully for his awkwardness and unusual and not very attractive appearance. He could out-talk them all in his rich syrupy voice with its Irish intonations, while compared with the healthy young products of the English public schools he was sophisticated and knowledgeable, altogether considered rather a remarkable fellow and in a mild way a 'character'. That he had already learned from Miles and Gower something of the humour and scandal and vivid vocabulary of the homosexual underworld was not known in his college, even to Kitten or Bouncer, for to Oscar, as to most young men when they first hear of that underworld, it seems bizarre, even comic, a subject for esoteric conversation to be exchanged with a few adventurers, an improbable if seductive aspect of the life which awaited him after Oxford.

Meanwhile he worked hard for his degree and played his part in helping to entertain and charm the parents and sisters of Kitten and Bouncer when they visited Oxford.

Later, when he lectured in America, he made a great deal of his association with John Ruskin who was at that time Slade Professor of Art. Hesketh Pearson thinks he may have been among those who assisted in Ruskin's disastrous attempts at road-making, but this picturesque supposition is highly improbable,[1] and when ten years later Wilde wrote Ruskin one of the gushing letters he addressed to eminent men, enclosing a copy of his first professionally published book *The Happy Prince and Other Tales*, one does not feel from the terms he used that Ruskin had influenced him in any significant way. Wilde, in fact, wrote to J. M. Stoddart, an American publisher, that his preface for Rennell Rodd's poems was most important "signifying my new departure from Mr Ruskin and the Pre-Raphaelites", somewhat pretentious words to use of a short preface to another man's book. He may, like other undergraduates interested in artistic matters, have had walks and talks with Ruskin but these were certainly not, as he claimed in his letter to the Slade Professor, 'the dearest memories of my Oxford days'.

Walter Pater, Fellow and Tutor of Brasenose College and author of *Studies in the History of the Renaissance*, paid far more attention to young Wilde, though not perhaps so much as he paid to the football- and cricket-playing undergraduates for whom he gave lunches, those 'simple good-looking youths of the sporting fraternity' whom William Rothenstein noticed in his rooms when he was sketching him. Pater was a highly interesting figure, secretive and paradoxical. If, like John Addington Symonds, he had left an introspective and self-revealing journal, it would be one of the books most worth reading of its time. Only a man of intense feeling, of emotions that writhed out of sight, could have written *Marius the Epicurean*, yet even those who knew him best thought Pater, particularly in his later years, a dull stick, a shifty-eyed reticent scholar who had no words to waste on mere

---

[1] Wilde boasted of his roadmaking efforts in one of his American lectures. But in that he only did what was expected of him.

conversation. They proposed facile explanations for his dreary isolation—his ugliness, his parsimony, his self-dedication to scholarship. Scarcely a word he spoke has been recorded, and such anecdotes as there are stress nothing but his reserve. He was not even a misanthrope with a spirited hatred for mankind who shut himself away; on the contrary, he seems to have been willing to receive those who wanted to see him, though without much graciousness. He lectured conscientiously, but when his students sought in private to provoke or persuade him to reveal at least some spark from the embers they suspected to exist, they were repulsed, and his admirers received courteous, chilly answers to their enquiries. Yet this was the man who had taught them to burn always with a hard gem-like flame.

That he encouraged Oscar in his first literary efforts, or what Oscar told Bouncer was his 'first art-essay', can be seen from the following letter:

Dear Mr. Wilde, Accept my best thanks for the magazine and your letter. Your excellent article on the Grosvenor Gallery I read with very great pleasure: it makes me much wish to make your acquaintance, and I hope you will give me an early call on your return to Oxford. I should much like to talk over some of the points with you, though on the whole I think your criticisms very just, and they are certainly very pleasantly expressed. The article shows that you possess some beautiful, and, for your age, quite exceptionally cultivated tastes: and a considerable knowledge too of many beautiful things. I hope you will write a great deal in time to come. Very truly yours, Walter Pater.

The terms used were sufficient to let Harris invent his whole ridiculous story about Pater and Wilde.[1] But Oscar certainly did value Pater's praise and took the trouble to copy out his letter rather than trust the original of it to the post when he wanted to

[1] See, if you think it worth while, Harris's *Oscar Wilde: His Life and Confessions* (1915).

send it to Bouncer. Whether the man himself meant much to Wilde is doubtful; his work certainly impressed him at this time, and he wrote in prison of 'Pater's *Renaissance*—that book which has had such a strange influence over my life.' He kept in touch with Pater after coming down and took Bosie Douglas to call on him when the two spent a week-end in Oxford. But Wilde as an undergraduate was far too much of an extrovert to try, as others had done and failed, to probe behind Pater's nervous façade.

8

In April 1877 Wilde went with Mahaffy, his former Tutor at T.C.D., to Mykenae and Athens, having written from Corfu to his Tutor at Magdalen, Rev. H. R. Bramley, to warn him that he might miss ten days at the beginning of term ('Seeing Greece is really a great education for anyone').

Whether or not he was educated by his visit to Greece there is nothing to tell us, for though he spoke throughout his life of Grecian culture as a synonym for all that was beautiful, and called Bosie 'so Greek and gracious', he does not seem to have described his emotions at the sight of Athens. All we have is a photograph of Oscar dressed, like so many visiting queers, in Greek drag, including the pleated skirt, ornamental boots and cap with a foot-long tassel. This is reproduced in Vyvyan Holland's *Oscar Wilde, A Pictorial Record* (1960). It would be interesting to me (since I have that kind of mind) to know who lent him the costume and whether Mahaffy knew about the photograph. In the meantime, amid so much solemn talk of Oscar being 'absorbed in the Greek ideals of beauty' when he visited the Acropolis, this little snapshot seems to have reality and humour. Wilde would think so, too. He was perhaps vain, but he was not a prig.

In returning to England, he 'took Rome in on his way back' as he had promised Kitten. There he met Bouncer and Dunskie (Hunter-Blair), also Julia Constance Fletcher (1858–1938) who wrote novels under the name of George Fleming.

For those who delight in coincidences and reflexions on the smallness of the world, it may be remarked that one of the friends with whom Wilde passed several days in Rome was a certain Hartwell de la Garde Grissell, a somewhat religious queer who, like other English Catholics of good family, had been appointed a Chamberlain of Honour to the Pope. Oscar mentioned him at this time in a letter to Bouncer. He seems to have remained in Rome throughout several decades until Oscar returned in the last year of his life and found Grissell still there and given to furtive contacts in public lavatories. He had that holier-than-thou attitude not unhappily infrequent in those homosexual Christians who become unnaturally devoted to rites and ceremonies. He tried to intimidate Oscar, who with a characteristic mixture of sincerity and flippancy reported to Ross that he had received a Papal blessing on a number of occasions. Grissell apparently protested at this. "I am horrified at what you tell me about Grissell: its impertinence, its coarseness, its lack of imagination: I should really write to him if I were you. He who seven times sought and seven times received the blessing of the Holy Father is not to be excommunicated on postcards by the withered eunuch of the Vatican Latrines. (By 'He' I mean myself.)"

Oscar reached Oxford a month late and was rusticated for the rest of the term and fined £47 10s. which made him write to Kitten about 'the wretched stupidity of our college dons'.

9

Wilde enjoyed no special popularity and his friends belonged to much the same set as Bouncer and Kitten, pleasant young men, mostly of the upper classes, who came from public schools and wealthy homes and were bound for undistinguished but satisfactory careers. There were the Peyton brothers Algy and Tom, the first of whom would inherit his father's baronetcy, the second become a Canon of Ely. There was Nicholas 'Julia' Tindal with whom Wilde stayed in London—he afterwards became a barrister

—and John Burton 'Jack' Barrow who was also called to the Bar. David Hunter-Blair was a rather more intimate friend who enjoyed the nickname Dunskie, from the name of his father's Irish estate. He was a convert to Catholicism and afterwards became Abbot of Fort Augustus. He encouraged Oscar's interest in the idea of conversion at that time, and persuaded him to hear Cardinal Manning and seek an interview with Newman, but achieved no more. Perhaps a late sequel to Hunter-Blair's efforts came in Wilde's thrill at seeing the Pope seven times when he was in Rome in the last year of his life.

Other friends were 'Hammond', R. S. B. Hammond-Chambers and 'Gussy', probably—as Hart-Davis says—Cresswell Augustus Cresswell, like all the rest a Magdalen undergraduate. Oscar slyly notes the arrival of others: "Some rather good demies have come up this term, Fletcher an Eton fellow, and Armitage, who has the most Greek face I ever saw, and Broadbent." This was to Bouncer; to Kitten he said more confidentially, "The freshmen *in it* are Gore, a great pal of Tom Peyton's lot, Grey a nice Eton boy—and we have all suddenly woke to the idea that Wharton is charming. I like him very much indeed and ran him in for the Apollo lately." But no one took the place of Bouncer and Kitten and they remained loyal to one another even after Bouncer (the first to go down) left the other two in 1876. On this occasion Wilde and Kitten joined to buy him an inscribed ring, of which Hart-Davis says that it "is now in Magdalen Library. It is a thick gold band in the form of a buckled strap engraved on the outside Μνημόσυνον Φιλίας αντίφιλοντὶ φίλοι which can be roughly translated 'A memento of friendship, from two friends to a third', and on the inside 'O.F.F.W. & R.R.H. to W.W.W. 1876'."

Perhaps among these friends should be mentioned a girl Wilde knew during vacations in Ireland, Florence Balcombe. She was a neighbour in Dublin and far too shrewd to take Oscar seriously when he obviously only wanted a pretty girl to boast about to his friends and, when she became engaged to Bram 'Dracula' Stoker, to part from with quite sick-making old-style-melodrama letters. Later when he knew Ellen Terry, and when Bram Stoker had become business manager of the Lyceum Theatre and Florence was in the company, Wilde wrote a letter which, like most of his attempts on paper to be tragically emotional, is exceedingly funny. It is addressed to 'My dear Nellie'. "I send you some flowers—two crowns. Will you accept one of them, whichever you think will suit you best. The other—don't think me treacherous, Nellie—but the other please give to Florrie *from yourself*. I should like to think that she was wearing something of mine the first night she comes on the stage, that anything of mine should touch her. Of course if you think—but you won't think she will suspect? How could she? She thinks I never loved her, thinks I forget. My God how could I!" This was three years after he had written to Florrie: "We stand apart now, but the little cross will serve to remind me of the bygone days, and though we shall never meet again, after I leave Ireland, still I shall always remember you at prayer. Adieu and God bless you."

We have already seen how Wilde's friendship with Bouncer faded into the light of common day; that with the Kitten was more unfortunate. In the first year or two after coming down from Oxford, Wilde, who had joined a club—the St Stephens on Victoria Embankment, quite an expensive institution of which membership cost Wilde £42—wrote to Kitten from there addressing him as 'dear Reggie'. His letter sounds rather grand and has a touch of impatience with what Oscar may have seen as an immature and bourgeois relationship. It certainly suggests that Wilde was aware of his new status as a man about town. "I was only in Cambridge for the night with Oscar Browning[1] (I wish he was *not* called Oscar) and left the next morning for the Hicks-Beach's in Hampshire, to kill time and pheasants and the *ennui* of not having set the world quite on fire as yet. I will come some day and stay with you, though your letters are rather what boys call 'Philippic'. I am going tonight with *Ruskin* to see Irving as Shylock, and afterwards to the *Millais* Ball. How odd it is. Dear Reg, ever yours, Oscar. Remember me to Tom Peyton."

The Kitten, never a very industrious correspondent, felt that someone who answered what may have been a pressing invitation

---

[1] A well known homosexual of the time whose career is sketched in my *Feasting with Panthers* (1967).

c

to Devonshire with a promise so casual, 'I will come some day and stay with you', was scarcely worth the effort necessary for keeping in touch, so relations between the two of them unhappily lapsed and were never resumed.

THREE

Sharing Rooms in London

Lord Ronald was not interested in Frank Miles solely for his looks but because he was such a gay and amusing creature. The easily bored Gower was quite ready to spend money on him, take him about—it will be remembered that Ronald and Frank planned to take Oscar with them to Rome in 1876—and introduce him to relatives and useful friends. But Frank's dominating mother disapproved of the situation without fully understanding it and insisted on his working seriously at his profession. So Frank and Oscar decided to join forces and took rooms in Salisbury Street, at a house called Thames House; 'untidy and romantic' Oscar considered it.

This arrangement was very much in the tradition of the time—the shared 'cribs' of Du Maurier's characters and the Pre-Raphaelites. But Frank and Oscar, conscious of their social as well as their artistic ambitions, demanded something far more elegant than the studios of bearded bohemians, and meant to make their rooms a meeting-place for famous people, chiefly women whom Frank would paint and Oscar flatter with sonnets. The rooms they found were suitable for the ambitious scheme; they had a very large sitting-room, panelled in white, on the first floor and their bedrooms were above it. The house belonged to or was rented by a pleasant family who lived on the ground floor and provided them with breakfast which was brought up to their rooms by a fifteen-year-old Christ's Hospital (Blue-Coat School) boy. At five o'clock or so, the two young men prepared their studio to entertain carefully chosen guests for afternoon tea, and when they had persuaded a number of famous actresses and artists' wives and a few of Lord Ronald's circle to attend these informal 'at homes', they really thought they were getting somewhere.

Perhaps they were. Attracted either by Frank's portraiture, or Oscar's wordy adulation, some very well-known and much-courted women became frequent visitors at 13 Salisbury Street, perhaps the greatest triumph of the two young men being the beautiful Mrs Langtry, the Jersey Lily, of whom Frank did many portraits and to whom Oscar wrote a sonnet *The New Helen*, which appeared in the London magazine *Time*. But there were others, Ellen Terry, Mrs Alfred Hunt, the original of Tennyson's 'Margaret', and her daughter Violet who was to be known to another literary generation, Genevieve Ward, Mrs Bancroft, Lady Lonsdale. It was small wonder that Oscar felt able to invite men to 'tea and beauties at five-thirty'.

Oscar's mother was usually promised to the guests and referred to as 'Mamma' or 'Lady Wilde' according to the occasion. Oscar was evidently proud of her at this time and spoke of her with pride to the end, though she never appeared at his home in Tite Street. In *De Profundis* he rather wistfully claimed for her that 'intellectually she ranked with Elizabeth Barrett Browning and historically with Madame Rolland'. "Any Saturday you are in London", he wrote in 1879 to Harold Boulton, a friend who had edited *Waifs and Strays* at Oxford, "I hope you will call and see my mother who is always at home from five to seven on Saturday. She is always glad to see my friends, and usually some good literary and artistic people take tea with her. Her address is Lady Wilde, 1 Ovington Square, S. Kensington."

"I send you a—rather soiled—copy of my mother's pamphlet," he told James Knowles the editor of the *Nineteenth Century*. "You probably know my mother's name as the 'Speranza' of the *Nation* newspaper in 1848. I don't think that age has dimmed the fire and enthusiasm of that pen which set the young Irelanders in a blaze. I should like so much to have the privilege of introducing you to my mother—all brilliant people should cross each other's cycles, like some of the nicest planets. In any case I am glad to be able to send you the article. It is part of the thought of the nineteenth century, and will I hope interest you."

Wilde still had a small share of his patrimony and the joint establishment in Salisbury Street seemed to promise a great future. He and Frank worked hard at entertainment, and Oscar had a few copies printed of an excruciatingly bad melodrama he had written called *Vera or The Nihilists* and sent them to Madame Modjeska, the Polish actress just then starring in a version of *La Dame aux Camélias*, and to Ellen Terry. To the last-named he wrote: "Perhaps some day I shall be fortunate enough to write something worthy of your playing." But he certainly could offer nothing then and began to grow impatient for success.

Tea-parties and chit-chat might produce commissions and popularity for Frank Miles, but for Oscar there was no more than congratulation on his being a successful host to a number of lovely women and his vague reputation for cleverness and aestheticism. His brother Willie on the *World* newspaper did what he could to boost Oscar in both capacities, but as yet there was very little to boost.

2

So Oscar, like other young men trying to break their way into literature, wrote a great many poems and posted them off to a great many editors. 'Mr Oscar Wilde begs to enclose a sonnet for the approval of the Editor of *Macmillan's Magazine*'—this was one of his unsuccessful approaches, but a few were not sent back, and when Oscar got a bite he knew how to follow up the editorial acceptance with flattery. Thus Clement Scott, who was editing *The Green Room*, a supplement to *Routledge's Christmas Annual* for which Oscar's 'translation' of a Polish poem by Helena Modjeska had been accepted, was told:

Your letter has given me very great pleasure: whatever beauty is in the poem is due to the graceful fancy and passionate artistic nature of Madame Modjeska. I am really only the reed through which her sweet notes have been blown: yet slight as my own work has been, and of necessity hasty, I thank you very much for your praise, praise really welcome, and giving me much encouragement, as coming from a real critic.

Your own poems I know very well. You dare to do, what I hardly dare, to sing of the passion and joy and sorrow of the lives of the men and women among whom we live, and of the world which is the world of all of us.

When I read your poem some weeks ago on the clerks, I remember thinking of the praise Wordsworth gave to Burns for having shown how 'Verse may build itself a princely throne on humble truth'. For my own part I fear I too often 'trundle back my soul five hundred years', as Aurora Leigh says, and find myself more at home in the woods of Colonus or the glades of Arcady than I do in this little fiery-coloured world of ours. I envy you your strength. I have not got it.

Altogether Oscar succeeded in storming ten editorial fortresses with his offers of poetry during his two years in London, though a glance at some of his lines today is embarrassing. 'Fair as Sebastian and as early slain,' he apostrophizes Keats, writing on *The Grave of Keats* in the *Burlington*, while *Pan* accepted his villanelle about 'the Goat-foot God of Arcady'. *Time* featured *The Conqueror of Times*, 'The woes of man may serve an idle day,' and the *World* published Oscar's sonnet to Sarah Bernhardt ending with 'The loveless lips with which men kiss in hell.'

The rest of his successes were with Dublin papers—in the *Illustrated Monitor* a sonnet *Urbs Sacra Aeterna* 'O Rome what sights and changes hast thou seen!'; in the *Dublin University Magazine*, *A Chorus of Cloud Maidens* 'And the sun in the sky never wearies of spreading his bright rays around', *The Irish Monthly* had *Lotus*—

> Not so; such idle dreams belong
> To souls of lesser depths than mine;
> I feel that I am half divine;
> I know that I am great and strong.

This brought him a parody from *Punch*, his first attention in that paper, 'by Oscuro Wildegoose'.

Then in *Kotobos*, the T.C.D. paper, appeared *The Rose of Love* with the stanza

> O twining hands! O delicate
>   Fair body made for love and pain;
> O House of love! O desolate
>   White lily, overdrenched with rain!

While Wilde was still at Oxford in 1875 he had published *Graffiti d'Italia* with his recognition of the Pope

> O joy to see before I die
>   The only God-anointed King,
>   And hear the silver trumpets ring
> A triumph as (h)He passeth by.

The Pope was also recognized, but not quite so dutifully, in the sonnet *Easter Day* which Wilde contributed to Harold Boulton's *Waifs and Strays*

> Priest-like he wore a robe more white than foam,
>   And king-like swathed himself in Nero's red;
>   Three crowns of gold rose high above his head:
> In splendour and in light the Pope passed home.
>
> My heart stole back across wide wastes of years
>   To One who wandered by a lonely sea,
> And sought in vain for any place of rest.
>   Foxes have holes, and every bird its nest,
>   I, only I, must travel wearily,
>   And bruise my feet, and drink wine salt with tears.

If it may seem that Wilde, both as a poet and host, was given to trimming his sails, it must be remembered that scarcely a writer, from Shakespeare onwards, had not in his youth done much the same.

It did not make for much success. Edmund Yates, the editor of the *World*, wrote to Willie Wilde: "I wish you would put me *en rapport* with your brother the Newdigate man, of whom I hear so much and so favourably," but 'the Newdigate man', as he told Kitten, had not 'set the world quite on fire as yet.'

3

Verses at a guinea, or sometimes less, in semi-amateur publications were not very profitable and Frank Miles was too much of a playboy to work over-industriously himself or persuade Oscar to work. The two decided to look for cheaper and perhaps less centrally situated rooms, and they found these at Number One, Tite Street. Since a Miss Elizabeth Skeates had once lived here and the house was called after her, Wilde ingeniously named it Keats House, and printed the words at the head of his notepaper.

Soon after they moved in, Frank got into trouble through some indiscretion in his nocturnal wanderings, and an attempt was made to arrest him. The incident has been hopelessly misunderstood and distorted, Sherard even supposing Frank's vice was small girls so that he could, Sherard told Hesketh Pearson, 'have shaken hands on a common taste with Victor Hugo'. Poor Sherard simply could not believe such a thing as homosexuality existed outside lunatic asylums. There are further absurd elaborations—Wilde holding the door against 'three six-footers, experts in the removal of obstacles', till Frank escaped over the roof, and so on. But in spite of these, proofs of Sherard's ability to make a few paragraphs out of anything, there does seem to have been some basis for the story and it is, after all, a likely one remembering Frank's habits of cruising the West End with Ronald Gower.

Oscar was more discreet. Now and for the next six or seven years, he looked for sentimental attachments with actors, undergraduates, gentlemanly and not too effeminate queers, and was either too cautious or too unaware of his true nature to look for 'rough trade', the sort of youths whom Gower and Miles picked up in the bars. Later he was to realize himself and develop this side of his nature, but at Salisbury Street and afterwards in Tite Street, his contacts were with more or less cultured young men like Harold Boulton and—a new friend—Norman Forbes-Robertson.

With the last of these, the younger brother of Johnston Forbes-Robertson, Wilde's friendship started with a bang—"I don't know if I bored you the other night with my life and its troubles. There seems something so sympathetic and gentle about your nature, and you have been so charming whenever I have seen you, that I felt somehow that although I knew you only a short time, yet that still I could talk to you about things, which I only talk of to people whom I like—to those whom I count my friends. If you will let me count *you* as one of my friends, it would give a new pleasure to my life." It continued till 1890 when Norman went into management and asked Oscar for a play, already half-promised. Oscar was at the height of his success and brought an end to the friendship, much as he had done to that with Kitten, by refusing to collaborate and adding some rather haughty advice: "Speaking quite generally, I think that as a manager you will find it good economic policy to pay a good price for good plays: the play is always 'the thing'. Everything else is nothing."

But before this happened in 1890 Oscar wrote Norman a number of amusing and affectionate letters, including some from the United States during his lecture tour. "Here from the uttermost end of the great world I send you love and greetings, and thanks for your letters which delight me very much. But, dear boy, your hair will lose its gold and your cheek its roses if you insist on being such a chivalrous defender of this much abused young man. It is so brave and good of you." In 1886 Oscar showed by a letter full of rather bitchy nonsense that Norman was in with Raffalovich and his crowd and in sympathy with Oscar in his moods of outrageous camp. "I will dine with pleasure with Stephen Coleridge on Sunday. Will you tell him so? How agitated little André was last night! His introducing Eric to Frankie[1] was a masterpiece. . . . Augusta's party was a great success, but there was a virgin of some ninety winters who hid haggard blushes behind a tattered fan! She was quite dreadful, and must not be asked again." Altogether we are justified in adding Norman to the company of charming young men Oscar cultivated at this time, predecessors of Bosie and Ross.

4

At Keats House, Oscar decided to pay for the publication of a book of verse as many other poets, keen to start somewhere on the road to fame, have done and do today, among them several of those with a great future and others whose beautifully printed collections have emerged shyly and never been heard of again. He wrote to a publisher named David Bogue, who issued books on commission and had done so for Samuel Butler, amongst others. (Wilde was not lucky in his publishers. Both Elkin Mathews and John Lane did rather worse than pass by on the other side when his trial came, and David Bogue, like Leonard Smithers, later went bankrupt and committed suicide.) "I am anxious to publish a volume of poems immediately," wrote Wilde in May 1881, "and should like to enter into a treaty with your house about it. I can forward you the manuscript on hearing that you will begin negotiations. Possibly my name requires no introduction." Within the month a contract had been signed whereby Wilde undertook the expense of printing 750 copies which were to be issued in three 'editions' of 250 each; further 500 copies were printed in the next year of which 220 remained to be re-issued in a new binding by Matthews and Lane ten years later. So that it can be said that Wilde got rid of, by sale or gift, about a thousand copies of his *Poems*, which was no small achievement, even though, having printed his work to advertise himself, he made a very lavish distribution of free copies.

In Hart-Davis's edition of Wilde's *Letters* are a number that he

[1] I.e. Eric Forbes-Robertson to his sister Frances.

wrote to accompany copies of this book, and we find that like other young writers he sent it with eulogistic phrases to poets and politicians. To Robert Browning: "Will you accept from me the first copy of my poems—the only tribute I can offer you for the delight and the wonder which the strength and splendour of your work has given me from my boyhood." To Matthew Arnold: "Will you accept from me my first volume of poems . . . of the constant source of joy and wonder that your beautiful work was to all of us at Oxford . . . for I have only now, too late perhaps, found out how all art requires solitude as its companion, only now indeed know the splendid difficulty of this great art in which you are a master illustrious and supreme." To W. E. Gladstone: "Will you do me the honour of accepting my first volume of poems—as a very small token of my deep admiration and loyalty to one who has always loved what is noble and beautiful and true in life and art, and is the mirror of the Greek ideal of statesman."

One need not be cynical to suppose that there were a great many more recipients of such letters, besides copies sent to potential reviewers like Oscar Browning and Bouncer—'a review in a Bristol paper might cause a sale in that lovely old town.'

Wilde seems to have been fairly successful. Reviews appeared in *Academy*, *Athenaeum*, *Lady's Pictorial*, *Punch*, *Saturday Review* and *World*, a fair bag. At least in London and Oxford circles Wilde was becoming known, though not so well or for the reasons which some of his biographers have supposed.

The great mistake of these, in over-estimating Wilde's reputation at that time, is to suppose that in several *Punch* jokes or F. C. Burnand's play *The Colonel* or in Scott Ramsay's *Where's the Cat?* or in *The Charlatan*, a caricature depicted was specifically that of Wilde. It was not. Wilde was emerging as *an* aesthete, yes, but he was not *the* Aesthete. Du Maurier's drawing and joke about living up to blue china were not directed at Wilde but at the anonymous long-haired aesthete of the time, a much derided figure in the *Punch* humour of the '80s. Wilde was elegant in appearance but not outrageous, he was effusively witty with women but not yet a famous epigrammatist, interested almost exclusively in his own sex but not, even in London, notorious.

He worked hard in 1881, not only to promote his *Poems*, but to secure a production for his play *Vera or the Nihilists*. We have seen how he sent this to Ellen Terry and it seems certain that he offered it wherever he saw a possibility—certainly to Clara Morris, an American actress, and to Herman Vezin (who also gave Wilde lessons in elocution). At one time it looked as though it was going to be produced (on 17 December 1881) at least for a morning performance at the Adelphi Theatre, with Mrs Bernard Beere in the principal part. But three weeks before the date it was cancelled, supposedly, but not probably, owing to the assassination of the Czar Alexander II which had happened as long ago as the previous March.

Oscar's disappointment was tempered by a new and promising prospect which had just been opened to him. He had been offered the chance of a lecture tour in the United States.

5

In preparation for this, and not because of an imagined quarrel between Oscar and Frank Miles, Oscar prepared to leave Keats House and did so shortly before he sailed for New York on Christmas Eve. It would not have been surprising if the two had quarrelled, for they had lived together for more than two years and the arrangement for young men of their temperaments cannot have been without strains and stresses. Poor Frank died ten years later, having spent the last four years of his life in an asylum. With Ronald Gower, Oscar remained on friendly terms and in 1888 went down to Stratford-on-Avon to propose his health when Ronald's statue of Shakespeare was unveiled in the gardens of the Memorial Theatre.

FOUR

On Show in America

Perhaps no episode in Wilde's life has been so plastered with legends and improbabilities as his tour in America. Wilde's whole life was improbable, and it is a pity that his most sensational achievements have been lost to view behind a mass of silly anecdotes, crudely invented scenes and impossible reports. Here, for instance, he had one of his most remarkable triumphs and the nature and scope of it has been completely lost while any fool remembers the costume he wore.

It happened like this. In April of that year (1881) *Patience*, perhaps the most lively of the Gilbert and Sullivan operas, was produced by Richard D'Oyly Carte at the Opéra Comique in London and in October was moved to the newly built Savoy Theatre. Carte had decided to produce it in America, where it appeared in September.

Patience satirized the so-called Aesthetes, the Fleshly Poets, the Pre-Raphaelites, and the character of Bunthorne was modelled in part on Rossetti, considered the chief of these. Some bright publicity-minded adviser, probably W. F. Morse, Carte's American director, suggested to D'Oyly Carte that American public interest in *Patience* could be enhanced by a Bunthorne, a genuine real-life aesthete, lecturing at the same time, someone who would dress the part and behave in a sufficiently precious way to show Americans what the opera was satirizing. It appeared that the 'Aesthetic movement', being scarcely heard of across the Atlantic, was found rather a vague subject for such outright comedy as Gilbert provided, and Morse felt that it should be pointed up.

Who shall we send, and who will go for us? 'Here am I,' said

Oscar. 'Send me.' And Carte did. It seems likely that the solicitor George Lewis and his wife, friends of D'Oyly Carte, had something to do with the choice of Wilde as the protagonist of this publicity scheme; certainly Oscar thought so. "For this and nearly all my successes, I have to thank your dear husband," he wrote to Mrs George Lewis from New York.

So D'Oyly Carte and W. F. Morse, known in the Dickensian manner as Colonel, signed a contract with Oscar. Its exact terms unfortunately are not known, but it provided for Oscar's expenses, the costumes he agreed to wear and for his lecturing fees, one-third of which he would receive. It sent him across to New York on the *Arizona*, a little apprehensive about the whole scheme which had so suddenly been wished on him, but determined to work out his own salvation. At least they would not shoot him— one can imagine Carte and Morse deciding—and a little ridicule would do Oscar no harm, especially as with his long hair and the elaborate drag he adopted for the tour he would seem to the Americans to be asking for it.

Here one has a glimpse of the man's character. After his long university career—three years at Trinity College, Dublin, and four at Oxford—and three years of independence in London, he had the courage to accept this challenge, to be projected into a country which to Englishmen of that time was still the America of *Nicholas Nickleby*, and he prepared to stand before it wearing drag and spouting about beautiful things. He was twenty-six years old and was aware of the homosexuality in him and aware probably of the hostility it aroused; he was also magnificently conscious of his own ability to defeat that hostility. He went alone and was prepared to face the jungle without supporters and without much encouragement from anyone.

Those who have depicted Wilde as already a considerable celebrity, already sporting 'aesthetic' costume, give small credit to this fearlessness and enterprise and must find it hard to understand his reckless behaviour fifteen years later.

His reception was well-arranged. No chance was to be missed in making a public figure of Oscar, or, failing that, a public laughing-stock. Whether he ever made that many-times repeated reply to the Customs officials, 'I have nothing to declare but my genius,' or that smiling remark to the pressmen, 'I was disappointed in the Atlantic,' or whether these have been cooked up since, it is impossible to judge. If he used this kind of smart Alec reply at that time, he had thought it out during the crossing, for he was not yet the master of spontaneous repartee he afterwards became. He may, on the other hand, have been trying to live up to the role assigned to him by Carte. One can scarcely imagine anyone declaiming that sentence unrehearsed to a busy Customs officer.

He was thrilled by his reception and wrote to Mrs George Lewis, 'It is delightful to be a *petit roi*.' So far, all was going well for the promoters. Oscar had attracted plenty of attention and apparently felt it was only what was due to him as a poet, an aesthete, an artist and a remarkable young man.

Then something happened which alarmed the promoters. Oscar on his own account, and by sheer force of personality, made a hit. The material of his lectures was not remarkable but he, even in that ridiculous get-up of knee-breeches and the rest, had a sensational success.

This was not what Carte and Morse had intended. They had engaged, and supposed that they had brought to America, a 'Miss Nancy', in the American term of the time. They found they had caught a Tartar. The public was expected to laugh their heads off at Oscar, and book their seats for *Patience* in order to see more of that kind of comedy. Instead, they listened enrapt to Oscar and cheered him to the echo while another lecturer named Archibald Forbes, also promoted by D'Oyly Carte, found his public drifting disastrously away. These assertions would be presumptuous were they not supported by a letter which Sir Rupert Hart-Davis has published in his edition of Wilde's *Letters*, written by Dion Boucicault, the actor and dramatist, to Mrs Lewis, a letter which sums up the situation most convincingly. "I cannot help feeling that so long as Carte and Forbes thought Oscar was only a puppet —a butt—a means of advertising the Opéra Comique of *Patience*— they were charming, but when Oscar's reception and success threw Forbes into the shade, Forbes went into an ecstasy of rage, and 'went back' on Wilde, behaving more like a wild bull than a gentleman. Carte escaped all responsibility, turned Oscar over to a subordinate and left him at the mercy of the Press, making a market of their caricatures to advertise him in connexion with *Patience* and Bunthorne."

Forbes was a professional bore, such as would only have been tolerated on an American lecture circuit in the '80s. He made of his experiences as war correspondent the usual Munchausen rigmarole; on the platform and in the photographer's studio he wore three rows of medals and a foreign Order. With his thick iron-grey moustache he looked a fine military type, and in previous years had held his own as a lecturer. Now he was galled by the Aesthete's success and tried to introduce a note of humour at Oscar's expense. It is again to Sir Rupert Hart-Davis that we owe this extract from his lecture:

I glanced down at my clothes, which I had not changed for a fortnight, and in which I had ridden 150 miles. Now I wish it understood that I am a follower, an humble follower, of the aesthetic ecstasy, but I did not look much like an art object then. I did not have my dogskin knee breeches with me, nor my velvet coat, and my black silk stockings were full of holes. Neither was the wild, barren waste of Bulgaria congenial to the growth of sunflowers and lilies.

On seeing newspaper reports of this, Oscar behaved almost as humourlessly as Forbes. Instead of ignoring the feeble gag, Oscar, as later he was to do most fatally with another childish insult, rose to it and wrote a grand remonstrance, thus giving Forbes the opportunity of replying somewhat solecistically:

With the knowledge I have, and which you know I have, of the utterly mercenary aim of your visit to America, the possibility of my accepting your pretensions put forward in the same letter as follows: 'I have something to say to the American people, something that I know will be the beginning of a great movement; and all foolish ridicule does a great deal of harm to the cause of art, refinement and civilisation here.' It is no affair of mine to whom else you may choose to advance these pretentions; but I must utterly decline to allow you to address them to me.

There could be no doubt of the 'utterly mercenary' aim of both men's visits to America, and it was foolish of Oscar to write to a fellow entertainer that *he* had something to say to the American people and all the rest of it. But Forbes came out of the fracas badly. He had wanted to play the bold, virile rough-rider ridiculing the effeminate art-lover. He had found, by the only measure important to both of them—the amount of the gate-money—that Oscar easily outmanoeuvred him. Carte could do nothing to help him, became ill and soon after left for England. Morse somewhat grudgingly continued to arrange Oscar's lectures, and Oscar continued to draw good houses even in out-of-the-way places in the West.

What Forbes said to the Carte management and his own associates can well be imagined. It was the baying of jealous hounds which would follow Wilde for the rest of his life. There would be plenty of successors of Forbes, who now huffily left for Baltimore, all his medals jingling.

Wilde's reception in Canada was mixed, to say the least of it. Mr Kevin O'Brien who writes an article *Oscar Wilde and Canadian Artists* in a recent number of a university review,[1] while falling into the common error of supposing that Wilde was already the 'comic rage of England', digs out some curious details about this visit. He says that excited boys chased Wilde's carriage in Toronto, shouting 'Oscar, Oscar is running Wilde.' He recalls that a correspondent in the *Halifax Chronicle* called Wilde a charlatan and described him as 'a narrow-headed, spindle-shanked, shaky, ungraceful specimen of mankind'. More abusive was the French-Canadian poet Louis Frechette, though he kept his most spiteful

[1] *The Antigonish Review*. Nova Scotia, Winter 1971.

outbreak till Wilde was in prison and publicly disgraced. He remembered Wilde, according to Mr O'Brien, as a great lout of a fellow dressed like a street-organist's monkey, considering him unctuous, soft and mincing, with a sop-like countenance and hermaphroditic face.

Much of this scurrility came from jealousy of Wilde's prosperous appearance at that time in a country which ignored or starved its own writers, or from the official reception at Government House accorded to Wilde. But Oscar should have become aware of this kind of hostility and prepared for it to manifest itself later. He always underrated his enemies, being himself without malice. 'How absurd!' he would say of John Lane, André Raffalovich, W. E. Henley and the rest who released their spleen when he could no longer defend himself, even if he wished to do so. And certainly 'How absurd!' he would have said of Louis Frechette.

What was important about all this in the life of Oscar was that this time he had defeated, one might say routed, a conspiracy of the hearties to make him look ridiculous. He had won his first battle in that war which was to last the rest of his life against the bourgeoisie he affected to despise, the commonplace type with a stick and a pipe and a half-bred black-and-tan, whom he never, like other writers of the day, exalted, preferring in life as in literature sinister criminals and picturesque labourers when he was not caricaturing the aristocracy. It may have been somewhat too easy, this victory; not all his enemies would be as indifferent as Carte to everything but the all-over success of his enterprises, not all his rivals would be petty bores of the calibre of Forbes. Oscar would find that showing good-nature in his contemptuous attitude to the public was not enough. In the meantime he could congratulate himself.

It is not from newspaper accounts published during his tour that a caricature of Oscar has been handed down to us. The American press was only just emerging from the mad sensationalism and prosy sermonizing of the earlier nineteenth century, but the press gave Oscar credit for some real successes and ridiculed his audience more than him. It is during the years since then that there has grown up the familiar monster who has been called Oscar Wilde, that over-dressed and exotically coiffured person, who roused himself from elaborate attitudes only to voice some devastating witticism, and took the United States—as later he was supposed to have taken Paris and London—by storm.

If during that tour he had in fact made all the replies, many cut from the comic columns of the time, some incredibly banal, others vulgarly smart, which have been attributed to him by his biographers in the years since 1882, the poor young man would not have had time or even breath for any normal conversation.

That he was very much more than the 'funny man' frequently depicted may be seen from his letters to Norman Forbes-Robertson which are full of the humour and gentle self-mockery which characterized his letters to Robbie Ross fifteen years later, when alone and ruined in Paris he laughed at his own successes among the boulevard boys:

Great success here: nothing like it since Dickens, they tell me. I am torn in bits by Society. Immense receptions, wonderful dinners, crowds wait for my carriage. I wave a gloved hand and an ivory cane and they cheer. Girls very lovely, men simple and intellectual. Rooms are hung with white lilies for me everywhere. I have 'Boy'[1] at intervals, also two secretaries, one to write my autograph and answer the hundreds of letters that come begging for it. Another, whose hair is brown, to send locks of his own hair to the young ladies who write asking for mine; he is rapidly becoming bald. Also a black servant, who is my slave—in a free country one cannot live without a slave—rather like a Christy minstrel, except that he knows no riddles. Also a carriage and a black tiger who is like a little monkey. I give sittings to artists, and generally behave as I always have behaved—'dreadfully.'

On the other hand, one may wish to believe that sixty Harvard undergraduates attended Oscar's lecture wearing aesthetic costume

[1] Slang word for Champagne.

and regalia, to be humiliated by Oscar, wearing evening dress, with 'as a college man I greet you!' and other bright remarks, or that the same joke was played a week or two later by the undergraduates of Yale, to be crushed by the same retorts. Or one may wish to credit the scene painted by Hesketh Pearson when Oscar was invited by a number of hearties who meant to make him drunk: "Eventually all but himself were drunk and he led them, staggering and drooping, to the street, where he helped them into hansom cabs and then walked back to his hotel. But he still had not completely vindicated his masculinity, and one evening at a club several youths suggested a round of brothels. Wilde was perfectly game, and proved that he could take his woman, as he had taken his whisky, like a man." Or this one from Philippe Jullian: "Denver and Leadville were full of excitement over his arrival. The saloons were decorated with peacock feathers and the 'scarlet women', who were the usual attraction, dispensed with their ringlets, their low-cut dresses and their high-heeled boots and donned virginal headbands and the tunics of the *Demoiselles Elues*. To the stupefaction of their clients, they carried lilies in their hands, and the Sheriff stated that at this rate he would be obliged to plant sunflowers in the prison yard."

3

Oscar sold an idea for an historical play to Mary Anderson, then a successful young actress of twenty-three to whom he gushed—"I want you to rank with the great actresses of the world. I desire your triumph to be for all time and not for the day merely and having in you a faith which is flawless as it is fervent I doubt not for a moment that I can and will write for you a play which, created for you, and inspired by you, shall give you the glory of a Rachel, and may yield me the fame of a Hugo. The dream of the sculptor is cold and silent in the marble, the painter's vision immobile on the canvas. I want to see my work return again to life, my lines gain new splendour from your passion, new music from your lips."

Mary Anderson seems to have responded to this, and terms were arranged between Oscar and her manager and stepfather Hamilton Griffin by which Oscar would receive $1,000 down and $4,000 on delivery which, Oscar promised, would be in the following March. Miss Anderson eventually declined the play, as we shall see. 'The play in its present form, I fear, would no more please the public of today than would *Venice Preserved* or *Lucretia Borgia*,' she wrote to him, but the 3,000-word letter which he sent to Mary Anderson, outlining the promised play, showed that Oscar, though deficient in stagecraft and as a playwright not yet very original, had plenty of enthusiasm; and it is not surprising to find that in the following year he sold to an American actress named Marie Prescott the rights in his long-hawked *Vera: or the Nihilists* which he had brought out from England with him. He was, of course, a born playwright, and although in the years that followed he did much other work, including a novel, his eye was always on the stage.

Apart from the theatre people he met and made much of, Oscar did not neglect Literature in America but dined with Oliver Wendell Holmes, breakfasted with Longfellow and met again Julian Hawthorne (son of Nathaniel) and his wife—also the Alcotts, Godfrey Leland, Julia Ward Howe and others.

But his most notable contact was with Walt Whitman. It is always interesting to know how the literary queers of the last century on both sides of the Atlantic handled their public relations. Samuel Butler, Herman Melville, Edmund Gosse were discreet about it, some so discreet probably that they are not even named here. Others, like Henry James, Walter Pater and Edward Lear, sublimated it. A few 'did not care who knew' and argued and wrote interminably about it, like John Addington Symonds. One or two like Edward Fitzgerald kept out of the way of gossip, but had no secrets from themselves. Others like Wilde and Ronald Gower tried to have the best of both worlds, Gower succeeding and Oscar only failing by his own irresponsibility. But in none of these categories can be counted Walt Whitman, in some ways the least inhibited of them all with his passionate and almost public love-making with a horse-bus conductor, who yet wrote to

Symonds when almost cornered by Symonds's persistent enquiries about the Calamus section of *Leaves of Grass*: "That the Calamus part has ever allowed the possibility of such construction as mentioned is terrible. I am fain to hope that the pages themselves are not to be even mentioned for such gratuitous and quite at the time undreamed and unwished possibility of morbid inferences—which are disavowed by me and seem damnable." The only explanation seems to be that offered by Gosse: "I don't believe in those 'children'! (Whitman claimed to have six illegitimate children.) For reasons, of course precisely opposite to those put forward by the servers of pillows to all armholes. The real psychology of W.W. would be enormously interesting. I think the keynote to it would be found in a staggering ignorance, a perhaps wilful non-perception, of the real physical conditions of his nature. But the truth about him (the innermost truth) escapes from almost every page for those who can read." Whether or not Whitman was, as Gosse thought, staggeringly ignorant of his own nature, he was scarcely likely to come out with any open confessions when called on by this Oxonian dandy and eloquent lecturer. Yet the two seem to have got on well together, becoming slightly pickled on elderberry wine or milk punch, Whitman saying that Oscar was a 'great big splendid boy' and Oscar writing to Whitman, parodying the old poet's manner: "There is no one in this wide great world of America whom I love and honour so much." Was that, I can't help vulgarly wondering, all?

4

Another early affair of Oscar's comes to light through events at this time which would not otherwise have been revealed. He had met an Oxford undergraduate, four years younger than himself, and fallen for him so hard that the two had in the previous summer set off by themselves on a walking tour down the Loire, of which Wilde wrote on his return to a boy of twelve, the son of his friends George and Betty Lewis. "I had a very charming time in

France, and travelled among beautiful vineyards all down the Loire, one of the most wonderful rivers in the world, mirroring from sea to source a hundred cities and five hundred towers. I was with a delightful Oxford friend and, as we did not wish to be known, he travelled under the name of Sir Smith, and I was Lord Robinson. I then went to Paris—a large town, the capital of France—and enjoyed myself very much."

They had an idyllic holiday. They were both poets, or imagined themselves to be, both in excellent health and spirits. Young Rennell Rodd was a goodlooking boy, only a mite feminine in appearance and manner, and he deeply admired Oscar. He was intended for a diplomat's career and became British Ambassador in Italy in 1908 and Lord Rennell of Rodd before he died just after the First World War, but in that summer of 1880 he was nothing but a handsome youth whose head was full of facile poems.

Of these poems Rennell Rodd had published a collection in London under the title *Songs in the South*, and now Oscar set about persuading an American publisher to issue it with a preface by him. He had met J. M. Stoddart, who held the rights in the Gilbert and Sullivan operas and had given a reception for him after his lecture in Philadelphia. He now approached him on the subject of Rennell Rodd's book. With a preface by Wilde, or as it was decided an *envoi* by Wilde and dedicated to him, it was to be issued under the title *Rose Leaf and Apple Leaf* suggested by Wilde—an improvement on Rodd's own title *The Daisy*.

Oscar, feeling no doubt that but for his intervention the book would not have been published in America at all, grew very proprietary about it, asked Stoddart for £25 to be divided equally between him and Rodd, and abolished the dedication to Rodd's father, substituting, 'To Oscar Wilde, "Heart's Brother", These Few Songs and Many Songs to come.' Unfortunate, that. Receiving the book, Rodd complained to Stoddart that the dedication was too effusive, and asked for it to be removed. This abruptly ended another of Wilde's idealistic friendships with young men, and a year later he was writing of Rodd as 'the true poet and the false friend'.

Years later, in a book published in 1922,[1] Rodd wrote with patronising pomposity of Wilde—"In those early bohemian days I saw a great deal of that brilliant but unhappy man, and as a year or so later we quarrelled irretrievably and met no more I feel the greater obligation to do justice to certain aspects of the man as I knew him." He fulfils this obligation by speaking of Wilde's 'genial and kindly nature', but the Rt Hon. Sir James Rennell Rodd, G.C.B., as he then was, does not mention that happy walking tour along the Loire.

Wilde told Dion Boucicault—"Let me gather the golden fruits of America that I may spend a winter in Italy and a summer in Greece amidst beautiful things."

As he came to the end of his tour, the profits that had accrued seemed to him to promise that he would be able to accomplish this much, but not much more. He sailed on the *Bothnia* on 27 December 1882, a year almost to a day after his arrival.

---

[1] *Social and Diplomatic Memories 1884–1893.*

FIVE

Paris and an English Lecture Tour

For his return to Europe Wilde had acquired two assets, the sum of one tohusand dollars from Mary Anderson with perhaps some smaller amounts saved from his lecture fees, and a handsome fur coat. This coat has given rise to various fables and elaborations, one biographer picturing Wilde in 'fur-lined coats made of green cloth and faced with braid'. There was, in fact, only one fur coat and Oscar gave its history to Robert Ross from prison. "Also, I would take it as a great favour if More would write to the people who pawned or sold my fur coat since my imprisonment, and ask them from me whether they would be kind enough to state where it was sold or pawned as I am anxious to trace it, and if possible get it back. I have had it for twelve years, it was all over America with me, it was at all my first nights, it knows me perfectly, and I really want it." It was a splendid article, probably acquired during his brief journey from the States into Canada, and it appears in several of his photographs. It caused Whistler, perhaps jealously, to write: "Oscar—how dare you? What means this disguise? Restore those things to Nathan's and never again let me find you masquerading the streets of my Chelsea in the combined costumes of Kossuth and Mr Mantalini!"

The thousand dollars from Mary Anderson was for the play he was to write for her, and he decided to go immediately to Paris to work on this. 'Winter in Italy and summer in Greece' would have to wait till the play was finished and producing riches for its author; in the meantime he would do what he had long wanted to do, take literary Paris by storm as (he felt) he had taken literary London and unliterary New York. Before January (1883) was over, he had installed himself in the Hotel Voltaire on the Left Bank. It was an inexpensive bourgeois hotel and only the bemused Sherard would have called it 'one of the most charming spots in Paris', as he does in his book about an unhappy friendship.[1]

But Paris had a tradition of resistance to such storming, and Oscar was viewed without notable enthusiasm by his realistic French fellow writers. Or as Sherard said—'Oscar Wilde, who appeared to me the most wonderful talker that the world had ever seen, achieved in this respect no notable success in Paris.'[2] Edmond de Goncourt described him in his *Journal* as 'an individual of doubtful sex who talks like a third-rate actor', and the general impression was not much kinder. Fur coats and stories of the Wild West were amusing, and Oscar was a quaint and no doubt talented fellow (though there was not much printed evidence of this as yet), but on the whole he failed to produce thunder-claps.

He did as he had done in London—sent copies of his *Poems* to many of the best-known French writers with a number of fulsome letters, some of which have survived, like this to Edmond de Goncourt:

Monsieur, Daignez recevoir mes poèmes, témoignage de mon admiration infinie pour l'auteur de *La Faustin*.

Je serai bien content de penser qu'il y aura une place, peut-être, pour mes premières fleurs de poésies, près de vos Watteau, et de vos Boucher, et de ce trésor de laque, d'ivoire, et de bronze, que dans votre *Maison d'un Artiste* vous avez pour toujours immortalisé.

He received in return formal invitations to the *salons* of those who had them; Victor Hugo, who dropped off to sleep during the interview; and Alphonse Daudet, whose son Léon, then a boy of sixteen, remembered meeting him and did not care for him—'his voice was at once pallid and fat, the words came tumbling out of his frightful slack mouth and when he had finished he would roar

---

[1] Robert H. Sherard, *Oscar Wilde: The Story of an Unhappy Friendship* (1902). Popular edition, 1909.   [2] Ibid.

with laughter like a fat, satisfied, gossipy woman.' He also met Mallarmé and Henri de Regnier. He did not get on with Zola and found Verlaine rather too much. But he bought himself a monkish white dressing-gown and carried an ivory cane, both in imitation of Balzac. He settled down to write his play, *The Duchess of Padua*, for Mary Anderson, finished it and sent it off to America in April.

In the meantime he had met Robert Sherard and in him made a new friend, not one who would accept his *congé* after a brief affair, but a real clinger, a self-consciously loyal prosy man who hero-worshipped Wilde to distraction and continued to see himself as Fidus Achates for thirty years after Wilde was in his grave and he had only the shadows of Wilde's old enemies to contend with. The mixture of appreciation and exasperation which this roused in Wilde during his lifetime has only once been perfectly expressed, and that by Browning in *Time's Revenges*:

> I've a Friend, over the sea;
> I like him, but he loves me.
> It all grew out of the books I write;
> They find such favour in his sight
> That he slaughters you with savage looks
> Because you don't admire my books.
> He does himself though,—and if some vein
> Were to snap to-night in this heavy brain,
> To-morrow month, if I lived to try,
> Round should I just turn quietly,
> Or out of the bedclothes stretch my hand
> Till I found him, come from his foreign land
> To be my nurse in this poor place,
> And make my broth and wash my face
> And light my fire and, all the while,
> Bear with his old good-humoured smile
> That I told him 'Better have kept away
> 'Than come and kill me, night and day,
> 'With, worse than fever throbs and shoots,
> 'The creaking of his clumsy boots.'

Sherard was a paralysing bore, as Oscar came to know long before he began to discourage his visits to his hotel during the last days in Paris, but Oscar did not realize this at first. Sherard was twenty-two years old, with straight very blond hair, a clear complexion and a sound body, and his passion was literature. A clergyman's son from the Lake District, he was at first a little shy of Wilde, of whom he had heard as a rising figure in what was still called the artistic world, but when Oscar smiled encouragement, he fell at his feet. He was—it becomes clear with time—utterly uncomprehending of homosexuality, and if Wilde attempted to seduce him, Sherard must have been painfully shocked, though such was the charm, the fame and the self-confidence of Wilde that Sherard may easily have acceded in a whatever-are-you-doing? way.

There is not—how could there be?—the smallest evidence that anything of the sort took place, but I find the notion irresistibly amusing in view of Sherard's solemn disapproval of what he always called 'aberrations'. Certainly Sherard protested too much to be easily believed. "During twenty years of communion with the world, of commerce, by profession and standing, with men and women in every rank of life, in many parts and places, I never met a man more entirely pure in conversation, nor one more disdainful of vice in its vulgarity and uncomeliness. Never there came the faintest suggestion of an unclean thought from those eloquent and inspiring lips; no coarse word ever soiled them; and if behind the wonderful eyes a demon was indeed crouching, madness here too allied itself with such supreme cunning of dissimulation, that for me, till the very end, he remained the *beau idéal* of a gentleman in all that that word implies of lofty and serene morality." Certainly Oscar began to cultivate him after he had heard Sherard claim to be a Philistine at a dull and pretentious dinner party, walking him out into the Parisian night. 'Before he left he invited me to dine with him on the morrow at the Hotel Voltaire,' says Sherard. And certainly Constance Wilde thought Sherard a taking young man. 'Today,' she wrote in a letter to her brother, 'we had a young Mr Sherard here to breakfast; he has a romantic story and a romantic face: I thought Chatterton was walking in when he appeared. When I knew him a little I remarked on this resemblance and he told me he had so many traits of character like him.'

Whatever may have happened it could only have been very early in Wilde's acquaintance with Sherard. Wilde perceived that he had committed a blunder when he made a conquest of that hetorosexual commonplace nature, a blunder whose consequences, though at the moment they amused him, would choke him when he realized that they were there for the remainder of his life.

At first, yes, Oscar wrote to Sherard in the terms he used to other artistic young men who roused his interest—'I think of you often wandering in violet valleys with your honey-coloured hair' —and accepted the dedication of Sherard's first book of poems called *Whispers*.

As for the dedication of your poems, I accept it: how could I refuse a gift so musical in its beauty, and fashioned by one whom I love so much as I love you?

To me the mirror of perfect friendship can never be dulled by any treachery, however mean, or disloyalty, however base. Individuals come and go like shadows but the ideal remains untarnished always: the ideal of lives linked together not by affection merely, or the pleasantness of companionship, but by the capacity of being stirred by the same noble things in art and song.

But later in the year when Sherard arrived broke in London and Oscar felt bound to put him up for a while in his smart apartments, there was not quite the same enthusiasm, and by 1888 when Sherard (now married) sent a copy of a play of his for Wilde to show to Wilson Barrett, or certainly by 1894 when Sherard wished to interview Wilde for *McClure's Magazine* without payment to Wilde, the friendship began to wear thin and, in prison and afterwards, became an embarrassment. Meanwhile, here was tall fair-haired Bob showing Oscar about the Paris he knew well, his suspicions of Wilde not at all roused by such a blatant piece of getting-off as Sherard later described in his *The Real Oscar Wilde*.

"After his hour in Verlaine's company at the Café François Premier, we were walking down the Boulevard St Michel, when we were accosted by a young acrobat, an exceedingly graceful and handsome young fellow. He was carrying a red carpet, and he asked us to patronise him, for, he said, '*Je travaille très bien*,' 'I like that,' said Wilde; 'I like his "I do fine things." That is what every artist ought to say about himself. This lad quite takes the taste of Verlaine, with his hideous squalor and his bagnio humility and self-derogation, out of my mouth. I will patronise this lad.' So he sat down on the *terrasse* of a café on the Place St Michel and bade the acrobat perform, bestowed largesse on him, and afterwards made him sit at our table, where he let him order what he liked, and carried on an animated conversation with him for a very much longer time than I thought necessary or wise. And this in spite of the fact that the spectacle of this elegantly dressed and remarkable-looking man sitting in front of a café at the same table with a tumbler in spangled trunks attracted the attention of all the passers-by. He did not seem to mind being noticed under such circumstances, any more than later on he had no hesitation in showing himself at public places of entertainment with the extraordinary companions who afterwards testified against him."

Sherard also recounts in the same book "I remember how one night Oscar Wilde fell into conversation with a young Latin Quarter *souteneur* who was known as 'Le Petit Louis' and who had attracted our attention by the grace and vigour with which he had danced the can-can." "I had offered Petit Louis, who was exhausted after his quadrille performance, a *bock* of the nasty Bal Bullier beer and Oscar Wilde began to talk to him. He learned from Petit Louis that he was heartily sick of the shameful life he was leading in Paris and wanted to get back to Brittany, there to enlist in the navy. But he had no money for the journey, and it was impossible for him to go to the recruiting office *de la Marine* in the clothes—the only suit he possessed—which he was wearing, clothes which at a glance betrayed his method of living. Oscar Wilde listened to his story with deep interest and then asked him several questions. In the end he said: 'Come to the Hotel Voltaire, Quai Voltaire, tomorrow at half-past twelve and I will see if I can do anything for you.' " This was successful, and Sherard continues: "And there in the sitting-room of Wilde's suite in the Hotel Voltaire, for the joy of his emancipation from the horrors of his life in the depths of Parisian vice, did *Le Petit Louis*, former *souteneur* and *marsouin* (marine) to be, execute in the fulness of his heart, and for the delectation of Oscar Wilde and Maurice Rollinat, poets, and of myself, a *pas seul* or *pas de cavalier* of amazing grace and agility." Petit Louis duly joined the Navy and appeared some years later as 'a fine sturdy bronzed boatswain' asking for Wilde, whose name he had unfortunately forgotten and who was then in prison. Sherard, with elephantine tact which would have infuriated Oscar, replied solemnly 'I too have forgotten his name.' He seems to congratulate himself on this idiotic retort.

No one else has unwillingly produced such lively and authentic snapshots of Wilde as poor Sherard in his blessed naïvety. It was typical of his general unluckiness that all his early letters from Wilde were stolen by the police going through his papers when he was under suspicion as a Dreyfusard, but in his recollections there are other sublimely ingenuous absurdities. "I was aware of his admiration of youth. His writings abound in allusions to his preference for young people to those whom in one of his plays he spoke of as 'of the usual age'. The *homme d'un certain age*, as the middle-aged man is described in France, was, perhaps unfairly, censured by Wilde as necessarily tedious." Sherard not only recorded conscientiously those six weeks of his first acquaintance with Wilde, but later filled the best part of three books by highly coloured accounts of their incidents. "With regard to his un-English habit of embracing his friends, of which I heard but never witnessed, the jury were perhaps unaware that it is—especially amongst the Latin races—a custom all over the Continent. I remember my indignation when calling at Naples, on a former Dresden school-mate of mine—who had since those early days blossomed into a portly and prosperous hotel-keeper—my friend, *coram populo* on the landing-stage at Sorrento, threw his arms round my neck and embraced me on either cheek. It was un-English and repellent to me, but no harm whatever was meant. And I don't believe that Oscar Wilde meant any harm either,

when he followed this effusive Continental method of salutation."
Even Wilde's new hair-do only seemed to Sherard one of those
little 'mannerisms and eccentricities which irritated the literary
men', and he described the change in his hearty way. "Then there
was that custom of his of having his hair curled. This is common
enough amongst the French proletariat, indeed no French work-
man would think of going to his wedding without first paying a
visit to a *coiffeur-friseur* (hairdresser), but it is not usual *dans le
monde*. He had acquired this custom after his return from America
and a visit to the Louvre Museum, where the coiffure of the
Emperor Nero, in a bust, had attracted his attention, at a time
when, having discarded the long hair of the aesthetic period, he
was considering in what style to have his really beautiful *chevelure*
arranged. He wrote me from London: 'Society must be amazed,
and my Neronian coiffure has amazed it. Nobody recognises me,
and everybody tells me I look young.' "

    One simply has to go on quoting from Innocent Bob. "When
I first met him in Paris he was dressing—apart from his use of fur
coats and rather showy jewellery—like an ordinary French gentleman, silk hat, redingote and so on. . . . He was not, however, long
content to remain in the current fashion; he desired to be distinc-
tive and noticeable; and during the first weeks of our acquaintance
he was debating what style of dress to adopt. He hesitated between
the mode of 1848 (Paris) and that made fashionable by Beau
Brummel. In the meanwhile he revived the fashion of shirt-cuffs
which turned back over the cuffs of the coat, a revival for which
the laundress of the Hotel Voltaire was heard to bless him. In the
end and on his return to London in 1883—as was duly announced
in *The World* by his friend, Edmund Yates—he adopted the
costume of Beau Brummel." Sherard adds, "Towards the end of
his life he abandoned all foppery and contented himself with the
cheap clothes of the middle-class tailors." This, like much else
that Sherard observed, is true, and dismisses yet another crop of
lies. When Wilde came out of prison, his fur coat pawned
irretrievably by his sister-in-law or brother, and economy in
clothes a necessity, for the first time he dressed like an unostenta-
tious British business man on holiday in France or Italy, as can be

seen from photographs. In other words it was not when he was approaching death that he tarted himself up (as one woman has asked us to believe) but at this period when he was young, ambitious and conscious of the value to him of publicity, supposing it was best achieved by a noticeable appearance.

There can be no doubt that in Paris as later in London there were sophisticated observers like Edmond de Goncourt who called him 'an individual of doubtful sex', who knew exactly what it was all about and thought Oscar a big cissy with his curled hair and jewelled walking-stick. But it was not, fortunately for Oscar then, a sophisticated age, and most people thought him a bit of an eccentric or 'one of these aesthetes you hear about'. The Victorians, by a happy misunderstanding, habitually took an effeminate man, a dressy perfumed giggling man, for 'a devil with the women', an elegant Lothario rather than a queer. W. S. Gilbert himself seems to have been under this impression when he wrote *Patience*; his virile Englishness of thought would not have let him even *caricature* a homosexual if he could have recognized one. This provided a certain amount of cover for men like Oscar, and it was noticeable that at the time of the trials, many who had watched his most indiscreet cavortings in the West End of London were astounded when the prosecution witnesses were produced and told their story.

2

Wilde may have charmed Robert Sherard in the belief that his blond good looks and ready smile made him accessible physically rather than sentimentally; Sherard found in Wilde all he had in his provincial way dreamed that a writer should be, polished, a little eccentric, lively and satirical in conversation, a frequenter (as Sherard believed) of all the most exclusive salons, above all a man of the world, as poor Bob was not. "Less a mortal than a demigod" Sherard described him then, "a brazier filled with the unquenchable fire of genius." I like the picture of the two of them lunching together at the Café de Paris in the Avenue de l'Opéra, ('a house

D

reputed to be exclusively patronised by millionaires', Sherard said with awe), Wilde wearing what Sherard called his 'abundant jewellery', or at chez Bignon, 'luxurious and expensive' where 'coffee made itself on the table between us'. The indifference with which Oscar 'discharged the formidable bill' confirmed Sherard in his conclusion that Oscar was a man of wealth, and may have led him to touch Oscar, as he did for £15 with which to go to London to sit for an examination 'because his bank had disappointed him.'

Sherard was capable of jealousy of Wilde too, then and for the rest of his life. It will surprise no one who is familiar with that slightly maudlin, heterosexual type, forever watching the smiles bestowed on someone more desirable than himself, though unable to compete with readier offers, that Sherard looked on with bitter heart-burning at the pleasure with which Wilde received a handsome young sculptor named John Donoghue whom Wilde had known in Chicago.

"In the early days of my friendship with Wilde," he wrote huffily, "Donoghue was always butting in." He had made a medallion of Wilde which, Sherard said, 'was not a very satisfactory piece of work.'[1]

John Donoghue was a striking-looking young man now just thirty years old, who had written appealing to Wilde while he was lecturing in Chicago, saying that poverty and neglect were preventing him from achieving any success as a sculptor. Wilde went at once to call on him in his studio, and such joy ensued that Wilde made references to Donoghue in his lectures, which brought success overnight. To Charles Eliot Norton he wrote ecstatically—"I send you the young Greek: a photograph of him: I hope you will admire him. I think it is very strong and right, the statue: and the slight asceticism of it is to me very delightful. The young sculptor's name is John Donoghue: pure Celt is he."

Any word of interest from you would be very cheering to him. I feel sure he could do any one of your young athletes, and what

[1] Sherard The Real Oscar Wilde.

an era in art that would be to have the sculptor back in the palaestra, and of much service too to those who separate athletics from culture, and forget the right ideal of the beautiful and healthy mind in a beautiful and healthy body. I can see no better way of getting rid of the mediaeval discord between soul and body than by sculpture. Phidias is the best answer to Thomas à Kempis, but I wish you could see the statue itself, and not the sun's libel on it.

Donoghue showed his gratitude by making a bas-relief of Wilde, and it was through the publicity that Wilde had given him that Donoghue had been enabled to come to Paris and meet Wilde there, since the Chicago Institute (largely on the strength of Wilde's recommendation) had purchased the sculptor's *Sophocles*.

"Donoghue used to profess great affection for and gratitude towards [Wilde]," wrote Sherard acidly,[1] "but when troubles came, Donoghue was not one of those who stood by his former friend and benefactor." This was a particularly bitchy reflection since in the year of Wilde's 'troubles' Donoghue had what must have seemed to him as cruel a tragedy of his own. Sir Rupert Hart-Davis says: "His greatest project, a colossal winged statue of 'The Spirit', was designed for the Chicago World's Fair of 1892–1893, but Donoghue was too poor to pay the freight charges from Europe, and after the statue had lain some time in the Brooklyn docks, it was dumped in the sea. The sculptor never recovered from this blow, but declined upon spiritualism and melancholia, and eventually drowned himself."

But in the meantime, to anticipate for a moment from Sherard's jealousy in 1883 to the next year, that of Oscar's marriage, Sherard must have been chagrined when the handsome John Donoghue turned up again to spoil poor Bob's proprietary enjoyment of the honeymoon couple's visit to Paris.

"Very different but also interesting is the young sculptor Donoghue whom I have seen several times," wrote Constance Wilde to her brother. "Very handsome Roman face but with

[1] Sherard *The Real Oscar Wilde*.

Irish blue eyes. He has done a lovely bronze bas-relief for the Salon, a seraph: a nude figure full profile of a boy playing a harp, perfectly simple and quite exquisite in line and expression."[1] On the next evening the Wildes gave a dinner party for 'Miss Reubell, Mr Sargent (the American artist) Mr Donoghue and M. Bourget'. There is only one further reference to Donoghue in Wilde's letters—two years later he wrote to A. P. T. Elder "I am sure you will be glad to hear that one of the most beautiful things in last year's Salon was a bas-relief by your marvellous fellow-townsman, and my dear friend, young Donoghue." But Wilde was like that. He did not care for Polonius's advice and it took a great many hoops of steel and a lot of grappling to keep his soul constant for more than a season or two, as Sherard himself was to discover.

After three months the money which Wilde had salvaged from his American trip ran low, and when Mary Anderson wrote refusing *The Duchess of Padua*, it was time for Oscar to return to London. He did so and for some months was extremely hard up.

It would not be fair to say that he was living on his wits but like most young men in similar situations, he waited somewhat impatiently for something to turn up. He felt that Paris (as a place in which to earn a living) had for the moment failed him. Meanwhile he found and kept what was called at the time 'a good address'.

This was Number 9, Charles Street, Grosvenor Square, where a Mr and Mrs Davis kept lodgings 'for single gentlemen of distinction'. The street was transformed, according to Sherard in 1902, and became Carlos Street. Wilde had scarcely time to settle in there before he decided to go to New York for the first night— at last—of *Vera or The Nihilists* which Marie Prescott was having produced at the Union Square Theatre. It ran for a week only and provoked a fiendish press—'a foolish, highly-peppered story of love, intrigue and politics' (*New York Tribune*), 'unreal, long-winded and wearisome' (*New York Times*) and 'long-drawn dramatic rot' (*New York Herald*). There was an attempt to save Oscar's face in the *New York Mirror*:

[1] Rupert Hart-Davis *The Letters of Oscar Wilde*.

If Oscar Wilde desired any vindication for the abuse, ridicule and contempt with which he was met on his first visit to this country, it was handsomely secured to him by the triumph of his play in the face of such adverse conditions as seldom beset an author whose purposes are serious and honest . . . It is not the first instance in history of the crucifixion of a good man on the cross of popular prejudice and disbelief.

But in spite of that friendlier piece of criticism Wilde sailed for home on the *Arizona* on September 11 and never returned to America. On this second visit he had been exactly one month in New York, a very rapid return journey for those days.

Wilde had received one thousand dollars from Marie Prescott ("an inferior actress who can only scold on the stage and off it" said the *Pilot* nastily) and was to have had fifty dollars for each performance. It cannot have left him much balance when his travelling expenses were paid.

3

Sherard was broke, too, a not unusual state of affairs since he was attempting to make a living by one of the hardest of methods then as today, as an untalented free-lance writer. He had returned to England from Paris and had been staying at Eller Howe, Ambleside, Westmorland, where he had friends or relatives. Hart-Davis[1] says 'friends' and Sherard's connection with the Lake District is unlikely to have had more than a coincidental relationship with the fact that Sherard was a great-grandson of Wordsworth. His father, however, the Rev. B. Sherard Kennedy, may have had some kindred living at Ambleside.

Wilde and Sherard corresponded while Sherard was in Westmorland and then met 'by hazard' as Sherard writes[2], on Clapham

[1] Rupert Hart-Davis *The Letters of Oscar Wilde.*
[2] Sherard *The Real Oscar Wilde.*

Junction station. "If I remember rightly," says Sherard with rather over-written casualness, "my position at that time was a very bad one. I was to leave the house where I had been staying as a guest on the morrow, and hardly knew where to go."

This was a curious confession from a man who told Constance Wilde (and perhaps had also told Oscar) that his father was a millionaire but that he (Sherard) 'starved in a garret and lived in dreamland always'. But Wilde accepted the story. Wilde had just secured for himself a lecturing job, a tour of the English provinces, and expected to be away from his digs in Charles Street a good deal. Sherard could stay there, which would 'at least give me shelter until I had found something to do'.

This was characteristically kind of Oscar who, one may gather from a few of his reported remarks at that time, had ceased to be attracted by Sherard. It was fortunate because it enables us to know something of Wilde's life after he had left Paris in May 1883 until he was married just a year later.

The landlord and landlady, Mr and Mrs Davis, were according to Sherard excellent people. "Mr Davis had been a butler in good families; his wife had been a cook, and a real *cordon-bleu* she was. Mr Davis used to go out to banquets in the city to superintend the waiting, and had a standing arrangement with the Governors of the Bank of England. They were both devoted to Oscar Wilde, though he was often in their debt, and could not speak too highly of his cleverness, kindness and consideration." "Oscar's rooms were on the top floor, an oak-panelled sitting-room, with a small bedroom opening out of it. When Oscar was at home, I used to sleep in a bedroom on the ground floor, when he was *en voyage* I was allowed to use his bedroom. I remember that the bed was no sybaritic couch; it was a particularly hard camp bedstead, and reminded me of those we had at Oxford. There was no bathroom in the house, an inconvenience which troubled Oscar Wilde but little. He was not addicted to the daily bath. At the same time he had a veritable *cultus* for his body, and took great pride in his personal appearance." "He was fond of his body, he used to stroke and pet himself. When he was reading he was usually seen to be caressing his nose or gently pulling his ear. Sometimes with his nail he would scrape off some piece of dead skin, which he would roll up, afterwards contemplating the pellet—which had been part of himself—with admiring interest. I remember how once, when a new overcoat was delivered to him in Paris, and he had put it on, he manifested quite a childish pleasure in the comfort it gave him. 'So warm, Robert,' he said, folding his hands across his breast like a child. The arrangements at the lodgings in Charles Street were distinguished and comfortable. Our newspapers were invariably aired before they were brought, with the early cup of tea, to our bedsides. The valeting was what one is accustomed to in the best houses. As to the catering, it was incomparably the best I have ever met with in any lodgings. We used to *déjeuner* in the French fashion about eleven o'clock, and it was as good a breakfast-lunch as any that could be got anywhere in London. The Davises had some excellent claret." "We generally dined *en ville*. Oscar was usually invited out; I dined where I could, not infrequently with Duke Humphrey. Sometimes we went to the Café Royal, and on more than one occasion Whistler was with us. He was not very prosperous in those days, and used to order the very cheapest claret to take with his frugal grill. Oscar Wilde showed him the greatest deference. 'Like the grand Virginian gentleman that you are,' he sometimes said to him. Whistler seemed to me always to be nurturing a grievance, either against some individual or against the social collectivity. I remember once saying to Oscar that the pre-prandial conversation with Whistler was an excellent substitute for bitters as an *apéritif*, and so indeed it was. His remarks were the cascara sagrada of conversation. I was promptly snubbed by Oscar for my observation. 'One does not criticize a James McNeill Whistler,' he said."

Of how long this arrangement lasted there is no record and Sherard is deliberately vague, but he had certainly left Charles Street to return to Paris before Oscar met, or rather met again Constance Lloyd when his lecture tour took him to Dublin in November.

That lecture tour had, like Wilde's American one, been arranged by Col. W. F. Morse who had left D'Oyly Carte and become the London manager for J. M. Stoddart and the Encyclopaedia

Americana. Lecturing, before its attraction had been made to seem tedious and old-fashioned by the cinema and later by broadcasting and television, was a profitable business, far more so than it is today, and Morse wrote to Wilde "I can foresee a good season's work and fair prices—not large. From ten to twenty-five guineas per night is all they will pay." It seems to have satisfied Wilde. "I am hard at work lecturing and getting rich," he wrote to Lillie Langtry. Oscar lectured on *The House Beautiful* and Sherard attended a lecture at the Prince's Hall—"The attendance was a fair one, and most of his points were appreciated. His manner was supremely easy; he dominated his audience. He seemed to realise that what he was saying was both new and interesting, and that it was for his listeners to appreciate that fact and feel pleased and proud at being lectured to by him." "I understood that he had been carefully coached in his stage manner and deportment, and that by no less an actor than Mr Hermann Vezin."

Wilde continued to lecture at intervals after his marriage and until 1885, when he decided that it would be better and in the long run more profitable for him to obtain a post as a school inspector. With this object he approached George Curzon with whom he had nurtured a friendship since he had met him at Oxford in 1882. 'My dear Curzon,' he wrote with slightly facetious diffidence but obvious sincerity of intent:

I want to be one of Her Majesty's Inspectors of Schools! This is ambition—however, I want it, and want it very much, and I hope you will help me. Edward Stanhope has the giving away and, as a contemporary of mine at Oxford, you could give me great help by writing him a letter to say (if you think it) that I am a man of some brains. I won't trouble you with the reasons which make me ask for this post—but I want it and could do the work, I fancy, well. If you could give me and get me any help you can I will be so much obliged to you, and I know how the party think of you— you brilliant young Coningsby! I hope to get this and to get it with your approval and your good word. I don't know Stanhope

personally and am afraid he may take the popular idea of me as a
real idler. Would you tell him it is not so?

Curzon, who had been the perhaps unwitting cause of Oscar
Browning's dismissal from his post as an Eton housemaster, duly
wrote the letter and another to Sir Henry Holland, when the Vice-
Presidentship of the Council of Education had changed hands.
But nothing came of it and soon after Wilde was writing in
January or February from the Central Station Hotel, Glasgow: "I
am away in the region of horrible snow and horrible note-paper!
Lecturing and wandering—a vagabond with a mission."

Those lecture tours certainly gave Wilde poise and what is
called experience and provided almost his only glimpse of the
provinces of Britain. He may have worn his fur coat a trifle
haughtily as he strode into the great hotels of the Midlands and
North of England but he was able to charm the dullest lecture
organizers and leave a slightly scented and eccentric, but none the
less likeable, aura behind him. One feels this from the letter he
wrote to the Librarian of Worcester Public Library: "I have most
pleasant memories of my morning in Worcester with you, and of
all the lovely things you showed me from the blue and white
Worcester china down to the gilded King before the altar. I will
hope to lecture at Worcester again and hope you will do me the
honour of arranging it for me." What adventures he may have
found in Glasgow or Carlisle or elsewhere, nothing remains to
suggest, though Sherard's stories of this period, already quoted,
show that Oscar was already a skilled picker-up of likely-looking
young men. In this respect, the rest of his life is more adequately
chronicled.

SIX

Marriage and Editorship

The difficulty about the story of Wilde is not only the many encrustments of legend that have to be pared away but the search for an appropriate idiom in which to recount it, particularly as one approaches his marriage and at the same time his frivolous pursuit of young men. In speaking of what is called—at the best loosely—'normal sex' we take much as said and understood, but when it comes to describing less conventional attachments we are expected to speak, in terms like 'homosexual' and 'perverted' which are in fact almost meaningless. We do not think it necessary, except in pornographic novels, to state in detail what brought a man and woman to cohabitation and propagation, or to particularize their methods. We simply say they fell in love, were married and had children. But when the promiscuous relationships of a man of less stereotyped habits are discussed we are expected to allude to them either with euphemisms and analogies —'he became very fond of the boy', 'he formed an indiscreet relationship with him'—or to proceed with a quite unnecessary and often inaccurate bluntness—'he buggered him', 'he showed himself to be a sodomite'. Both of these are absurd, for with a little goodwill even the least understanding readers, the kind who talk about 'filthy perverts' and say 'I'd like to shoot the lot of them', or those who consider homosexuality frightfully mysterious and interesting, should at least be able to follow the argument put in quite simple language without coarseness or coyness or pseudo-Greek scientific terms.

Wilde met Constance Lloyd[1] when his finances were at a low ebb. He liked her, discovered that she had a private income and began to see what he could make of her as a charming and personable expression of his own aesthetic ideas, the 'châtelaine of the House Beautiful' as someone in fact called her. That he afterwards 'did his duty by her as a husband' was shown by the prompt births of two baby sons, and that for a long time he was fond of her and made her happy, without denying himself the pleasures of his private life, is without question.

What he felt about it himself is unguessable, but I do not believe that he ever intended to interrupt his own easy-going comfortably self-centred life in order to make some exhibitionistic sacrifice to the ideals of marriage which Constance had inherited. I do not suppose—indeed the idea is far-fetched—that Wilde said 'now I shall forget my own sex and take pleasure only in this pretty little female I've married'. The most he may have resolved at first was, 'I will give her a square deal. I will make her talked of, a notable hostess, a woman distinguished by clever clothes and famous associates; I will give her children—in fact I long for them —and make love to her with the most romantic words as I, better than anyone else, am able to do.'

What he could not give up is what he called his 'art' and with it his 'artistic associations'. But in the early years Constance had no reason to be disturbed by that.

From the very first Oscar made it clear to Constance that the 'artist' must lead his own life unencumbered by domesticity. They went for their honeymoon to Paris which Oscar always regarded as a convenient Babylon just across the Channel. He does not seem to have made any very serious effort to make Constance feel that his life was entirely hers, for immediately the young men began to appear. "Of course I need not tell you that I am very happy, enjoying my liberty enormously." This, surely, was a rather odd way for a recently married woman to congratulate

---

[1] It took Frank Harris, supported in this case by Robert Ross, to discover and disclose the fact that her father, Horatio Lloyd Q.C., had been charged with indecently exposing himself to nursemaids in the gardens of the Temple.

herself on her new state and we are not surprised to learn that 'Oscar is out so I can give you no message from him'. Oscar was again 'out' when she wrote three weeks later and Constance (fleetingly no doubt) was "thinking of becoming correspondent to some paper or else going on the stage: *qu'en pensez-vous?* I want to make some money: perhaps a novel would be better."

Whatever its realities were, the relationship between Wilde and Constance did not lack verbiage from Wilde to make it out-wardly an ecstatically happy one. "I am going to be married", he wrote to Lillie Langtry, "to a beautiful girl called Constance Lloyd, a grave, slight, violet-eyed little Artemis, with great coils of heavy brown hair which make her flower-like head droop like a blossom, and wonderful ivory hands which draw music from the piano so sweet that the birds stop singing to listen to her." To Waldo Story he was less poetic. "We are, of course, desperately in love. I have been obliged to be away nearly all the time since our engagement, civilizing the provinces by my remarkable lectures, but we telegraph to each other twice a day, and the telegraph clerks have become quite romantic in consequence." To Constance herself: "The air is full of the music of your voice, my soul and body seem no longer mine, but mingled in some ex-quisite ecstasy with yours. I feel incomplete without you."

That all the rest of Oscar's letters to Constance must have been destroyed by herself or her family we are justified in believing with Sir Rupert Hart-Davis, but their destruction leaves us nothing, not even third-party assessments, to indicate how Oscar and his wife lived and talked and entertained together. We are reduced to generalities and precedents.

These mostly suggest a reasonably happy marriage between them. A man of predominantly homosexual proclivities—absurd series of syllables but my meaning emerges somehow—frequently makes a superlatively good husband for an intelligent and im-aginative wife. He has ideas on house decoration and entertain-ment, he responds to her articulate and not over-demanding urges with romantic if not quite realistic gusto, he may even when a certain detached comradeship has been formed between them discuss sympathetically and perhaps enviously her love affairs. He is usually an excellent father and a standby in the case of illness. He designs his wife's clothes and is charming with her friends without giving her cause for jealousy. If after all that he demands an occasional night in a Turkish bath or a holiday with a male friend, the wife probably realizes that she would be a fool to complain. That was the kind of marriage, it may be confidently surmised, though with divergences here and there, which existed between Oscar and Constance Wilde, and Sherard, with blundering tactlessness, revealed it when he said of Wilde's honeymoon: "I think that it was during his stay in Paris at this time that he visited with me the haunts of the lowest criminals and poorest outcasts of the city, the show-places of the Paris Inferno,—Père Lunette's and the Château-Rouge,—which everybody who wishes to know the depths of darkness which exist in the City of Light goes to see."[1]

"I must write and thank you for your great kindness to Constance," Oscar writes to his friend Emily Thursfield, "who has come back perfectly charmed with her visit, enchanted with you all, and looking extremely well—much better than when she went away." He dedicates one of the stories in his collection of fairy stories to Constance, he writes to Lady Mount-Temple to say that Constance seems very happy in France, he tells Frances Forbes-Robertson that Constance is in Rome with her aunt. Such casual asides are almost all we have from Wilde's letters, and the few men and women who knew the pair and have left any sort of record are not much more helpful. What, for instance, can one make of this—Sherard's only approach to a descriptive passage? "I frequently met Constance at her house, and admired her very much. She was beautiful and gracious, kind-hearted, and devoted to her husband, for whose great cleverness she had the highest admiration. In the awful tragedy which befell the house in Tite Street, it was for her that one felt the deepest sorrow. I was glad that I was able to be of some service to her in those days, though the hope that I had entertained, that in the end things might yet be adjusted between them, proved itself a vain one." Vyvyan Holland's *Son of Oscar Wilde* gives not one single glimpse among

[1] R. H. Sherard, *Oscar Wilde: The Story of an Unhappy Friendship* (1909).

his childhood recollections of his parents together. Frank Harris, who according to Lord Alfred Douglas never met Constance Wilde, gives—for what it is worth—an embittered picture of the marriage. "As soon as the dreadful load of poverty was removed, Oscar began to go about a great deal, and his wife would certainly have been invited with him if he had refused invitations addressed to himself alone; but from the beginning he accepted them and consequently after the first few months of marriage his wife went out but little, and later children came and kept her at home." Bosie Douglas is far more revealing, though somewhat from his own point of view. He says:

I was always on the best of terms with Mrs Wilde. I liked her and she liked me. She told me, about a year after I first met her, that she liked me better than any of Oscar's other friends. She frequently came to my mother's house and was present at a dance which my mother gave during the first year of my acquaintance with her husband. After the *débâcle* I never saw her again, and I do not doubt that Ross and others succeeded in poisoning her mind against me, but up to the very last day of our acquaintance we were the best of friends. The last time I saw her was two nights before the proceedings taken by Oscar Wilde against my father at the Old Bailey, when we all three had dinner in a restaurant and went on to a box at the St James's Theatre, where Oscar's play, *The Importance of Being Earnest*, was running to crowded houses. She was very much agitated, and when I said good-night to her at the door of the theatre she had tears in her eyes. I felt dreadfully sorry for her, for though I then believed Oscar would beat my father, and had not the slightest anticipation of the frightful catastrophe that was imminent, I knew that at the very best the whole business must be a terrible ordeal for her. Honesty compels me to say that Oscar during the time I knew him was not very kind to his wife. He certainly had been (as he often told me) very much in love with her, and the marriage was purely a love match. At the time when I first met him he was still fond of her, but he was often impatient with her, and sometimes snubbed her, and he resented, and showed that he resented, the attitude of slight disapproval which she often adopted towards him. Towards the end of the time before the catastrophe (and they never met again after he came out of prison) the relations between them were distinctly strained.[1]

No one else who knew both Oscar and Constance has anything more to say about them and as usual there is nothing but the usual dribble of secondhand gossip.

Meanwhile in default of any authoritative report, we are justified in making a few assumptions. We can see Oscar, tall, dressed rather showily in the frock coat of the eighties, his brown hair no longer elaborately curled but naturally waved, pacing impatiently round to Tite Street where (with Constance's money) they had taken a house which they were re-decorating. We can see him, wrapped in his fur coat, being seen off by Constance as he left for one of his lecture-tours in the North. He was still just under thirty years old; and having, as Harris somewhat spitefully but probably truthfully said, 'earned a respite from care by his marriage', he was free to disport himself on lecture platforms, to indulge in epigrammatic slanging-matches with James McNeill Whistler in the pages of The World, and generally without doing anything concrete to further his reputation as a writer, to advertise himself as a practical aesthete, one who gave lectures on 'the house beautiful', a man of ostentatious taste and witty opinions. He had quite a reputation for these things and never missed a chance of adding to it, though his strictly literary achievement was still almost nil. He 'knew a lot of people' and although he and Constance could not afford to entertain as much as he wished—since entertaining meant chiefly formal and elaborate dinner-parties—they both appeared at Lady Wilde's eccentric 'At Homes' and Wilde never missed a Private View. Small wonder that after a time Constance found herself unable to 'keep up with Oscar' and gradually began to let him go his own 'artistic' way. There is no record of any public or private disagreement between them—they seem simply

[1] The Autobiography of Lord Alfred Douglas (1929).

to have resolved to lead each his own life, Constance that of small conventional tea-parties and At Homes with her family and friends, shopping excursions for which Oscar's advice was always available, domestic cares and later the bringing-up of her children; Oscar that of ambitious contacts and some 'artistic' work and friendships with young men at which he was becoming adept.

The words 'artistic', with 'art' and 'artist' became obsessions with Wilde. He could scarcely speak or write without using them. A few, a very few from the many thousands of examples of that time, can be quoted: 'You carry with you the sympathy of all who love *art*', which Wilde wrote to Henry Irving. 'It is always a privilege to number any *artists* in one's audience,' to an unidentified correspondent. 'The marvellous development of your *art*,' to Mary Anderson. 'The *art* that appeals to laughter and the *art* that appeals to beauty are different things,' to an editor, in reproof for his having included a parody in the same issue as a poem by Wilde. 'Anyone with a real *artistic* sense must see the value and repose of pure colour,' he lectured W. A. S. Benson, an architect, and 'the whole afternoon was charming and *artistic*', he told Norman Forbes-Robertson of a matinée performance. 'Ask of *Art* to sacrifice herself for you and a bitter disappointment may come to you,' he told an unidentified correspondent, and 'write and tell me what things in *art* you and your friends love,' he commanded H. C. Marillier. '*Art* and Liberty seem to me more vital than any creed,' he told William Sharp, while to Marillier again he wrote that 'the *artistic* life is a long and lovely suicide'. So on for the rest of his London life, till in prison the trick reached absurdity in his *De Profundis* letter: 'You did not realize that an *artist* and especially such an *artist* as I am,' etcetera; 'you were proud, and quite naturally so, of being the intimate friend of an *artist* so distinguished, but you could not understand the conditions requisite for the production of *artistic* work.' 'We had, not unnaturally indeed, differed on the question of the *artistic* value of your translation of *Salome*.' 'Your desires and interests were in Life not in *Art*.' 'You had the rudiments of an *artistic* temperament.' 'You were the absolute ruin of my *Art*.' 'One half-hour with *Art* was always more to me than a cycle with you.' 'Nothing really at any period of my life was ever of the smallest importance to me compared with *Art*.' 'My position in the world of *Art*. . . .' 'What did interest them (the French) was how an *artist* of my distinction . . . could have brought such an action.' 'The difficult and beautiful *art* of literature.'

This continued, though less noticeably, during the first few months after Wilde left prison and finally, in his letters from Paris and Rome during the last years of his life entirely died out.

But for the first three years after his marriage, when he was in fact least of all occupied with attempts to write, the 'artist' and his 'Art' were perpetually being referred to by Oscar.

3

This is ironic, for creatively speaking they were the most un-satisfying of his years. He continued to lecture, quoting a fee sometimes as little as five guineas. He took a great deal of interest, both financial and artistic, in the decoration of his house in Tite Street by Edward William Godwin, the architect, stage designer and interior decorator who had lived with Ellen Terry for a number of years and was the father of Edith and Gordon Craig. He joined with an authoritative tone in correspondence in news-papers which touched on the subjects of his lectures, and he formed a number of new friendships, particularly among titled women. He wrote occasional articles for the *Pall Mall Gazette* including criticisms of Whistler which brought him into public conflict with that prickly artist in the columns of *The World*.

It was not, however, until late in 1885, after he had been settled in Tite Street for a year and his son Cyril was six months old, that Wilde gave evidence for the first time since his marriage of his easily awakened interest in young men who came his way. He received a letter from Henry Currie Marillier who was then just twenty years old and was at Peterhouse, Cambridge. He wrote to remind Wilde that five years ago, as a pupil at Christ's Hospital, then still in London, he had brought Wilde's coffee in to him in

Salisbury Street and Oscar, in a most revealing letter, wrote on 5 November:

Of course I remember the blue-coat boy, and am charmed to find he has not forgotten me.

Your letter gave me great pleasure and if possible I will come down to see the *Eumenides*—which I suppose will look like Hamlet surrounded by the witches of *Macbeth*—but you have not told me the date of the production yet, so I cannot say if I will be really free.

I have a very vivid remembrance of the bright enthusiastic boy who used to bring me my coffee in Salisbury Street, and am delighted to find he is devoted to the muses, but I suppose you don't flirt with all nine ladies at once? Which of them do you really love? Whether or not I can come and see you, you must certainly come and see me when you are in town, and we will talk of the poets and drink Keats's health. I wonder are you all Wordsworthians still at Cambridge, or do you love Keats, and Poe, and Baudelaire? I hope so.

Write and tell me what things in art you and your friends love best. I do not mean what pictures, but what moods and modulations of art effect you most.

Is it five years ago really? Then I might almost sign myself an old friend, but the word old is full of terror.

On receiving this, Harry Marillier immediately came up to London and spent the day with Wilde, who was forced to leave in the evening for Newcastle-on-Tyne where he was lecturing. From there he wrote on 8 November:

Harry, why did you let me catch my train? I would have liked to have gone to the National Gallery with you, and looked at Velasquez's pale evil King, at Titian's Bacchus with the velvet panthers, and at that strange heaven of Angelico's where everyone seems made of gold and purple and fire, and which, for all that, looks to me ascetic—everyone dead and decorative! I wonder will it really be like that, but I wonder without caring. *Je trouve la terre aussi belle que le ciel, et le corps aussi beau que l'âme.* If I do live again I would like it to be as a flower—no soul but perfectly beautiful. Perhaps for my sins I shall be made a red geranium!!

And your paper on Browning? You must tell me of it. In our meeting again there was a touch of Browning—keen curiosity, wonder, delight.

It was an hour intensely dramatic and intensely psychological, and, in art, only Browning can make action and psychology one. When am I to see you again? Write me a long letter to Tite Street, and I will get it when I come back. I wish you were here, Harry. But in the vacation you must often come and see me, and we will talk of the poets and forget Piccadilly!! I have never learned anything except from people younger than myself and you are infinitely young.

Three weeks later, when Wilde returned from his tour in the North he went down to Cambridge and according to Mrs Claude Beddington, who reproduced Wilde's letters to Marillier in her book *All that I Have Met* (1929), sketched out the story of *The Happy Prince* to an audience of undergraduates and later wrote it in Harry Marillier's rooms. Marillier himself, on a visit to Wilde in Tite Street, afterwards wrote some verses about 'Rainbow dreams On a lapis lazuli lawn'.

After the visit to Cambridge Wilde wrote again to Harry; a letter which, as they say speaks for itself:

Does it all seem a dream, Harry? Ah! what is not a dream? To me it is, in a fashion, a memory of music. I remember bright young faces, and grey misty quadrangles, Greek forms passing through Gothick cloisters, life playing among ruins, and, what I love best in the world, Poetry and Paradox dancing together!

Only one evil omen—your fire! You are careless about playing with fire, Harry.

And my book? Where is it? I must have it now. How delightful it would be were everything in one's house a gift! However, one's friends are always a gift—θεόδωροι. It seems to me you were rather horrid to *your* friend, the poet in exile. Ever yours, Oscar.

In the following January Wilde replied again to Harry Marillier, the last of his letters that have been preserved:

Dear Harry, I am away in the region of horrible snow and horrible note-paper! Lecturing and wandering—a vagabond with a mission! But your letter has reached me, like a strain of music wind-blown from a far land. You too have the love of things impossible—ἔρω ἰῶν ἀρυνᾶῑων—*l'amour de l'impossible* (how do men name it?). Sometime you will find, even as I have found, that there is no such thing as a romantic experience; there are romantic memories, and there is the desire of romance—that is all. Our most fiery moments of ecstasy are merely shadows of what somewhere else we have felt, or of what we long some day to feel. So at least it seems to me. And, strangely enough, what comes of all this is a curious mixture of ardour and of indifference. I myself would sacrifice everything for a new experience, and I know there is no such thing as a new experience at all. I think I would more readily die for what I do not believe in than for what I hold to be true. I would go to the stake for a sensation and be a sceptic to the last! Only one thing remains infinitely fascinating to me, the mystery of moods. To be master of these moods is exquisite, to be mastered by them more exquisite still. Sometimes I think that the artistic life is a long and lovely suicide, and am not sorry that it is so.

And much of this I fancy you yourself have felt: much also remains for you to feel. There is an unknown land full of strange flowers and subtle perfumes, a land of which it is joy of all joys to dream, a land where all things are perfect and poisonous. I have been reading Walter Scott for the last week: you too should read him, for there is nothing of all this in him.

Write to me at Tite Street, and let me know where you will be. Ever yours,   O.W.

Of Harry Marillier in later life we learn something from a note by Sir Rupert Hart-Davis in his edition of the Letters:

Classical scholar of Peterhouse, Cambridge, 1884–87. Became an engineer: for some years partner in W. A. Benson's metal works. Took to literary and art journalism: wrote for *Pall Mall Gazette* from 1893. Edited *The Early Work of Aubrey Beardsley* (1899) and published books on various subjects, particularly tapestry, on which he became a great expert.

But so far as his connection with Wilde is concerned these four letters are all we have.

4

Wilde made one more attempt to obtain an appointment as an Inspector of Schools, a totally unsuitable job one would have thought for one of his temperament and reputation. He wrote to Mahaffy in February 1886:

I want you, if you would do it for me, to write to your friend Lord Spencer, who is now Lord President of the Council, to make a recommendation of me as a suitable person to hold an Inspectorship of Schools. My name has been on the Education List for some time but a word from you as to my capabilities would go far towards getting me what I want. I know Spencer has a great admiration for your powers and judgment.

Nothing more was heard of this and within a year it was rendered unnecessary by Wilde's having obtained from the already powerful publishing firm of Cassell's the editorship of a woman's paper which had been in existence for less than a year called *The Lady's World*, a title which Wilde considered to have 'a certain taint of vulgarity about it' and insisted on changing to *The Woman's World*.

Once again, as in America, Wilde surprised those who had chosen him for his reputation rather than for his abilities, supposing that the mere name of Oscar Wilde, the lecturer on aestheticism, the self-advertised poet and expert on men's and women's dress, at the head of their magazine would make it controversial and profitable. They found that they had engaged a remarkably able editor, fertile in his suggestions and practical in his ideas. From his first letter to Wemyss Reid, the general manager of Cassell's, laying out the general changes and plans he proposed for the periodical, it was obvious that he was no dilettante when it came to editorial work. He was, of course, completely inexperienced in this but he very quickly showed his grasp. He wanted, he said, to make his paper deal 'not merely with what women wear, but with what they think, and what they feel'.

It should be made the recognized organ for the expression of women's opinions on all subjects of literature, art, and modern life, and yet it should be a magazine that men could read with pleasure, and consider it a privilege to contribute to. We should get if possible the Princess Louise and the Princess Christian to contribute to it: an article from the latter on needle-work for instance in connection with the Art School of which she is President would be very interesting.

The list of potential contributors he submitted was so remarkably comprehensive that even Sir Rupert Hart-Davis is intimidated by it and finds it 'unnecessary to provide notes for this regiment of literary ladies'—which is a pity. Wilde's plan continued:

It seems to me also that just at present there is too much money spent on illustrations, particularly on illustrations of dress. They are also extremely unequal; many are charming, such as that on page 224 of the current number, but many look like advertisements and give an air to the magazine that one wants to avoid, the air of directly puffing some firm or *modiste*. A new cover also would be an improvement: the present one is not satisfactory.

Wemyss Reid appears to have been impressed by these suggestions, and Wilde was duly appointed editor with freedom—not, one would have thought, usual at that time—to choose his own contributors, though for their fees he was limited to £1 per page. He himself wrote a page of Literary and Other Notes and he seems to have entered into the task with gusto.

Before he took the modest editorial chair in a small office of Cassell's premises in La Belle Sauvage, he had begun reviewing regularly for the *Pall Mall Gazette*. This had come about through his entering into correspondence over women's dress and gradually qualifying as a paid critic. He continued to contribute regularly until the middle of 1889 and thereafter at intervals till his imprisonment.

Now too he was doing what he called beautiful work in Art, but which might less pretentiously be termed writing a number of clever short stories, which he published in popular magazines like the *Court and Society Review* and *Blackwood's*. Also he wrote the first of his fairy stories, which were published as a collection, *The Happy Prince and Other Tales* in 1888. This was his first professionally published book, and there are critics who consider it his best. It was illustrated by Walter Crane and Jacomb Hood and published by David Nutt[1] who was famous for his finely printed and illustrated books.

In these fairy tales and the others which followed them, Wilde

[1] Yet another of Wilde's publishers who came to an unnatural end. The firm had been inherited from the founder, David Nutt, by his son Alfred Trubner Nutt who in 1910 was drowned trying to rescue his invalid son from the Seine.

seems to reveal most clearly his Irish origins. William Wilde, Oscar's father, 'had a good deal more native Irish blood in him than most of the Anglo-Irish could claim', Hesketh Pearson says, but it is difficult, from a first glance at Oscar Wilde's work, to decide where and how this Irish blood came out in it. Like so many of his compatriots, like Goldsmith, Sheridan, Synge, Shaw, O'Casey and the rest, he was a natural playwright, but essentially a drawing-room playwright, sophisticated and witty rather than romantic. His poetry is scarcely less metropolitan and polished and is totally unrelated, one would think, to the wild Galway landscape in which some of Oscar's youth was passed, while in his one novel, *The Picture of Dorian Gray*, a critic would find it difficult to name one scene, one figure of speech or one narrative touch which seems to owe anything to the imprints left by Wilde's upbringing. But *The Happy Prince* and all the rest are fairy stories, and but for an occasional touch of culture and self-consciousness, they are as much fairy stories as the tales told to children in the West of Ireland to this day. It was not for nothing that Oscar listened to the stories of Frank Houlihan, a Galway man who worked for his father at Moytura and whose son has added stories about Oscar himself to his mythological repertoire. Wilde's stories were spoken first and written later, as most of his wisecracks were, and it was the Irishman in Wilde, to the end of poor Oscar's life, who loved to draw an audience round him to appreciate this spoken art.

As he had done with his *Poems* seven years earlier Wilde sent complimentary copies of *The Happy Prince* with flattering letters to a number of distinguished men—to W. E. Gladstone, 'one whom I and all who have Celtic blood in their veins must ever honour and revere'; to John Ruskin, 'it is a dear privilege to offer anything to one to whom I am indebted as I am to you.' To Walter Pater who wrote:

I am confined to my room with gout, but have been consoling myself with *The Happy Prince*, and feel it would be ungrateful not to send a line to tell you how delightful I have found him and his companions. I hardly know whether to admire more the wise wit of 'The Wonderful (Remarkable) Rocket', or the beauty and tenderness of 'The Selfish Giant': the latter certainly is perfect in its kind. Your genuine 'little poems in prose', those at the top of pages 10 and 14, for instance, are gems, and the whole, too brief, book abounds with delicate touches and pure English.

Of *The Happy Prince* Hesketh Pearson (often more perceptive about Wilde's work than about his life) has this to say: "Like all who have expressed themselves in stories or plays for children, from Hans Andersen to James Barrie, he was emotionally un-developed. Even Dean Swift, who must have been revolving in his grave ever since Gulliver became a favourite in the nursery, was strangely immature in that respect and has delighted children for two centuries in spite of himself. Wilde answered a critic of his second book of fairy tales with the words 'I had about as much intention of pleasing the British child as I had of pleasing the British public.' True; but he had thoroughly pleased an Irish child: himself." This may have been the case, yet the impression is irresistible that during those years Oscar was, outwardly at any rate, becoming a mature and less conspicuously erratic man, an editor with an office in the city and the father of a family. He attracted no attention as he took the Underground from Sloane Square to Charing Cross, and thence walked to Ludgate Hill. He attracted little or no attention at first nights, for he had not yet had a play produced and although he was pointed out to the young men who used The Crown in Charing Cross Road and similar pubs and so-called bohemian meeting-places, it was as other mildly notorious figures were pointed out, and not yet as a phenomenon.

But this comparatively discreet manner of existence during the years following his marriage was disturbed by a number of factors in 1889 and 1890, including Wilde's wilful and deliberate rash-ness in publishing a short story of homosexual interest called *The Portrait of Mr W.H.* in *Blackwood's Magazine* and following it by a complete novel with a similar tendency called *The Picture of*

Dorian Gray which appeared serially in *Lippincott's Monthly Magazine* in 1890. The first, a fictional version of an old theory by which the Mr W.H. of the dedication to Shakespeare's sonnets is held to be a certain Will Hews, a boy actor of women's parts in Shakespeare's company, would have passed (as it did for Samuel Butler) if it had been put forward as a serious and rather boring literary theory, but to make a delightful spree of Shakespeare's homosexuality was unforgivable in the 1880s. It might fool the editor of *Blackwood's* who saw in it nothing but quaint antiquarian theorising, but it could not fool more knowing readers, who considered that Wilde was suggesting that England's greatest poet was a bugger, and doing so by introducing as narrator 'one of the pretty undergraduates who used to act girls' parts in College plays', according to Andrew Lang in the *Daily News*.

The story raised a stink but not nearly so much as did *The Picture of Dorian Gray*. In this most of the principal characters had their homosexual counterparts in real life—Basil Hallward, the painter who in a rather sickly way is in love with Dorian in the story, was Charles Shannon, the artist who lived for many years in marital bliss with Charles Ricketts, and Lord Henry Wotton, the cynical rich epigrammatist who steals Dorian from Hallward was Lord Ronald Gower, Wilde's friend since Oxford days. Dorian himself was a composite portrait but no doubt is left in the reader's mind about his amorality, which is in fact the theme of the book; and in Dorian Wilde gave the most audacious expression to his theory of 'the artist' being free from the obligations and exigencies of life, a theory sometimes miscalled art-for-art's-sake. It was, as we have seen, largely a personal concept adapted from many others, but with *Dorian Gray* he formulated it as a doctrine. It was caught at desperately and followed by the minor literary figures of the time whose lives were often vicious and feckless. It is true that Dorian's superiority to mere human ethics is finally punished and that right is made grudgingly to triumph. But in the meantime Wilde obviously enjoys himself describing the life of a man who has escaped a sense of guilt, who experiments with all the 'strange sins' in the list, who exploits his own lavish and extraordinary taste in all the arts—particularly that of the jeweller—who imperiously flouts all notions of decency and those who respect them, who smiles with infuriating loftiness at bourgeois efforts to reclaim him, who commits crimes for their kicks and ruins lives to watch the effect, all with a fastidiousness and elegance suggesting des Esseintes. The reader is left in no doubt as to where Wilde's sympathies lie.

The book is grossly over-written. The word 'strange' is used fifty-one times in it, 'wonderful' forty-one, 'curious' forty, 'horrible' thirty-five, 'hideous' twenty-two and 'monstrous' twenty. Its melodrama is clownish, its attempts at realism slapstick, its style novelettish. Its most artificial character, Lord Henry Wotton, is the only one with any life—the rest are dummies. Yet it has a certain drive behind it, even a certain power, which explains its appeal at the time it was published and its continuing popularity. If the decadents of the '90s existed as a clique, this was their oracle.

Wilde prefaced it with a number of maxims culminating in his unattributed rendering of Gautier's '*la peinture, la sculpture, la musique, ne servent absolument à rien*'. Moreover in letters to the editors of various daily newspapers whose critics had attacked the book, he reiterated quite brilliantly the opinion, which now seems an obvious one, that no work of art should be criticized on ethical grounds. "I am quite incapable", he wrote to the editor of the *St James's Gazette*, "of understanding how any work of art can be criticized from a moral standpoint. The sphere of art and the sphere of ethics are absolutely distinct and separate; and it is to the confusion between the two that we owe the appearance of Mrs Grundy, that amusing old lady who represents the only original form of humour that the middle-classes of this country have been able to produce." Some of his retorts to newspapers were read at the trial of Queensberry by Wilde's counsel, Sir Edward Clarke, when Carson put in the book as evidence.

The book had immediate impact. "Even in the precincts of the Savile nothing but praise of *Dorian Gray* though of course it is said to be very dangerous," wrote Robert Ross ecstatically to Wilde. "I heard a clergyman extolling it: he only regretted some of the sentiments of Lord Henry as apt to lead people astray.

Spriggie tells me that Lippincott's has had a phenomenal sale. Eighty copies were sold in one day at a Strand booksellers, the usual amount being 3 a week in that part."

"*Dorian Gray*, with all its faults, is a wonderful book," wrote W. B. Yeats. It was moreover a fateful one, for Wilde himself and for a number of young writers who accepted its barren hedonism.

From the moment of its publication Wilde seemed to assume. the mingled characters of Dorian and Lord Henry. He took to peppering his conversation with wisecracks, to lounging gracefully in long chairs, smoking innumerable cigarettes like Lord Henry and openly indulging his penchant for 'strange sins' like Dorian, or at least posing as one who did, which to Victorian England was nearly as distasteful. The Tite Street householder, the Fleet Street editor became less and less recognizable in him, and as he advanced towards his fortieth year with growing success, which was to turn to the public triumph of his first modern play, he became over-confident, over-dressed and overwhelming to all whom he considered his inferiors.

Nor was Harry Marillier the only young member of a university whom Oscar met at this time in somewhat—since it *was* Oscar—ambiguous circumstances. Later in the year of his last known letter to Harry he received a call at Tite Street from two undergraduates, aged twenty-one and twenty respectively, who shared rooms at Oxford, having been at Eton together. They were Douglas Ainslie and Lord Albert Edward Godolphin Osborne and they invited Wilde for a production of the Oxford Union Dramatic Society, of which they were both founder members. Oscar, with that phraseology which he made a habit of using in his letters to young men at this time, as we have seen in those to Marillier, replied:

Dear Douglas, I have lost your note. What is your address, and what day have you asked me for? I am really 'impossible' about letters: they vanish from my room. I don't think Constance will be able to come, but I will certainly manage some day. I hope you and Osborne are reading hard. He is quite charming, with his low musical voice, and his graceful incapacity for a career. He is a little like the moon.

You were very sweet to come and see us; we must have many evenings together and drink yellow wine from green glasses in Keats's honour.

Nothing further is known of this tripartite friendship. Ainslie became a diplomat and translator into English of Benedetto Croce. He wrote an autobiography named *Adventures Social and Literary* and Sir Rupert Hart-Davis quotes from it a story of Wilde's saying, " 'I will turn you to stone,' said Pallas Athene, 'if you harken not to the words of my wisdom.' 'Ah, but I am marble already,' said Osborne, little Osborne, and passed on."

In that same year (1886) there began another friendship of Oscar's with a Canadian boy of seventeen which was to become one of the most important for the remaining fourteen years of Wilde's life. No attempt was later made by either of them to conceal the fact that it started as a love-affair or that Robert Baldwin Ross, the boy in question, was a sophisticated and practising young queen whom, according to Frank Harris, speaking in the last bitter years of his life, Wilde had met in a public urinal. Ross, in fact, seems to have been proud of their relationship and once told Harris, inaccurately of course, that he was the first boy Oscar ever had. 'Do you observe that I have fallen in love with you again? Our Indian Winter,' Wilde wrote to Robbie Ross seven months before his death. More interesting and indicative is it that within two years of their meeting Wilde and Ross were using the terms of high camp in letters and doubtless in conversation "I have been speaking at Stratford about Shakespeare," wrote Wilde to Ross in October 1888, "but in spite of that enjoyed my visit immensely. My reception was semi-royal, and the volunteers played God Save the Queen in my honour." The occasion was the unveiling of statues of Shakespeare and four of his characters of which the sculptor was Wilde's friend Ronald Gower. The statues are good Victorian monuments, and represent Philosophy (Hamlet), Tragedy (Lady Macbeth looking like Dame Sybil Thorndyke),

Comedy (Falstaff), and History (Prince Hal represented as a beautiful boy in tights). Wilde proposed Gower's health and it was small wonder that the band played God Save the Queen in his honour.

Nor was Wilde denied some Transatlantic hero-worship at this time, and showed his response to it. He received a number of gushing letters (still preserved in the William Andrews Clark Memorial Library at the University of California) from William Clyde Fitch, then a young man of twenty-four and afterwards a successful playwright. 'We must make merry over a flagon of purple wine, and invent new tales with which to charm the world,' Wilde wrote to him, while another American, Edgar Saltus, ten years older than Fitch, sent him his book *Mary Magdalen*, which Wilde called 'so pessimistic, so poisonous and so perfect'. "You have given me that *nouveau frisson* I am always looking for," he told the author.

Saltus was a curious character who wrote a number of breathless books about imperial Rome. He responded to Wilde's alliterative description of his book by saying that vice had to be 'perfumed, pagan and private' to interest Wilde, and telling a rather silly story claiming that *Salome* had been written in competition with his own *Mary Magdalen*. His widow wrote a hair-raising book, full of baby-talk, called *Edgar Saltus the Man*, in which she refers to him throughout as 'Mr Saltus' and includes several photographs of herself looking like an actress in an early silent film. One is captioned 'Marie Saltus, Sitting at the Table on which her husband wrote his books, burning incense before a Siamese Buddha, and meditating on a Stanza from the Blagavad-Aida.'

SEVEN

'Bosie' Douglas

In the six years between 1888 and the end of 1894 Oscar Wilde achieved his whole literary output. But for the two early attempts at drama, *Vera* and *The Duchess of Padua*, and the undergraduate exercises in verse which he had printed as *Poems*, there was only the last effort at prosody, *The Ballad of Reading Gaol*, outside those few years of production in which everything he had to say in traditional forms was said. True there remain the letters, including the long letter called *De Profundis*, and it is the present author's contention that the letters of his last years are the most entertaining and revealing works of Wilde's life. But his reputation, both in Britain and abroad, was not created by them, since they could not be published in their entirety till 1962 and the exaggerated importance of Wilde in the minds of some Continental and English critics rests on the works of these years.

During them he was certainly prolific, writing with a facile grace that was the envy of such as W. E. Henley or the more laboriously comic Jerome K. Jerome. There was a glibness and readability about the essays he collected in 1891 under the title of *Intentions*, and a neat twist in each of the tales in *Lord Arthur Savile's Crime and Other Stories* in the same year. Meanwhile he followed up his book of fairy stories by *A House of Pomegranates* with Designs and Decorations by Charles Ricketts and Charles Shannon, who lived and worked and, as a contemporary said, 'did everything together'.

In February of that year Wilde had published in Frank Harris's *Fortnightly Review* an article called *The Soul of Man Under Socialism* of which the *Spectator* said not unjustly: "All these literary bullets are shot out in defence of the thesis that men should be themselves, in contempt it would seem, not merely of the public, but of all law which restricts their individualism. The article, if serious, would be thoroughly unhealthy, but it leaves on us the impression of being written merely to startle and excite talk."

The word 'unhealthy', which seems to be somewhat misapplied to Wilde's essay on socialism, had already been used with more effect in connection with *The Picture of Dorian Gray* and was to haunt Wilde for the rest of his writing life.

Towards the end of that year, 1891, after the publication in book form of four books, *The Picture of Dorian Gray*, *Intentions*, *Lord Arthur Savile's Crime* and *The House of Pomegranates*, Wilde found time to go to Paris to polish up, with the aid of French writers, the biblical drama of *Salome*, which he had written in French. In the following year he persuaded Sarah Bernhardt to appear in it in London but found it banned by the Censor on the grounds that the subject was biblical. In spite of some sulky threats to become a French citizen and take up residence in Paris he had by this time seen the success of his first modern English play *Lady Windermere's Fan* and from that his career as a successful playwright was uninterrupted till the public scandal of his action against Queensberry.

2

Meanwhile he had found a whole series of successors to Harry Marillier, Norman Forbes-Robertson, Douglas Ainslie and 'Little Osborne', some doubtless friends of Robbie Ross but others who approached Wilde directly, or met him in The Crown public house, or later through his connection with the stage. There was for instance W. Graham Robertson, an artist and writer then twenty-one years old who later became famous as a designer of stage costumes and the author of *Pinkie and the Fairies*, an annual children's play almost as popular in its time as *Peter Pan*. Again the special phraseology used by Wilde to young men is evident. "Someday you must do a design for the sonnet: a young man looking into a strange crystal that mirrors all the world. Poetry should be like a crystal, it should make life more beautiful and less real. I am sorry you are going away, but your narcissus keeps you in my memory. What do you allow your friends to call you? 'W'? or 'Graham'? I like my friends to call me Oscar." Wilde introduced Graham Robertson to Arthur Clifton, another young queer who was a friend of Robbie Ross's. He wrote to Graham at the house in which he lived with his mother till her death nearly twenty years later.

Do you really live at Sandhills, Witley? Surely not Sandhills! You are made for olive-groves, and for meadows starred with white narcissi. I am sure this letter will be returned to me by the post office.

I have written to you at Rutland Gate to tell you how sorry I am you have missed Paris, and how much more sorry I am that I did not keep you to your promise. I should have loved to have been with you—Sandhills or no Sandhills.

I send this letter into the air! Will you ever get it? I suppose not. Ever yours, O.W.

It was probably through Graham Robertson in 1889 that Wilde met Charles Ricketts, for he wrote to him: "My dear Graham, I am so sorry you are going away. Don't let the olives and the myrtles keep you too long. I called to see you on Saturday, and will try my chance tomorrow between five and six. I saw Mr Ricketts on Saturday, and he is most grateful for your cheque. He seems very cultivated and interesting." Oscar also obtained for Graham the task of designing the costumes for Sarah Bernhardt's production of *Salome* which was banned. But by April 1893, when *A Woman of No Importance* was being produced, the usual wearing thin of one of Oscar's friendships after a few years began to manifest itself. "I send you a stall for the first night of my play. I wish I could send another for your mother, but the rush for seats has been so enormous that we had to refuse Royalties and bigwigs, and

E

for my own friends I have only had a very few stalls, and have been obliged to refuse many dear and delightful people." Graham Robertson lived till 1948 and claimed considerable friendship with Wilde in his book of reminiscences *Time Was* (1931).[1] It seems likely however that he was gently dropped by Wilde, like so many other young devotees after the first flush of enthusiasm.

He did not however, like Raffalovich, live to abuse the memory of Wilde in later years. There must be many people living who remember him, a somewhat prissy old gentleman who still had some of the good looks of the youth whom Sargent had painted in 1893. In an introduction to his *Letters* (1953) Kerrison Preston speaks of his 'noticeable purity' and says it was not mere negative sexlessness but 'more like the protective chastity of a woman'. But Robertson never denied, indeed spoke quite proudly of having been, with all it implied, a favourite boyfriend of Oscar Wilde.

Like a youth called unpropitiously George Herbert Kersley, though in his case Wilde professed not to have forgotten him after six years. Graham Robertson was an artist and writer, George Kersley combined the arts of poetry and acting in a youthful ambitious way. He published books of verse including *Early Flight* with a tribute to his 'noted friend Mr Oscar Wilde'. Wilde promised to speak to 'Charlie Hawtrey' about him if he saw him, and when George obtained a walking-on part in *An Ideal Husband* Wilde wrote characteristically: "I am cheered to know that you will at any rate be a part of my play, so that I shall have an opportunity of seeing you. You must not think that I have forgotten you: friends who are also poets are never forgotten: memory keeps them in rose-leaves: but Life—coloured, turbulent Life—rushes like a river between oneself and those whom one likes, too often."

This, presumably, was the brush-off, since Kersley's name does not occur again in the record, but it was a gentler one than most.

A slightly older young man, for he was twenty-five when he met Wilde, was Harry Melvill who lived to be a notorious old

---

[1] "Another sedative was a series of eleven readings he gave on radio of Graham Robertson's beautifully written book *Time Was*"—Compton Mackenzie *My Life and Times: Octave Ten* (1971).

queen caricatured by both Osbert Sitwell in *The Machine Breaks Down* and by Michael Arlen in *The Green Hat*. "What a charming time we had at Abbots Hill," Wilde wrote to Melvill. "I have not enjoyed myself so much for a long time, and I hope that we will see much more of each other, and be often together."

A young actor, the brother of W. B. Maxwell—afterwards a well-known novelist—and the son of Miss Braddon who wrote *Lady Audley's Secret*, was Gerald Maxwell, in whom Wilde seems to have taken some, though not a very lasting, interest. He apologizes for not being able to go down to Bournemouth to see Gerald play and promises to do so when he is nearer town. 'You seem to have thrilled the great Bournemouth school of criticism.' At the end of three months of acquaintance Oscar says—'Anything I can do for you I will' and hopes that 'next time you write you will remember that I have a Christian name. Yours ever.' But three years later Oscar has become 'Yours sincerely' and asks formally, 'Pray remember me to your people', and that, so far as Gerald Maxwell's name in letters is concerned, is the end.

Among these letters only one was addressed to a young actor called Otho Stuart, but it was obviously not the first Oscar had written or, unless there was a sudden calamitous falling-out, the last!

I must send you a line to congratulate you warmly and sincerely on your beautiful and poetic rendering of Oberon last night. Of course you looked quite wonderful—like a marvellous Dionysos—and you moved with infinite grace, but it was your treatment of the verse that really fascinated me. To speak poetry well is so rare an accomplishment that it was a delight to listen to your lovely voice, with its fine sense of music and cadence and rhythmical structure. You certainly have a delicate artistic sense of the way in which imaginative work should be treated, and I have not enjoyed anything so much as "Otho's Oberon" for a long time. Ever yours.

At the same time Oscar was writing to a certain Aubrey Richardson (unidentified by Hart-Davis):

What a pretty name you have! it is worthy of fiction. Would you mind if I wrote a book called *The Story of Aubrey Richardson*? I won't, but I should like to. There is music in its long syllables, and a memory of romance, and a suggestion of wonder. Names fascinate me terribly. Come and see me some Wednesday.

Another young actor to make a single appearance in the *Letters* and perhaps not much more lengthy one in Wilde's life was Roland Atwood to whom he wrote:

I send you your necktie, in which I know you will look Greek and gracious. I don't think it is too dark for you.

Since I saw you I have heard so much of your Silvius, and how romantic it was, and how beautifully that rich musical voice of yours rendered the poetry and the passion of Shakespeare's verse, so I am not surprised that you have had many offers. Do stay in town, and act for us. Affectionately yours.

3

This curious catalogue omits the name of one among the undergraduates, rather than among the actors, who took an important place in Wilde's life, not for his own sake but because on a summer afternoon in 1891 he brought together Oscar and Bosie Douglas, and this turned out to be a most fateful occasion for both of them.

Lionel Johnson was a diminutive Wykehamist, then at New College, Oxford. He lived in London and had already started boozing and talking with writers older than himself, and he frequently met Ernest Dowson, the poet, and Charles Conder, the artist, at The Crown.

The Crown was then the sort of pub frequented by vociferous young writers and a good many literary charlatans, painters and would-be painters, together with male prostitutes and servicemen looking for an addition to their miserable wages from one or another of the richer and older customers. It was not by any means exclusively a 'queer' pub, but having once gained a reputation for being lively, it was used by those who wanted to find a young sailor or an out-of-work stable boy, as well as by artists who may have been scarcely conscious of these activities. George Moore, for instance, then just forty and known chiefly for *A Midsummer's Wife*, was still to be seen there, and young men like Dowson, who had nothing in common with the male prostitutes about him, still came frequently. Lionel Johnson was delighted with the atmosphere. Stewart Headlam, the Christian-Socialist parson who was to be a noble friend to Wilde in the time of crisis, also came to The Crown, though he was older than most of the others, being born in 1847.

Lionel Johnson met Oscar Wilde during a visit Wilde made to Oxford early in 1890. "I was determined to meet you before I left Oxford," Wilde wrote to Johnson. "I hope you will let me know when you are in town." Johnson wrote of this on 18 February to his friend Arthur Galton:

On Saturday at mid-day, lying half asleep in bed, reading Green, I was roused by a pathetic and unexpected note from Oscar: he plaintively besought me to get up and see him. Which I did: and I found him as delightful as Green is not. He discoursed, with infinite flippancy, of everyone: lauded the *Dial*: laughed at Pater: and consumed all my cigarettes. I am in love with him. He was come to visit Pater; and to see *Strafford*.

Whatever may have happened between Wilde and Johnson that February by the end of the summer term Johnson was willing to introduce young friends to Wilde, and the most spectacular of these was his junior and fellow Wykehamist, Lord Alfred, known among his friends as 'Bosie', Douglas. He was an athlete, a poet and an aristocrat, singularly attractive in appearance with the 'honey-coloured' hair that Wilde adored. Johnson described him to Wilde as 'the most beautiful young man alive and a fine poet'. Johnson was not a silly, well-meaning little man, but a creature of vision and intuition who believed that these two were made for one another. In his later years, before and after the Wilde catastrophe, it was a grief to him that he brought them together for he never lost his devotion to Bosie and believed that Wilde was wrecking his friend's life. He directed at Wilde a sonnet which is among his best, 'I hate you with a necessary hate', before the scandal broke and he regretted it after. But at this time he saw only the older man, gay, sparkling and in search of young friends, and the younger uncannily handsome and full of charm, and believed that he was doing a kind act in promoting a meeting.

Having arranged time and place with both parties, Lionel Johnson called for Bosie at his mother's house in Cadogan Place and took him in a hansom to Tite Street. Though all three must have known that this was more than a casual introduction such as might be made in a club, the whole call was conducted with the greatest decorum. Bosie and Johnson were shown into the small sitting-room on the ground floor which had a Victorian bay window looking over iron railings to the street. This room was decorated in red and yellow—yellow walls and scarlet enamel—and there was a cast of the Hermes of Praxiteles. There were a few pictures, Beardsley's drawings of Mrs Patrick Campbell, a Simeon Solomon and a Monticelli, but most of the wall space was taken up with bookshelves.

Wilde made his entrance, splendid in frock coat and button-hole. Bosie has recorded, as others have, that the first impression he had was of someone rather 'comic-looking', but this was soon dissipated as Wilde began to talk. The practised artist, with a range of modulations for his rich and plummy speaking voice, and what Ross called 'one of the hundred artificial manners which he has for every person and every occasion', soon mesmerized the undergraduate. When Wilde asked Bosie to dine with him during the next few days at the Albemarle Club, Lionel Johnson must have been delighted with the success of his introduction.

Certainly both were dazzled, though by different qualities in the other. To Wilde, who was already surrounded by young men both of Ross's intelligent and artistic kind and occasionally by the sexually congenial but less presentable working boys he had begun to pick up, Bosie's combination of the poetic and athletic, his spectacular good looks and his title, must have been irresistible. To Bosie, to be flattered and listened to by the bulky and assured Irishman who talked so confidently and brilliantly of life, which he saw as a splendid drama whose acts were the three hundred and sixty-five days of the year, was the most exciting experience he had known.

Conventions, however, were maintained to the end and Bosie was taken up to the drawing-room on the first floor to be introduced to Constance Wilde. Here there was a more Oriental atmosphere—bulrushes in Japanese vases, bamboo chairs and (Whistler's idea) huge coloured feathers let into the ceiling. Bosie and Wilde's wife came face to face, and there is no reason to doubt Bosie's statement, maintained consistently through all his phases, that they liked each other at once and continued to like each other till the crash after which they never met.

The meeting with Bosie was the culmination of all Wilde's meetings with undergraduates and young actors, but as it was not the first of them, it was not to be the last.

There had been, for instance, almost two years before Wilde met Bosie, a quite memorable occasion in The Crown when Oscar had picked up and adopted as a friend a young man named John Gray. He was the eldest of the nine children of a journeyman carpenter. He was born in 1866 in Woolwich, where his father worked in the Docks or Arsenal. From the first he seemed something of a prodigy to his Scottish parents, but lovably so, a pretty and graceful child with a remarkable aptitude for learning and for what his family found esoteric and useless occupations. At thirteen years he was sent to work in the Arsenal as a metal turner's mate but determined to better himself, and being of a naturally artistic disposition he taught himself French and drawing and became a passable violinist. Ambitious for clerical rather than manual work as a means of livelihood, he passed an examination for a clerkship in the General Post Office and in his early twenties, working in the library of the Foreign Office, he was able to take a room in the Temple and spend his nights in the cheerful gas-lit streets and bars and music-halls of central London. There is no record of his returning to Woolwich or, except for his friendship with one sister who became a nun, of further association with his family.

By 1889 when he was twenty-three years old he had tuned his voice to his new surroundings, dropping the dialect as he had dropped the companions of boyhood, and had learned to dress and act the part of what he would doubtless have called a young man about town. He was writing short stories and poems in the manner popular at that time, translating from the French Decadents, and spending more money than he could afford on going to the theatre.

Wilde was enthusiastic about him, taking the chair for him at the Playgoers' Club when Gray read an almost inaudible lecture on 'The Modern Actor' and introducing him to a number of his unorthodox friends like Ricketts and Shannon who found Gray so irresistible that they published an essay of his, or like Frank Harris, Ada Leverson and Pierre Louÿs, none of whom could be considered conventional members of society. The cooling-off came for Oscar after he had met Bosie Douglas, when for a time none of his former friends had much appeal for him and even Robbie Ross took second place.

In 1892, however, Oscar was stricken with compunction at his tendency to neglect Gray whenever he could be with Bosie, and agreed to bear the whole cost of issuing Gray's first book of poems *Silverpoints*, which was accordingly taken to John Lane for publication in the following year. Gray was viewed with some suspicion by his earnest fellow poets for his association with Wilde and other smart and wealthy people. Though he assiduously attended meetings of the Rhymers' Club he was never made a member, and though he could be seen at The Crown, his dress, like Wilde's, had grown conventional but elaborate, and his

manner, which was confidently camp, was putting-off to penurious and alcoholic writers like Dowson, Lionel Johnson, Plarr and
the rest, who were mostly public school and university men
rejoicing in their new seediness. It was a difficult situation for
Wilde who had genuinely liked Gray and admired his good looks
but who was now infatuated with Bosie. It was solved by Gray
himself, who just after the publication of *Silverpoints* was adopted
by a richer and far more devoted sugar daddy, André Raffalovich
himself. It is doubtful whether Wilde ever met him again.[1]

4

From the first there was a strong element of exhibitionism on
both sides of the Wilde Douglas friendship. To Wilde, Bosie was
the apotheosis of all the handsome and cultured young men of the
past, someone to show off as men showed off their proprietary
relationship with a famous beauty of the stage or a royal mistress.
Proud of his own virile or at least male form of homosexuality,
to know that people turned to watch him entering a restaurant
with the dazzling young son of a marquess obviously attached to
him, gave him a rare pleasure and if the two of them had stood
side by side in the dock, admitting the love that dare not speak
its name for one another, it might not have broken Wilde's spirit,
whatever the penal consequences.

As for the sexual side of their relationship, it was sentimental
rather than lustful. Neither was the other's favoured type, for
Wilde increasingly wanted tough young criminals whom he could
tame by bribery, and Bosie was so nearly heterosexual that he
only liked feminine youths whom he could associate in his mind
with beautiful boys, famous in myth or history. Oscar and Bosie
went to bed together on a number of rather tipsy occasions,

[1] The sequel to this, almost the only 'happy ending' to a story of the '90s,
is told in my book *Feasting with Panthers* or more indulgently in a *Footnote to
the Nineties* by Brocard Sewell. Gray became a Catholic priest and Raffalovich,
following him into the Church, built for him Saint Peter's Church, Edinburgh,
where he became Canon Gray and died in 1934. Raffalovich, who occupied a
house nearby for the 27 years of Gray's priesthood, predeceased him by only
four months.

assuring one another that theirs was an eternal love which would withstand all the menaces of the world, including (later) those of Bosie's Philistine steeplechasing father. They took infinite pleasure in one another's society and in romantic love-making in talk and letter-writing. For their first two years together they were seldom bored and never quarrelsome, though there were occasional fore-warnings of future disagreements.

They did not become inseparable at once. After their meeting, Bosie went off to Homberg to stay with his Montgomery grand-parents, and Wilde seems to have been working on *Lady Winder-mere's Fan*. Early that winter Wilde went to Paris alone, as we have seen, to get help in polishing up his French play. (According to Wilfred Blunt, Wilde was ambitious to become a French Academician.) On his return he went to Oxford to stay a week-end in the rooms in the High Street which Bosie shared with Lord Encombe. This was an enchanting occasion for both of them. Bosie was at Magdalen, Wilde's old college, and Wilde took his protégé to see Dr Warren, the President whom he startled by facetiously threatening to present a colossal equestrian statue of himself to the college. They also called on Walter Pater whom Wilde regarded as the greatest living prose-writer. Bosie tried hard to appreciate both the man and his work but found the prose finnicking and the man a bore. "He had practically no con-versation and would sit for hours without saying more than an occasional word."

It is hard to imagine which of the two friends was prouder or the other as they re-visited Oscar's haunts—Bosie of the famous writer and poseur, or Oscar of the beautiful young man with the title 'like the name of a flower'.

5

But neither of them made any serious attempt at fidelity to one another. Wilde had to extricate Bosie (through the lawyer George Lewis) from some difficulty with a blackmailer at Oxford, and Wilde picked up his publisher's office-boy, Edward Shelley.

It happened like this. When Elkin Mathews and John Lane formed their partnership in January 1892, the first book that was to bear their joint imprint was *Poems* by Oscar Wilde. The edition was to be limited to 220[1] copies and signed by Wilde on his own insistence.

Although he was busy with rehearsals of his first play to be produced in London, *Lady Windermere's Fan*—'one of those modern drawing-room plays with pink lampshades', he called it— he found time to go down to the offices of Elkin Mathews and John Lane, 'At the Bodley Head', in Vigo Street to put his splaying signature in these 220 copies; and while doing so he noticed that the new firm had taken on a good-looking office boy.

Three years later this boy, Edward Shelley, was described by the press as a tall, heavy-framed young fellow with a square jaw and distinctly 'intellectual' face. But in spite of this disability and his passion for literature, expressed in hurried confidence at the office, Wilde liked the look of him and stopped at his desk to chat on a number of occasions.

It is interesting to notice that three-quarters of a century ago Londoners were not so ignorant of queerness that this could pass. "It would be a terrible thing for society at large", proclaimed Mr Justice Wills solemnly in this connection, "if it were considered unnatural for a man to ask a younger man of good character to dine with him." But the irreverent employees of Mathews and Lane were not easily deceived and pulled Shelley's leg mercilessly about it, calling him 'Miss Oscar' and 'Mrs Wilde'. Or perhaps Wilde's reputation had spread to Vigo Street. Or perhaps Shelley at eighteen was camp and obvious. Anyhow it caused quite a sensation when in the weeks that followed, Shelley showed his fellow clerks presentation copies of Wilde's books, and rather fatuously a copy of *The Sinner's Comedy* by John Oliver Hobbes (Mrs Craigie), inscribed 'From the Author to dear Edward Shelley'.

Wilde should have known better. Shelley was not, in any case, his type. Coming from a respectable home, a product of State education, he had literary ambitions and affected some refinement.

[1] The copies left in stock of Bogue's edition.

His brother was of sub-normal intelligence and had to be kept at home. Edward had what were known then as 'ideas above his station' and was put into a great flutter by Wilde's notice of him.

One day as Wilde was leaving the offices, he stopped and spoke to Shelley. Would he like to have dinner with him that evening? Oh, Mr Wilde! Thank you, Mr Wilde. Seven o'clock then, at the Albemarle Hotel.

They dined in the public room, and Wilde ordered champagne. Then they went to Wilde's suite and, after a whisky and soda, Shelley found himself kissed and taken to bed, as he must have anticipated. On the following night they went to a theatre together.

Wilde in the next weeks saw much of Shelley, taking him to the Earl's Court Exhibition, the Lyric Club, the Café Royal, Kettner's and to a first night at the Independent Theatre. He considered him presentable enough to be invited to Tite Street and introduced to his wife. And when the first night (20 February 1892) of *Lady Windermere's Fan* approached, he sent Shelley a ticket. The boy was to sit next to Pierre Louÿs, André Gide's friend who had helped Oscar draft *Salome* in French. '*Vous serez à côté d'Edouard Shelley*,' he wrote Louÿs, and some acquaintance may have sprung up between the two, for in one of Shelley's letters to Wilde he said that Louÿs was 'of the same opinion' about Wilde's work and added that he was 'a charming fellow'.

Shelley heard Wilde make his unfortunate curtain speech congratulating the public on the intelligence of their appreciation. He must have been in that group of 'admiring disciples' at the bar in the interval which Le Galienne noticed 'over whom (Wilde) towered head and shoulders'. Next day Shelley wrote Wilde a gushing letter

Dear Mr Oscar Wilde, I must again thank you for the 'House of Pomegranates' and the theatre ticket. It was very good of you to send them to me and I shall never forget your kindness. What a triumph was yours last night! The play is the best I have seen on the stage, with such beauty of form and wit that it adds a new phase of pleasure to existence. Could Lady Blessington live anew the conversations would make her jealous. George Meredith might have signed it. How miserably poor everything else seems beside it! Except, of course, your books—but then your books are part of yourself.

For the rest of that year they met at intervals, and when in the autumn Wilde took a farmhouse for his family at Felbrigg near Cromer—'excellent for writing and golf still better', Oscar wrote unconvincingly to Tree—he asked Shelley to come and stay. Shelley was still working for Mathews and Lane and had to refuse.

To think of Wilde in that year of his first success in the theatre, so famous that his every movement was followed in the press —his stay with Bosie at Homberg that summer and their address there were duly reported—taking his publishers' ambitious office-boy about with him must have been more discomforting to his friends than many of his later indiscretions. It was the year in which the Lord Chamberlain refused to license *Salome* after Sarah Bernhardt had begun to rehearse it and Wilde threatened to become a French citizen, to the delight of *Punch* who pictured him as a Legionnaire. It was the year when (at Homberg) Wilde first met the Prince of Wales. *Lady Windermere's Fan* made him a pot of money, and he was being extravagant in every sense of the word.

Shelley was intense, highly strung and demanding. Already that October he began to be tiresome.

My dear Oscar, Will you be at home on Sunday evening next? I am most anxious to see you. I would have called this evening but I am suffering from nervousness, the result of insomnia, and am obliged to remain at home. I have longed to see you all through the week. I have much to tell you. Do not think me forgetful in not coming before, because I shall never forget your kindness and am conscious that I can never sufficiently express my thankfulness to you.

He complained of the 'brutal insults' he was receiving in Vigo Street and the 'horrible harsh existence' he was leading there. He wanted money to live in Chelsea and read with a private coach, and when he finally lost his job and his parents complained of his idleness, he said he was 'eating the bitter food of charity and contempt'.

Wilde paid him various sums of money which were never demanded with threats but with hysterical appeals like 'God forgive the past. Do your best for me now'. It seems likely that Shelley told his father of the relationship and was forbidden to see Wilde since for nearly a year nothing was heard of him, but in April 1894 he reappeared. Wilde wrote to Bosie who was in Italy:

I had a frantic telegram from Edward Shelley, of all people! asking me to see him. When he came he was of course in trouble for money. As he betrayed me grossly I, of course, gave him money and was kind to him. I find that forgiving one's enemies is a most curious morbid pleasure; perhaps I should check it.

That Wilde wrote this flippantly has no significance, for Wilde at this time was always flippant, even when he was most deeply concerned. That an excitable young clerk who kept talking about the sins they had committed together,[1] kept making approaches, which were what Wilde called elsewhere a mixture of romance and finance, may have disturbed him as much as the open demands of a blackmailer. If so, he was right. He had Shelley to dinner at Kettner's after Queensberry had been charged

[1] "Shelley was in the habit of writing me many morbid, very morbid letters which I tore up. In them he said he was a great sinner and anxious to be in closer touch with religion." (Wilde's evidence at his first trial.)

with criminally libelling him, doubtless to obtain his promise of silence, but Shelley was at first one of the most dangerous witnesses against him, and since he was out of the circles covered by Queensberry's detectives in their researches, he may have volunteered his testimony.

6

Meanwhile the actors continued to find favour with Wilde. The time would come, and was not so far away, when only semi-illiterate working boys would attract him, but in the meantime here—in 1892 after the banning of *Salome*—is a twenty-one-year-old called Sydney Barraclough being given the usual initial flattery:

I must some day have you in a play of mine: your Ferdinand in *The Duchess of Malfi* was a really fine performance, with such rare qualities, a style and distinction wedded to power and passion, and mastering them. You brought with you the atmosphere of romance as you came on the stage, and the Italy of the Renaissance in its pride and cruelty moved gorgeously before us, and became mad and monstrous in its insolence of sin and its sudden horror of its sin. You have a great future before you, Sydney. Let me help you.

A month later, when Wilde had taken Lady Mount-Temple's house at Babbacombe for himself and his family, he wrote to Sydney: "I want you down here: it is a lovely place, and you need rest and quiet, and I need you too, and we will devise schemes and undermine the foolish Tree, who *must* engage you for my play." But Wilde failed to get Sydney the part he wanted in *A Woman of No Importance* which went to Fred Terry, although he wrote: "you know you are my ideal Gerald, as you are my ideal friend."

After that we hear no more of Sydney Barraclough, and we meet—momentarily in a letter from Babbacombe—a certain Oswald Yorke aged twenty-seven who also wants a part in *A Woman of No Importance*. But with him the actors fade out and Bosie Douglas occupies the centre of the stage.

7

The first year or two of the friendship were certainly the happiest and least neurotic ones. Bosie was still little more than a boy, enthusiastic about Oxford, athletics, poetry and Wilde, flatteringly spellbound by the famous and notorious author of *The Picture of Dorian Gray* and *Lady Windermere's Fan*. Wilde had not yet met the two men who were to offer him fatally his choice among the semi-criminal youths of the streets and bars and but for a few fairly respectable contacts like Gray and Shelley was usually satisfied with Robert Ross and his friends—and for moments of high romance, Bosie Douglas. Without restriction from Bosie's parents, since Queensberry had not yet been chaffed about the situation by his sporty friends, and Lady Queensberry saw no danger and liked Constance Wilde whom she invited to her home, and without so far as we shall ever know nagging or jealousy from Oscar's wife, the two could move about together not only in London restaurants and theatres, but to Homberg, to the farmhouse at Felbrigg and for the whole winter to Babbacombe Cliff, Lady Mount-Temple's home in Devonshire.

There was another very practical reason for their happiness in these first years. Bosie had not yet been deprived of his allowance from his father, and Oscar had begun to make money. Even before *A Woman of No Importance* had been a success, his *Duchess of Padua* had been produced in New York under the title of *Guido Ferranti* and several of his books were selling well. So Oscar and Bosie could make one another presents, surprise each other with clothes and jewelry, which they both loved, dine out pleasantly and conspicuously and—it must be admitted—exchange confidences about their latest young men. One can scarcely say 'conquests'; 'finds' rather. Wilde certainly told Bosie about Shelley—his later letters prove as much—and probably about Graham Robertson, Gerald Maxwell, Roland Atwood and the rest. Bosie described his own youthful acquaintances in Oxford and London. It was, they both felt in 1891 and '92, an ideal friendship which would last for all their lives.

Not, however, in the opinion or with the agreement of Robert Ross. For some five years he had been privileged to produce Wilde in gatherings of his friends, to attend him in public, to be invited to Tite Street, and he now found himself treated with friendly but abstracted politeness. Oscar seemed to Robbie to have no attention for anyone but Bosie. Bosie was taken to the Café Royal, Kettner's or the Savoy, and lived, as Wilde later maintained and Ross believed, almost exclusively on 'clear turtle soup', 'luscious ortolans wrapped in their crinkled Sicilian vine-leaves', 'amber-scented Champagne', 'pâtés procured directly from Strasburg', washed down with 'special cuvées of Perrier-Jouet'. There were no more gatherings at which Oscar scintillated for the benefit of Robbie, Reggie Turner, Arthur Clifton, More Adey, Maurice Schwabe and the rest of Ross's circle, for Oscar was now inseparable from Bosie. Ross had been kept in a particular compartment of Wilde's life, welcomed there and treated with kindness, but never encouraged to emerge into the white lights of Wilde's social magnificence. He now watched while Bosie as by natural right, was taken everywhere, introduced to everyone. Ross had been petted but patronised; Bosie was not only adored but revered. Ross had been a useful amanuensis, Bosie was a fellow-writer. Ross found himself taken for granted while Bosie walked over a ubiquitous red carpet laid by Oscar. While Bosie was introduced to the most distinguished people Wilde knew; Ross, to whom such things were of urgent importance, found himself being offered by Besant the unpaid sub-editorship of the house organ of the Society of Authors. While Bosie was to be given the distinction of translating *Salome* into English, Ross was reduced to making himself useful to Edmund Gosse and receiving the anxious confidences of Aubrey Beardsley's mother. He cannot have been pleased to receive from Oscar that summer a letter from the Royal Palace Hotel, Kensington saying, "Bosie is quite like a narcissus—so white and gold. He lies like a hyacinth on the sofa, and I worship him."

8

But in all those two years, perhaps in all Oscar's manhood life, there was no time happier, more irresponsibly mirthful and untroubled by cares of any kind than the four months he spent at the house at Babbacombe.

It was a house of the period when Morris and others—acclaimed in lectures by Wilde himself—had begun to introduce new schemes into household decoration. Babbacombe Cliff had been designed by Ruskin and decorated by Morris and Burne-Jones, for its owner Lady Mount-Temple was a friend of all the Pre-Raphaelites. It sounds unbearably folksy as we read of it today— rooms named after their wallpaper, the Marigold Room, the Lily Room and so on, and a bluebell wood between the house and the cliff in which pixies undoubtedly could be seen. Yet it was, says Vyvyan Holland in *Son of Oscar Wilde*, the first house in the West of England to have central heating installed, and it seemed that beneath its very windows the sea was sunlit and brightly blue.

Constance Wilde had often stayed there with the two boys, for she was a friend of Lady Mount-Temple, but when Oscar came during an absence abroad of the owner, the whole place seemed to be transformed by his gay presence. Unaccustomed to being out of London, he was at first whimsically homesick. "Are there beautiful people in London?" he asked Robert Ross. "Here there are none; everyone is so unfinished." But soon he was writing of it as 'a lovely place' and telling Bosie Douglas 'it lacks only you'. This was after Constance, surprisingly leaving Oscar in charge of the two boys, had gone to Italy.

When Bosie came to stay, all was perfect. The two men played with Cyril and Vyvyan, drove into Torquay where they were photographed together in a formal pose in a studio and laughed helplessly over the weakest jokes.[1]

The situation was further improved by the fact that Bosie had brought with him a good-looking young tutor, a friend of Lionel Johnson's, since Bosie had been rusticated for a term for his failure to pass Greats. This tutor, Campbell Dodgson, who afterwards and until 1932 became Keeper of Prints and Drawings in the British Museum, left a very happy account (in a letter to Lionel Johnson) of the household at Babbacombe Cliff which he found indolent though anything but dull. "Our life is lazy and luxurious; our moral principles are lax. We argue for hours in favour of different interpretations of Platonism. Oscar implores me, with outspread arms and tears in his eyes, to let my soul alone and cultivate my body for six weeks. Bosie is beautiful and fascinating, but quite wicked."

When Dodgon left them in February Oscar wrote to him and one learns that the private joke between them and Bosie, and perhaps the little boys, was to consider Babbacombe Cliff as a school—evidence, if any was needed, that Wilde remained a boy in mind and that the very basis of the humour of his plays was in this running flirtation with absurdity. "I am still conducting the establishment on the old lines and really think I have succeeded in combining the advantages of a public school with those of a private lunatic asylum, which, as you know, was my aim. Bosie is very gilt-haired and I have bound *Salome* in purple to suit him. That tragic daughter of passion appeared on Thursday last, and is now dancing for the head of the English public. Should you come across her, tell me how you like her. I want you to like her. All the boys of the school send their best love, and kindest wishes. Sincerely yours Oscar Wilde, Headmaster, Babbacombe School." To this is added a list of Rules, which is reprinted in *The Letters of Oscar Wilde.*

---

[1] Much of the humour of this period Bosie was able to remember in middle age and it did not sound to me much like the brilliant wit of a famous epigrammatist. But it was obvious that the two enjoyed themselves.

Rules:

Tea for masters and boys at 9.30 a.m.

Breakfast at 10.30.

Work 11.30–12.30.

At 12.30 Sherry and biscuits for headmaster and boys (the second master objects to this).

12.40–1.30. Work.

1.30. Lunch.

2.30–4.30. Compulsory hide-and-seek for headmaster.

5. Tea for headmaster and second master, brandy and soda (not to exceed seven) for boys.

6–7. Work.

7.30. Dinner, with compulsory champagne.

8.30–12. Ecarte, limited to five-guinea points.

12–1.30. Compulsory reading in bed. Any boy found disobeying this rule will be immediately woken up.

But all this amiable nonsense led to the first violent quarrel between Oscar and Bosie, and after what Oscar described in *De Profundis* as a revolting scene, Bosie left the house. On his way back to town, however, he repented and stopped at Bristol to send Oscar one of the many telegrams with which their friendship was punctuated. Oscar hurried to join him and the two went on to London, where they took rooms in the Savoy Hotel. When Bosie had returned to Salisbury where his mother was living Oscar wrote:

Dearest of all Boys, Your letter was delightful, red and yellow wine to me; but I am sad and out of sorts. Bosie, you must not make scenes with me. They kill me, they wreck the loveliness of life. I cannot see you, so Greek and gracious, distorted with passion. I cannot listen to your curved lips saying hideous things to me. I would sooner be blackmailed by every renter in London than have you bitter, unjust, hating. I must see you soon. You are the divine thing I want, the thing of grace and beauty; but I don't know how to do it. Shall I come to Salisbury? My bill here is £49 for a week. I have also got a new sitting-room over the Thames. Why are you not here, my dear, my wonderful boy? I fear I must leave; no money, no credit, and a heart of lead. Your own Oscar.

EIGHT

Plays and Playthings

The 'homosexual world of London', as its inhabitants too self-importantly are fond of calling it, has lost its limits since the Abse Act, limits which came into being with the Criminal Law Amendment Act of 1885 and scarcely changed between then and 1967. Nowadays that secretive yet exhibitionistic manner of life, that furtively proud fellowship of men who are attracted by other men, is no longer threatened by the Rabelaisian mockery or sinister self-righteousness of the police and has found a calmer and less self-conscious existence. But between the Acts, as one might well call the period which began ten years before Wilde was arrested, there were certain characteristics of the 'homosexual world' in London and other big cities in Britain which remained constant and were visible to the observing eye.

The recognized and—unfortunately—recognizable meeting-places changed from epoch to epoch. In Wilde's time they included the Alhambra, the Pavilion, a certain part of the Empire and the bar of the St James's, as well as certain bars used by guardsmen and other male prostitutes in uniform, many public urinals and doubtless a number of cafés, while, most curiously, there was a notorious skating-rink in Knightsbridge, a meeting place much favoured by Bosie Douglas.

The esoteric vocabulary also changed with the period. 'Queer' was 'So' in those days, and a youth later designated simply as 'rent' was a 'renter' then, though 'queen' and 'camp' were perennial words. Wilde knew most of these terms and used them in correspondence with Bosie and Ross. He also knew, and later made brilliant use of, the self-defensive humour with which queers then as today sought to protect themselves from the cruder ridicule of their enemies.

Another unchanging feature was the clique which centred round some particular hospitable queen, one of whom, Alfred Taylor, was to play an important part in Wilde's promiscuous life and downfall. 'Hostesses' such as Taylor were scattered about London, some relatively discreet who sought a respectable clientele, some like John Watson Preston who kept a club at 46 Fitzroy Street and openly gave transvestist parties, while some served as a meeting-place for renters and blackmailers. Modern counterparts in all these categories existed until the later 1960s, and in far less clandestine forms exist today, their covens reported not in the police news but in the illustrated supplements of important Sunday newspapers.

Habits in dress, too, have changed. No longer is it possible for young men to advertise their sexual characteristics by growing their hair long, using make-up and wearing showy jewellery or clothes in conspicuous colours. None of these are caste-marks any longer, and a city suit as well as a pretty scarf or tie may conceal an eager-to-meet nature. Complete transvestism is comparatively rare, as it was in Wilde's time, though drag parties and dances are still popular.

Wilde entered this entertaining and vicious metropolitan world of homosexuality through a certain Maurice Schwabe whom he had met through Ross. Schwabe occupied a position about midway between the respectable queers like Ross and Arthur Clifton and the classless procurers of working-class boys like his friend Alfred Taylor. Schwabe was a 'fat talkative queen with glasses and a pronounced giggle', according to an old Anglo-West-Indian bar-keeper in Tangier who had known him in 1910, and he was killed in the First World War. He took Wilde to Little College Street, Westminster, and introduced him to Alfred Taylor.

This was a somewhat pitifully gay character, and Wilde must have known from the first what his usefulness to himself could be. Alfred Waterhouse Somerset Taylor was the son of a wealthy cocoa manufacturer. He had been at Marlborough for a few terms only, but denied that he had been expelled. Now thirty-one, he was said to have got through a fortune of £45,000 in a few years, not an easy matter in the '90s, and had been through the bankruptcy court.

He was an empty-headed invert, gossipy and good-natured, a talented pianist, 'artistic' with all the awful implications of the word at that time, and he was to show later that he was capable of a selfless loyalty and courage which made almost everyone in the sorry prosecution of Wilde look mean and treacherous. But at the beginning of 1891 he was following a life of chattering fatuity. He had just taken rooms over a disused bakehouse in Westminster, camped them up with fans and artificial flowers, and covered the windows—it was almost enough to convict Wilde when it was made known in court that he had visited the place—with *three* sets of curtains through which *the light of day was never seen*. There was only one bed in the apartment, and instead of being a respectable brass-knobbed piece of furniture, it consisted of the spring-mattress only, slightly raised from the floor. As further signs of depravity Taylor burned scented pastilles or joss-sticks, had no servant and did his own cooking, asked young men to tea and opened the door himself and audibly called them 'dear'. Mrs Grant, who lived in the basement, didn't know *what* to make of it.

Taylor had been going round for years with a couple of queens, also of decent family. One was Ernest Macklin, who remains a somewhat dim figure who discreetly left the country before the Wilde prosecution, the other was Charles Spurrier Mason with whom Taylor had lived in the previous year. Mason, said Taylor proudly in court, was a very busy man with shares in a newspaper. He certainly wrote from a Fleet Street address to Taylor in November 1891, but it was not quite the letter one would expect from a newspaper proprietor, at least not in this century.

My dear Alfred, As soon as you can afford it do let me have some money and I will be pleased and obliged. I would not ask you if I could get money myself, but you know the business is not so easy. There is a lot of trouble attached to it. I have not met anyone yet. Come home soon, dear, and let us go out sometimes together. Have very little news. Going to a dance on Monday and to the theatre to-night. With much love, Yours always, Charlie.

Taylor used to tell, with a good deal of high-pitched laughter, how once Charlie Mason and he had gone through a wedding ceremony, Charlie as the bridegroom and he in a flowing wedding-dress. 'We had a wedding breakfast after it!' he would exclaim.

Taylor did a lot of 'cruising' in the more notorious streets and meeting-places, and 'frequently walked through Piccadilly' as he was induced to say in evidence to the horror of a London jury. He was known wherever homosexuals consorted and would ask the young men he met back to Little College Street for one of the tea-parties he benevolently gave to facilitate meetings between his friends. He had what he described as 'a fancy dress for a female, an Eastern costume' which he wore to carnivals at Olympia, Covent Garden and Queen's Gate, precursors perhaps of Lady Malcolm's Ball in the 1920s and '30s. He also—it was scarcely credible to the jury when they heard it—had 'lace knickers, and stockings under a long open cloak which fastened at the waist' and a wig made for him when he was going to a ball as Dick Whittington. A vapid innocuous queen, in other words, who under any sane system of legislation would be mildly derided perhaps, or accepted as a harmless anomaly. In most European countries he would have existed happily enough with his own kind, but in England in the '90s he was told by a learned judge that he was guilty of the worst crimes he had ever tried and sent to two years' hard labour.

The first introduction Taylor made to Wilde was a failure. He had found a young man named Edward Harrington who was wasting his time with a schoolmaster named Court. Harrington, a butch type, was attractive to Taylor but not to Wilde, which saved him from giving evidence later though he was produced in court to intimidate Taylor. Taylor next introduced a youth he had picked up at the Gaiety Theatre. This one was a cut above the criminals to come. His name was Sidney Mavor, and his nickname in Little College Street was Jenny Mavor—why is unknown; he would far better have been called Mavourneen. He was a tall, slim young man who lived with his mother in South Kensington. (In later years he became a Church of England parson.)

Schwabe gave a dinner-party at Kettner's for this introduction. Taylor had prepared Mavor by telling him he was to meet an influential man who might help him—'He likes young men when they're modest and nice in appearance.' When Mavor called for Taylor on the night of the dinner-party, Taylor was delighted with him. "I'm glad you've made yourself pretty," he said, "Mr Wilde likes nice clean boys."

When he arrived at Kettner's, where Wilde had been known since his Oxford days, they found a private room had been reserved, and Mavor had his first sight of luxury—pink-shaded candles, champagne on ice and a dinner-table spread in the over-crowded and ornamental way which passed for splendour at the time. When Wilde came in with Bosie and Schwabe, and Mavor was introduced to a 'real Lord', his cup must have been full, and it remained full all the evening. "Our little lad has pleasing manners. We must see more of him," said Oscar in his rich throaty voice when the dinner was over. He did—taking him to the Albemarle Hotel a few nights later and meeting him at intervals till shortly before the case.

It may be noted from this account of one of Wilde's dinner-parties in the private room of a restaurant to which Taylor brought an amenable young friend, that Bosie was present, as though to appraise the new discovery. This, barely two years after Wilde and Bosie had met, had become the accepted order of their friendship. They *adored* each other, but they were not ashamed to be seen with creatures of a very different kind. It was all a great outwardly humorous adventure.

It is not to be supposed that Wilde, either on a sudden impulse or by a deliberate resolution, decided to change his life when he began meeting Taylor and his friends. He had known long ago during his friendship with Gower and Miles the excitement of 'picking-up' in pubs and public places, and although he had abandoned this to devote his time more discreetly to actors and undergraduates, what Taylor provided was not a complete novelty to him. But as it developed with Taylor, it became for Wilde a sensational kind of pursuit by proxy, and Taylor's discoveries became more and more plebeian and eventually criminal.

As Wilde was proud to be seen in public with Bosie so, very soon, he found a new kind of exhibitionism in displaying the young ruffians he met at Taylor's. Like many another homosexual with a taste for 'rough stuff', he converted it in his mind into a noble kind of democratism. Had he not written that clever essay *The Soul of Man Under Socialism*? Surely this—this going about with Taylor and the rest—was democratic enough for anyone? He afterwards wrote in the *De Profundis* letter:

People thought it dreadful of me to have entertained at dinner the evil things of life, and to have found pleasure in their company. But they, from the point of view through which I, as an artist in life, approached them, were delightfully suggestive and stimulating. It was like feasting with panthers. The danger was half the excitement. I used to feel as the snake-charmer must feel when he lures the cobra to stir from the painted cloth or reed-basket that holds it, and makes it spread its hood at his bidding, and sway to and fro in the air as a plant sways restfully in a stream.

Wilde actually saw himself in the character of a friend to the poor and outcast, the criminal and anti-social, and he encouraged Taylor to bring him the lowest of their breed, though he did not lose his eye for a pretty face.

Frank Harris tells a story of Wilde, which although it may not be true in any literal sense, and although the background, the occasion and even the appearance of the persons concerned may be nonsense, yet has a certain horrible veracity about it which suggests that it was not founded on mere invention.

"I was in a corner of the Café Royal one night downstairs,

playing chess and, while waiting for my opponent to move, I went out just to stretch my legs. When I returned I found Oscar throned in the very corner, between two youths. Even to my short-sighted eyes they appeared quite common: in fact they looked like grooms. In spite of their vulgar appearance, however, one was nice-looking in a fresh boyish way; the other seemed merely depraved. Oscar greeted me as usual, though he seemed slightly embarrassed. I resumed my seat, which was almost opposite him, and pretended to be absorbed in the game. To my astonishment he was talking as well as if he had had a picked audience; talking, if you please, about the Olympic Games, telling how the youths wrestled and were scraped with strigulae and threw the discus and ran races and won the myrtle wreath. His impassioned eloquence brought the sun-bathed palaestra before one with a magic of representment. Suddenly the younger of the boys asked: 'Did you sy they was niked?' 'Of course,' Oscar replied, 'nude, clothed only in sunshine and beauty,' 'Oh, my,' giggled the lad in his unspeakable Cockney way. 'I could not stand it."

2

Another episode in which Wilde used the Café Royal as a meeting-place was that of a youth called Alfred Wood. This was a pleasant-seeming boy, fair-haired and frank-looking, who was in fact already a sneak-thief and collaborator with two professional blackmailers named Robert Clibburn or Cliburn (alias Carew, Collins, Harris, Robertson and Stephenson) and William Allen (alias Pea). These were hardened villains who used youths like Wood and Atkins to steal compromising letters with which they could blackmail the recipient or sender. Cliburn, a former telegraph boy in the post office, had already served a prison sentence for blackmail, having been convicted at Lewes Assizes in 1890.

Taylor found Wood delightful, as indeed the poor deluded creature found most young men, and like many another temporarily having nowhere to live, Wood went to stay with Taylor. Wilde still being absent at Babbacombe, Taylor introduced Wood to Bosie Douglas, which led to one of the most unfortunate episodes in the whole sequence.

Bosie at this time was no less crazy with the uninhibited pleasures of sexual curiosity than Wilde, though he did not regard them as strange purple sins. He was pagan, irresponsible and thoughtless of others, accepting Wilde's doctrine of the artist's right to amorality. He was also youthfully indiscreet or he would not have taken Wood to stay with him at Oxford.

During Wood's stay there ('at the Varsity' Wood called it) Bosie gave him a suit of clothes and according to Wood (who in fact probably stole them) Bosie carelessly left in one of the pockets a number of letters from Wilde which were written in Wilde's extravagant terms. Back in London, Wood showed these to Cliburn and Allen and at a conference it was decided that Wood should sell them back to Wilde or Douglas for the amount of his fare to America, but that Cliburn and Allen should keep one with which to levy further blackmail after Wood left for the New World. Cliburn made his selection—'This one's quite hot enough,' he said—and Wood wrote to Bosie who was staying with his mother at Salisbury. Bosie had already had some warning of Wood's intention, and now asked Wilde to deal with Wood. Wilde went up to London to meet Wood for the first time and secure the return of the letters. A meeting between Wilde and Wood at the Café Royal was arranged by telegram.

What followed, as one reads it today, has both comedy and pathos. Wilde, a lord of life and a lord of language, living on the crest of prosperity and fame, an artist above all considerations of discretion or caution, saw before him not a young blackmailer who had come to extort money from him for stolen letters, but an attractive boy. He had already put the case in the hands of George Lewis, his solicitor, and had probably lost sleep over it, but Wood's fair hair and frank smile made him forget all that. He invited the boy to dinner at the Florence, gave him the usual lavish hospitality, then took him back to his empty house in Tite Street where Wood stayed most of the night, leaving before the milkman, with his great brass urn and jingling harness, came to the door. A few nights later they met again by appointment at the corner of the street and after disposing of a cold fowl in the kitchen, they again went up to the bedroom. The little matter of the letters was arranged for thirty pounds at Taylor's a few days later and, after a farewell luncheon party at the Florence and an extra fiver, Wood left for America.

Wilde may have been startled when Cliburn and Allen appeared with the other letter—if so, he did not show it and refused to buy. The pair thereupon made copies of the letter and showed one to Beerbohm Tree who was rehearsing Wilde's second play, *A Woman of No Importance*. Tree handed this to Wilde with a mild comment, and when Allen called and asked for £10 for the original, Wilde refused 'as he already had a copy', but gave him 10s. for his trouble. Allen conferred with Cliburn round the corner and Cliburn brought the letter back, saying with a grin that it was evidently no use trying to rent Wilde and he might as well have it. "I'm afraid you are leading a wonderfully wicked life," said Wilde and Cliburn made a remark about there being good and bad in every one of us.

Wilde seems to have handled Allen and Cliburn with aplomb, however foolish he may have been over Wood, but he was more disturbed by the incident than he showed. He did not know how many copies of the letter had been taken and decided to carry it off by asking Pierre Louÿs to turn it into a sonnet which could be published in Bosie's Oxford magazine *The Spirit Lamp*. Louÿs obliged and his poem duly appeared in the May issue of *The Spirit Lamp* as an assurance against any further question about it. In this it failed.

3

'Jenny' Mavor was a mild beginning to Wilde's adventures through the agency of Taylor and Schwabe in the last three years before he was gaoled. Soon Schwabe produced a youth called Freddy Atkins who really was a bad hat and was later to figure disgracefully in the prosecution of Wilde. He had been associated with a man named James Dennis Burton who lived in rooms in Lennox Gardens, Chelsea. Burton's ostensible occupation was that of bookmaker or bookmaker's tout and he kept Fred Atkins at his home and called him his clerk, though Freddy at the time was barely seventeen years old. Burton's name on the racecourses was Watson, and Atkins called himself Dennis, St Denis or simply Denny.

It is possible that they went to race-meetings during the day but at night they were industrious blackmailers. There was nothing very original in their act, which consisted in Freddy going perhaps to the bar of the St James's, or in bad times on the streets or to the public urinals, and 'copping for a steamer', meeting a mug, or making contact with a prosperous-looking and responsive man. He would bring him home, and at the right moment Burton would appear, claiming to be Freddy's uncle, so that throughout the little world in which they were both notorious he was known as 'Uncle Burton'.

Freddy's only failing as a stool-pigeon was his uncertain complexion, for he was still at the age of pimples, but with his pale eyes, loose fair hair and pert profile he was attractive enough for Burton's purpose, Burton himself being 'So' in the language of that time. Occasionally Freddy dressed as a girl, 'wore drag', but realized that with his cheeky personality (Wilde thought him 'pleasant and good-natured') he was better off in showy male clothing. The two felt themselves suited to one another, and as Burton was a police-informer they were able to take chances that others avoided.

Burton had picked up Atkins some months earlier, probably when Freddy was a marker in a billiard saloon with ambitions common at that time to most off-stage female impersonators to 'go on the halls'. Their partnership was running well, but landladies, while not being 'particular' disliked disturbances in their rooms, and they had to move to Tachbrook Street, Pimlico, which they thought would be more central.

One night, soon after they arrived there, Freddy went out on the game, choosing the Alhambra as his beat. The area at the back of the circle at the Alhambra was for many years, before it became a cinema, a well-known meeting place, as well-known as the Empire Promenade was for ladies of the town, and one can see Freddy in his tight Victorian finery, his tall starched collar and flashy tie, ogling likely prospects among older men, more than one of whom wore evening dress. That night he soon found what he wanted and took his victim—known throughout the trials as 'the Birmingham gentleman'—back to Tachbrook Street.

But he had picked a wrong 'un. Freddy led the way to the bed and encouraged 'the gentleman' to undress, as he did. Uncle Burton made his usual appearance but not only did 'the Birmingham gentleman' refuse to hand over any money, but demanded the return of his watch and chain which Freddy had thoughtfully appropriated and passed to Burton. Birmingham gentlemen, it appeared, were not to be taken in by this sort of lark, and growing noisier and noisier, he threatened to call the police.

Burton and Atkins were doubtless prepared for scenes like this but they were not prepared for their landlady, who was 'respectable' and wasn't going to have goings-on in her house. She walked in, and seeing 'the Birmingham gentleman' and Freddy naked on the bed, sent her husband, or went herself, for the police.

Everybody's bluff was called now and a sorry procession including Constables 396A and 500A marched round to Rochester Row police station. Uncle Burton and Freddy had their story ready—it had all been a fight over a game of cards—and as the Birmingham gentleman and Freddy had had time to dress before the police arrived there was only the landlady's word for the more objectionable 'goings-on'. 'All I want is my watch and chain,' the Birmingham gentleman repeated, refusing to prosecute. Freddy agreed to return the watch and chain next day, and in view of the police intervention kept his word. So another midnight incident could be written off at Rochester Row until it was exhumed as evidence two years later in one of the most famous prosecutions of the century.

But Uncle Burton and Freddy were only momentarily discouraged. They took nearby rooms at Alderney Street, and their

George Francis 'Frank' Miles, the subject of Wilde's first known passionate friendship.
Victoria and Albert Museum

The mural with which Frank Miles decorated a wall of Wilde's fishing-lodge at Illaunroe when he stayed there in 1876. It is still visible nearly a century later.

Lord Ronald Sutherland-Gower, 'a mundane and talented man who followed the life of a promiscuous homosexual'.
Radio Times Hulton Picture Library

Lord Arthur Somerset, a victim of the Cleveland Street scandal.
Radio Times Hulton Picture Library

Moytura House near Cong on Lough Corrib, County Mayo, built by Wilde's father in 1865 and still bearing an inscription to that effect.

Illaunroe Lodge on Lough Fee, Connemara, Wilde's fishing-lodge. Except for some interior modernization it is unchanged from the time of Wilde's various visits.

Portrait of Oscar Wilde during English lecture tour, still wearing Neronian hair-do acquired during Paris visit. Perhaps Constance Wilde discouraged it when he married her that year? *R. W. Thrupp, Birmingham, 1883*

Lord Alfred Douglas, 'Bosie'.

Charles Hazlewood Shannon. Charles De Sousy Ricketts.

James Rennell Rodd, shortly after he had been Wilde's 'heart's brother' on a walking tour with him by the Loire, and had become 'the true poet and false friend'.
All Victoria and Albert Museum

CAPTIOUS CRITIC.

once again.
pale green, in.
dear, delig
rich with o
had cover
was about
the Prin
and hou
the true
and deli
came,
of
you
haired an
not the k
afloat o
practi
ha
joy
hair, World
a his
came
ta we are
th yman, at
se elmonico
cre captie
for etical
ow con
up t as
obli with
me b m. in
remna in I
dilly.

'ear as he was when we
'd him to America

*Frightful forshadowing of
our Oscar's future should he
continue to cut his hair and
resume the knee breeches*

offensive, compared with the Atlantic). Just one word more.
Should you continue to cut your hair, for dear life do not
resume the "*Patience* Advertisement Costume," or the result
may prove too terrible

Contemporary caricatures, the one in convict dress 1883 gruesomely prophetic.
Mary Evans Picture Library

FANCY PORTRAIT.

QUITE TOO-TOO PUFFICKLY PRECIOUS!!

Being Lady Windy-mère's Fan-cy Portrait of the new dramatic author,
Shakspeare Sheridan Oscar Puff, Esq.

["He addressed from the stage a public audience, mostly composed of ladies, pressing between his daintily-gloved fingers a still burning and half-smoked cigarette."—*Daily Telegraph.*]

Hitherto unpublished portrait of Oscar Wilde by Renée Thuyns, one-time art master at Portora Royal, Wilde's old school.

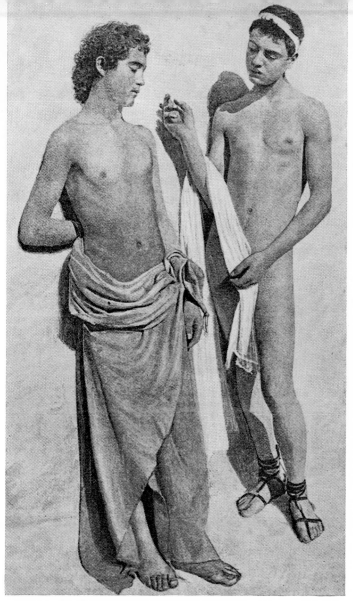

In *The Letters of Oscar Wilde* the following note appears referring to
the Baron von Gloeden: 'A German who settled at Taormina in the
nineties and died there in 1931. He acquired some reputation for his
photographs of Sicilian youths posed "noble and nude and antique"
in the guise of Theocritan goatherds or shepherds.' This is one of the earlier
studies, and Wilde probably saw it and others when he visited Gloeden
late in 1897. He afterwards sent him a copy of *The Ballad of Reading
Gaol*.

(*Opposite*) Portrait by J. S. Sargent of W. Graham Robertson as a youth.
'You are made for olive-groves, and for meadows starred with white
narcissi,' Wilde wrote to him. *The Tate Gallery*

Diaghilev as a young
man in Paris. 'There is a
young Russian here,'
Wilde wrote in May
1898. 'He is a great
collector and rich.'
The Mansell Collection

The Hon. Lionel Raleigh
Holland. 'He seems very
mad but quite brilliant,'
wrote Wilde in 1894.
*Radio Times Hulton
Picture Library*

fortunes were soon mended with a cheque for £200 made out to Mr Denis from another 'gentleman' whom Freddy had picked up while dressed as a woman.

Finding the curiosity of landladies irksome and blackmail more easily levied in hotels, they took respectable rooms in Buckingham Palace Road and worked from there with greater discretion. 'An elderly gentleman from the City' was invited back and robbed of his pocket case which enabled Uncle Burton to discover his address, call on him at his office and extort a large sum. Then there were two American gentlemen whom Freddy took to the Hotel Victoria in Northumberland Avenue where Uncle Burton, deeply shocked, found all three in *flagrante delicto*, and received compensation. This, and another douceur he got from a gentleman at Anderton's Hotel, Fleet Street, enabled him to take Freddy for a holiday to the South of France where they stayed at Gaze's Hotel, Nice, and had a day in Monte Carlo, but fell out, presumably over dividends from a profitable stroke while on holiday. It was more than a year before they worked together again.

It was during that year that Schwabe, at the Knightsbridge skating-rink, picked up Freddy Atkins. Schwabe took him to be a somewhat knowing youth but had no reason to see in this boy, less than eighteen years old, a hardened young villain with a police record. He took him about with him for some months, for Atkins, a tubby youngster with a ready grin, had a certain Cockney charm and talked amusingly about his experiences as a billiard-marker, a bookie's clerk and an entertainer in pubs—a recognized way of earning an occasional sovereign. His ambition was still to go on the halls. Schwabe became quite attached to him, and Freddy came to his rooms off Margaret Street almost daily but kept a room of his own in Pimlico. Freddy does not seem to have regarded Schwabe as a prospect but rather as friend, even a collaborator, for he spoke in court of a 'young fellow named Schwabe'. Schwabe introduced him to Wilde in October 1892.

Wilde was no less susceptible to Freddy's vulgar but sprightly personality. One can see the tall dressy Irishman in his elegant

F

frock-coat beaming down on the cheeky little street rat and in-dulgently promising to take him to Paris for a week-end, as so many Englishmen in the last centuries have promised so many new acquaintances, female and sometimes male. Freddy had passed through Paris on his way to Cannes with Uncle Burton, and wanted to see more of the exotic attraction which every young Englishman believed it to possess.

They travelled on the 'Club' train and went straight to an hotel at 29 Boulevard des Capucines where Wilde had discreetly en-gaged three rooms with communicating doors, for Schwabe was to join them on the following day. Next morning they lunched at the Café Julien and in the afternoon went to Pascal, the famous hairdresser under the Grand Hotel where Wilde had once had his hair done in what he called a Neronian style. Freddy was given the nineteenth-century version of a permanent wave. Wilde had to dine with someone connected with the publication of *Salome* and handed Freddy a sovereign with which to go to the Moulin Rouge. It was all very gay and enjoyable and they returned on Wednesday with Maurice Schwabe.

Unperturbed, perhaps even elated by the episodes of Wood and Atkins, Wilde kept in touch with Taylor and before long was rewarded by news that he had two new acquaintances—the brothers Bill and Charlie Parker, who had been introduced to him by Harrington in the notorious St James's bar. On the strength of Taylor's assurances Wilde engaged a private room at Kettner's and asked Taylor to bring the lads to dinner.

They were the sons of an employee in a racing stable at Datchet, and had been working in London, Bill as a groom, Charlie as a valet. Harrington had found them and brought them to the St James's to meet Taylor. Charlie, a dark, slightly built lad with a girlish face, had cheerfully remarked: 'If any old gentleman takes a fancy to me, I'm agreeable.' They were both without money.

Of all Wilde's dinner-parties at Kettner's, this, in the eyes of his guests, most absurdly parodied the kind of Roman feast Wilde dreamed it to be. If Mavor from South Kensington had been im-pressed, these two semi-illiterates who had been sleeping in doss-houses must have had their breath taken away. A large meal, champagne, Wilde talking about 'poetry and art and the old Roman days', as Charlie Parker put it, Wilde feeding Charlie with titbits and passing candied cherries from his lips to the boy's, brandy and cigars afterwards and at last Wilde's announcement as he put his arm round Charlie—'This is the boy for me!' Then, a trifle tipsy as he must surely have been, Wilde took Charlie back to the Savoy where he was staying. William was left with Taylor and had the consolation of hearing: 'Your brother is lucky. Oscar doesn't care what he pays if he fancies a chap.'

Whether or not Charlie was lucky seems doubtful. He afterwards stated in the witness-box that Wilde 'committed the act of sodomy upon me', which caused the prosecuting counsel, Charles Gill, to put one of the most asinine questions in the whole case. "With your consent?" he asked. Not surprisingly he received no reply. Charlie Parker also gave evidence about Wilde's approach to sex which would tell a psychologist all he needed to know about Wilde's sexual make-up. "I was asked by Wilde to imagine that I was a woman and that he was my lover. I had to keep up this illusion. I used to sit on his knees and he used to play with my privates as a man might amuse himself with a girl. Wilde insisted on this filthy make-believe being kept up."

This was the beginning of another of Wilde's intermittent relationships. He even took the boy about with him for a time, appearing in a box with him at the Pavilion. But when Wilde left London, having taken a house at Goring for the summer, Charlie was picked up by a rich man, mysteriously referred to as 'a famous operatic composer', who took him to Paris for some months. This may only have been a man named Harold Henry, a friend of Wilde's and Taylor's, who was in fact 'a clerk in a music publisher's in Putney'. Charles was to reappear later.

5

Meanwhile in that summer (1893) well provided for by his royalties from *A Woman of No Importance* which had opened most successfully on 19 April, Wilde took a furnished house on the river at Goring, and Bosie joined him there. After a time Constance Wilde went away with the children and the two friends were left together. They engaged as a servant a boy called Walter Grainger who had been employed in Bosie's rooms in Oxford, a 'peculiarly plain boy, unfortunately extremely ugly', as Wilde was to say tactlessly in evidence later. They shared the expenses of the establishment and lived modestly for some months, having on the river a Canadian canoe 'curved like a flower', as Oscar said.

It was while he was staying at The Cottage, Goring-on-Thames, that Wilde first corresponded with an interesting woman whom he called The Sphinx. Ada Esther Leverson was then thirty-one years old. Her husband, Ernest David Leverson, was the son of a diamond merchant and a man of some fortune. They were cultured and charming Jews. The Sphinx was one of the few of Oscar's friends who was not jealous of his friendship with Bosie, and the only communication known to be signed jointly 'Oscar and Bosie' was addressed to her. When others were raging at Wilde's return to Bosie at Naples after his downfall, he could write to her—"Bosie and I often talk over your delightful sayings." She wrote wittily, but not too wittily for *Punch*, and published several novels.

Oscar and Bosie had quarrels, and one which happened at Goring was bitterly recalled later by Wilde in *De Profundis*. Bosie went off one day after a violent scene with Oscar. Some of his Oxford friends had stayed the week-end and when they had left, the two stood 'on the level croquet ground with the pretty lawn all round' them and argued it out. The old, the perennial accusations between two lovers of the same sex trying to lead something like a married life were spoken angrily—they were ruining one another's lives, to part was the only remedy. After lunch Bosie 'sullenly' went up to London, to come back three days later, when there was the usual delightful reconciliation.

Yet Bosie always remembered that summer at Goring without bitterness, and spoke of the house and garden, and of Oscar on the river, and of their indolence and laughter. He wrote there two light-hearted lyrics, *Night Coming into a Garden* and *Night Coming out of a Garden* which are among the best of his early verses. Ornate and dated as they are, they show that the young man who wrote them did not have to go to his companion for poetic talent.

But neither of the friends wrote much that summer. Oscar was supposed to be writing *An Ideal Husband* but he got no farther than an outline. Bosie during the previous term had started translating Wilde's *Salome* back into English, in which Oscar had originally drafted it before he wrote it in French with the assistance of Pierre Louÿs and André Gide. Bosie now finished it, but this was not a difficult task, for the dialogue was of pseudobiblical simplicity. Oscar had probably asked Bosie to do it as a compliment to him as a writer and in order to have their names together on the title-page.

But it caused one of their fiercest quarrels when they were back in town. Robert Ross had become very friendly with Aubrey Beardsley and his mother, and persuaded Wilde to let Beardsley do the illustrations. Wilde and Beardsley disliked one another but Wilde gave Ross his way and Beardsley responded by including unkind caricatures of Wilde in the *Salome* drawings which Wilde described as "cruel and evil and so like dear Aubrey who has a face like a silver hatchet with grass-green hair". It needed all Ross's gifts of mediation and diplomacy to smooth this over, but when Wilde told him that he did not like Bosie's translation, he audaciously suggested that Beardsley should do one in its stead, which would be in every way better. It was probably the first time Ross had heard Wilde make the smallest criticism of anything Bosie did, and he wanted to take advantage of it. Then and thereafter Ross was always at hand when there was the hope of a quarrel between Oscar and Bosie, always hoping it was final and always disappointed by the inevitable reconciliation. This time he nearly succeeded, and if Beardsley's translation had satisfied Oscar, he would have had at least a temporary triumph.

But it did not. What Oscar wanted, of course, was his own original version and Beardsley's was farther from this than Bosie's. Finally, Oscar compromised, using his own version with some of Bosie's. Instead of the title-page planned, was one bearing the words, 'Translated from the French of Oscar Wilde: Pictured by

Aubrey Beardsley', while the Dedication would read: 'To My Friend Lord Alfred Bruce Douglas the Translator of My Play'.

Ross's part in this is shown by the letter Beardsley wrote to him about it:

I suppose you've heard all about the *Salome* Row. I can tell you I had a warm time of it between Lane and Oscar and Co. For one week the numbers of telegraph and messenger boys who came to the door was simply scandalous. I really don't quite know how the matter really stands now. Anyhow Bozie's name is not to turn up on the Title.

Later in the same letter he wrote:

By the way Bozie is going to Egypt in what capacity I don't quite gather; something diplomatic I fancy. Have you heard from either him or Oscar? Both of them are really very dreadful people.

After their stay at Goring that summer Bosie went to stay with his uncle George Finch at Burley-on-the-Hill while Oscar went off to Dinard for a fortnight on his own. Though the words he used to describe this in *De Profundis* were, like most of that book, theatrical and exaggerated one can see what he meant:

To be perfectly frank with you, I could not under any circumstances have let you be with me. We had been together nearly twelve weeks. I required rest and freedom from the terrible strain of your companionship. It was necessary for me to be a little by myself.

But on his way back from France he called at Guernsey and on his return wrote to Bosie who was in Devonshire for the marriage of his brother Percy. A reference to 'proofs' in his letter showed that he still affected to think of *Salome* as translated by Bosie.

6

All the incidents described in this chapter, the initial contacts and seductions, the procurements and carefully planned dinner-parties at which boys were produced for Wilde, took place within the twelve months from October 1892 when Wilde rented Babbacombe Cliff to October 1893 when he took rooms at 10 and 11 St James's Place, 'purely in order to work undisturbed' as he claimed in the *De Profundis* letter. Their background, as we have seen, was generally London, for Wilde could not stay away from the metropolis for long and came up frequently from Devon and Goring—for the production of *A Woman of No Importance*, for business talks, or merely (as in the case of Wood) to meet a boy. The first acquaintance with Taylor was in that year, and the production of 'Jenny' Mavor, the meeting and trip to Paris with Freddy Atkins, the dinner-party at which Wilde met the Parker brothers, and his taking of the younger of them back to the Savoy Hotel. It may well be understood that during that time, including what should have been productive periods at Babbacombe and Goring, Wilde did not do a stroke of work, or at least, more justly, got nothing down on paper.

For it was in that year that Wilde, let loose with plenty of money among the infinite possibilities of a London in which the poor were underfed, if not half-starved, and prostitution of every kind was scarcely concealed, became consumed with his passion for moving swiftly from one to another of the boys he met. Promiscuity such as his was not unusual and is the aspect of homosexuality which is most shocking to the uncommitted observer, perhaps because it is impracticable when two sexes are concerned. There is a fatal facility about it for homosexuals which produces cases like Wilde's that look like the ravening of wolves of unassuageable appetite but, viewed from another direction, are little more than cerebral excitement finding its outlet in an interminable series of rendezvous and brief encounters. Wilde was hypnotized not by any individual but by his conception of pleasure, of supermanship—a sultan, with all the world's delights to choose from, crying banally 'Bring on the dancing boys!' He was eating gluttonously, lunching at the Café Royal, dining at the Savoy and going on for supper at Willis's on most days, drinking too much at meals and between them. He regarded most of the young men who were brought to him by Taylor and Schwabe as figures in what he called painted pageants, paid them and gave no more thought to them than to the hansom cabs he hired. Fate, he thought, had cast him for the part of a Roman emperor, and he richly enjoyed it. He was, as he had always been, without the gift of self-criticism. He may have bemoaned his increasing weight—he could not see that his character was becoming gross, too. But as for his promiscuity—there was nothing exceptional in it. It was part of the life he had chosen.

It was also a part of London life in his day. Recent investigation has made doubly clear what has long been suspected, that under the righteousness of the Victorian exterior there flourished a life more vicious and harsh than that of any period in London's history. Young girls, often no more than children, could be bought and sold, as W. T. Stead proved and went to prison for proving. Poverty was so nearly general and so pitiless that the few who had gold sovereigns to chink in their pockets could choose what they liked of illicit pleasures, and though homosexuality itself did not increase in this or any other particular period, there was far more male prostitution. A redcoat having only a shilling or two a week to spend on beer or tobacco, and finding that he was an object of desire for inverts, was swift to make himself available, while a young apprentice, starved for sympathy or interest in his dreary life, if not for food, eagerly welcomed the attentions of middle-aged gentlemen ready to entertain him.

Such conditions doubtless existed in every big city from imperial Rome to the present, but when one comes to examine Wilde's life in the last year or two before his prosecution, and feels perhaps shocked by the variety of youths whom he procured, it should be remembered that some of them had not had an adequate meal for a long time—let alone dinner in a private room at Kettner's—and that work was difficult to find and exacting. There was plenty of temptation on both sides. Wilde was a highly-sexed and promiscuous man, like his father, but not a monster of incontinence. The boys were anxious to make money to relieve them from grinding necessity and monotony, and it is always difficult with their kind to decide where begging becomes blackmail. Although they gave evidence against Wilde spitefully enough later, they were bribed and threatened into doing so and were no worse than countless others of their kind in London.

7

There was some unpleasantness that year with Aloys Vogel, the manager of the Albemarle Hotel to which Wilde often took young men for the night—as he had taken Shelley—and this decided him to find a flat which would give him more freedom both for pleasure and work. Probably he really believed as he rented it, and probably he told Constance, that it was 'purely in order to work undisturbed', but when those he entertained at the flat came to be named by the Prosecution later, it is hard to see how Wilde can have convinced himself. For he was visited by Charlie Parker, Fred Atkins, a friend of Atkins named Harry Barford (said to be an actor), Sidney Mavor and Ernest Scarfe (known to Oscar and Bosie as Ernesto), a young clerk whom Taylor brought in unexpectedly, saying that he had come from the Australian gold-diggings. (Scarfe being a new acquaintance-ship was given his dinner at Kettner's and an inscribed silver cigarette-case. Taylor had met him at the Knightsbridge skating-rink through a man named Arthur Marling, alias Goff, a thoroughly bad lot who was associated with Cliburn and Allen.) All these visits were listed in court by an employee of the service flats in which Wilde had his apartment.

Thomas Price, a waiter at a private hotel at 10 St James's Place, said the prisoner Wilde had rooms there from October 1893, to April 1894. The rooms were on the ground floor, and consisted of a bedroom and a sitting-room communicating. He recognized the prisoner Taylor, and he had seen him at St James's Place on one occasion. Charles Parker came there five or six times. He used to ask for Mr Wilde, and was shown into Mr Wilde's rooms. He lunched there once. Witness knew Atkins by sight. He had called there twice. Scarfe called five or six times, and Barford about the same number of times. Mr Wilde had a latchkey, but never slept there more than a dozen times. (*The Trials.*)

It was not only young men of Taylor's circle he asked to his rooms in St James's Place, but male writers of fan letters who promised to be interesting. "Will you come and see me? Your handwriting fascinates me, your praise charms me," he wrote to someone called Ralph Payne, whom Hart-Davis has been unable to identify, while to Philip Houghton, an artist, he wrote: "Write to me about yourself; tell me your life and loves, and all that keeps you wondering. Who are you? (What a difficult question for any one of us to answer!) I, at any rate am your friend."

Meanwhile Bosie's mother was deeply anxious about him and his now publicly criticized association with Wilde, who was becoming notorious. She was determined to separate the two friends, especially since Wilde, in a somewhat disingenuous letter to her, professed to want the same separation. She called on the assistance of her parents and produced the only kind of scheme which might have a chance of success, a scheme which would appeal to Bosie himself. One of her most intimate friends from childhood had been Ethel Errington, who was married to Sir Evelyn Baring, 'Consul-General and Diplomatic Agent' in Egypt, who had just been given a barony and become Lord Cromer (afterwards first Earl of Cromer). Lady Cromer, appealed to by Lady Queensberry, at once invited Bosie to come and stay for some months at the Agency in Cairo with the idea that after this private experience of the diplomatic service, he might be found an attaché's post somewhere else. Bosie, who may have been feeling some of the strains of being Wilde's idol and playmate, agreed and left for Cairo in December.

But Lady Queensberry was still a little apprehensive of a possible move by Wilde and wrote to him one of her most kind and tactful letters, begging him not to 'meet Bosie abroad', by which she meant not to follow him to Cairo. She justified her letter by explaining that the friendship of such a distinguished man as Wilde was bad for Bosie's vanity, and association with Wilde and his friends had so educated the artistic side of Bosie's nature that he spoke of his elder brother as a Philistine.

Wilde, with the kind of thick skin his vanity gave him, again read this as criticism of Bosie and percipient praise of himself, and said he agreed with every word of it, adding grandly that he had not the slightest intention of meeting Bosie abroad.

But after Bosie's stay in Cairo, instead of taking up the duties of a post which had been offered him by Lord Currie, the British Ambassador in Constantinople, Bosie went, in the following spring, to stay with E. F. Benson (whom he had met in Egypt) in Athens. Why not? It was April and he had never seen the Acropolis. Lord Currie could surely wait.

Benson had rooms in Athens, and the young man who ended his life in Henry James's house in Rye, of which town he became Mayor, writing a series of chi-chi novels about Lucia and Miss Mapp, was an excellent host and cicerone.

Then—why not a week or two more? Why not telegraph to Oscar to meet him in Paris so that they could spend a few days together before Bosie took up his arduous work in Constantinople? He had already told Lord Cromer that he thought of running up to London, or at any rate Paris, before he reported for duty, and Cromer had raised no objection. The wire was sent to Oscar, and Bosie received an eager reply. This became in poor Wilde's disordered recollections in Reading Gaol a whole series of 'passionate telegrams' with which Bosie was supposed to have pleaded for a reunion. To De Profundis, too, we owe an account of the meeting in Paris which shows that Wilde's sense of humour failed him in prison, for before or after serving his sentence he would have been the first to find it comic:

When I arrived in Paris, your tears breaking out again and again all through the evening, and falling over your cheeks like rain as we sat at dinner first at Voisin's, at supper at Paillard's afterwards: the unfeigned joy you evinced at seeing me, holding my hand whenever you could as though you were a gentle and penitent child: your contrition, so simple and sincere at the moment: made me consent to renew our friendship.

Tears 'like rain' at Voisin's and Paillard's—how could Wilde, ever under the strain of prison, write like this?

Yet somehow, during that winter in the rooms in St James's Place, Oscar completed his third modern play, *An Ideal Husband*, a comedy which creaks with contrivance but which, when it would be produced nearly a year later, would be no less successful than the others.

NINE
The Enemy

"The father ranks in history with the good parents of moral tales: the son with the Infant Samuel: and I, in the lowest mire of Malebolge sit between Gilles de Retz and the Marquis de Sade." Thus Wilde wrote to Ross from prison concerning the public estimate of Queensberry and himself, and was so pleased with the concept that he repeated it a month or two later in the *De Profundis* letter to Bosie Douglas. It was true enough at the time of the trials and for some time thereafter, except among the few who could think objectively of the case and had a sense of justice. Queensberry was a hero. In spite of his publicly proclaimed atheism and his divorces he was seen as the man who had 'saved his son from that beast Wilde'.

But after the turn of the century, when both Oscar and Queensberry were dead, the pendulum began to swing to the other extreme until today the little ginger-headed Marquess, hard drinking and looking like a horse-trainer, has become the villain of the piece, the vindictive assailant of a man of genius, the hypocrite who pretended to protect his son in order to obtain publicity for himself and revenge on his family, the mean-spirited aristocrat who used his wealth to ruin a poor playwright. All the biographers of Wilde agree in their vilification of the man whom Wilde called the Scarlet Marquis.

But the truth lies, as usual, somewhere between the two extremes. Queensberry was an odious man, and what was worse in those days, a man of evil reputation. It is true that he was vindictive and that in his harassment of Wilde he looked for publicity for himself. But his motives should be better understood. With the creation of a public image of himself as an initiator of the Queensberry Rules of Boxing, a successful amateur jockey, a 'sporting peer' if ever there was one, Queensberry lived in fear of ridicule, and when he heard men in the horsy circles he frequented laughing at him for allowing his son to 'go about with a bugger', it roused his fury. Nor can all that vaunted concern for his son's welfare be quite dismissed as the merest hypocrisy. His wife had divorced him, his elder son had become a member of the House of Lords from which Queensberry was barred, and his youngest son sent him rude telegrams when he forbade him to associate with Wilde. Flesh and blood, he decided, could not bear it, and when he saw Wilde and Bosie not only going about together but choosing the most conspicuous occasions, the most fashionable restaurants, for their meetings, he became determined to step in and save not only his son's reputation but his own.

For a time although he was fed on scandalous talk, he was placated by Wilde himself. One day in the autumn of 1892, when he went into the Café Royal, he found Oscar and Bosie lunching together. He had not at this time actually spoken to Wilde and he was pleased to see that his son hurried across to his table and begged him to come and meet Wilde. With surly unwillingness, Queensberry agreed. Wilde gave him all he had of charm, brilliance and courtesy, and in ten minutes Queensberry was laughing and listening eagerly. At the end of lunch Bosie tactfully left them but he later heard from Oscar that they had remained together in friendly converse till past four o'clock and Queensberry had accepted an invitation to stay at Babbacombe early in the following year. This was confirmed by a letter which Bosie received from his father two days later. Queensberry wished to 'take back' all he had said of Wilde. He considered him charming and clever and did not wonder that Bosie was so fond of him. He had been told by his old friend Lord de Grey that Wilde was a friend of his and Lady de Grey's and was 'perfectly all right in every way'.

Bosie was delighted but Oscar refused to be impressed one way or the other. Queensberry to him was still no more than an irrelevance, someone whom Bosie took seriously both in attack and—when there was scope for it—friendliness, someone who gave Bosie an allowance. He did not wish to antagonise him but he, Oscar Wilde at the height of his fame, could scarcely be expected to make up to a man in style and taste and association so different from himself, and in all but rank so inferior.

At the point we have reached in the story of Wilde, little had happened to warn him of the future. Moreover he had not the least understanding of the characters of Bosie and his father, and could not perceive that underneath their mutual abuse and recrimination, the hysterical epithets they flung to and fro and the hatred they both believed they felt, Bosie and his father had a kind of unwilling love for each other. Bosie hated his father partly because he loved his mother (whom Queensberry undoubtedly wronged), partly because he loved Oscar, and partly because he believed his father hated him. Queensberry, the sour psychopathic misanthrope with an aching persecution mania, hated his son because he had once loved and now abhorred his wife, to whom Bosie was passionately devoted, because he believed that Bosie, like all his children—indeed like all the world —was against him, and because he was the kind of man in whom love and hatred were always mixed. But underneath these twin hatreds was the shy and tortured love of father for son and son for father. It was something which Wilde could never perceive. If he had done so and known how to take advantage of it, it would have saved him.

The invitation to Queensberry to stay with the Wildes at Babbacombe—a most unlikely occasion it seems now—led to nothing, and no more was heard of the Marquess during Wilde's stay at Goring or the time of his refuge in St James's Place. But in the spring of 1894, after Bosie's stay with the Cromers and his meeting with Oscar in Paris, they were once again lunching in the Café Royal when Queensberry joined them. The occasion was very unlike the previous one. Queensberry watched the two narrowly while he 'drank of' Oscar's wine, and they must have been in a defiant, ostentatious or perhaps merely flippant mood, for Queensberry, primed by gossip from fellow clubmen, was horrified. He stumped away and very soon began writing savage letters. After an exchange or two he wrote from Carter's Hotel in Albemarle Street on Sunday, 1 April 1894:

Alfred, It is extremely painful for me to have to write to you in the strain I must; but please understand that I decline to receive any answers from you in writing in return. After your recent hysterical impertinent ones I refuse to be annoyed with such, and I decline to read any more letters. If you have anything to say, do come here and say it in person. Firstly, am I to understand that, having left Oxford as you did, with discredit to yourself, the reason of which were fully explained to me by your tutor, you now intend to loaf and loll about and do nothing? All the time you were wasting at Oxford I was put off with an assurance that you were eventually to go into Civil Service or to the Foreign Office, and then I was put off with an assurance that you were going to the Bar. It appears to me that you intend to do nothing. I utterly decline, however, to just supply you with sufficient funds to enable you to loaf about. You are preparing a wretched future for yourself, and it would be most cruel and wrong for me to encourage you in this. Secondly, I come to the more painful part of this letter—your intimacy with this man Wilde. It must either cease or I will disown you and stop all money supplies. I am not going to try and analyse this intimacy, and I make no charge; but to my mind to pose as a thing is as bad as to be it. With my own eyes I saw you both in the most loathsome and disgusting relationship as expressed by your manner and expression. Never in my experience have I seen such a sight as that in your horrible features. No wonder people are talking as they are. Also I now hear on good authority, but this may be false, that his wife is petitioning to divorce him for sodomy and other crimes. Is this true or do you not know of it? If I thought the actual thing was true, and it became public property, I should be quite justified in shooting him at sight. These Christian English cowards and men, as they call themselves, want waking up. Your disgusted so-called father   Queensberry.

To this Bosie replied with a telegram which became mildly famous at the time of the trials but seems sadly facetious today. It would be interesting to know whether Wilde was amused by it or even knew that it was to be sent for somehow it suggests a silly joke shared between them. "What a funny little man you are," wired Bosie. Queensberry rose to this, writing by return:

You impertinent young jackanapes. I request that you will not send such messages to me by telegraph. If you send me any more such telegrams, or come with any impertinence, I will give you the thrashing you deserve. Your only excuse is that you must be crazy. I hear from a man at Oxford that you were thought crazy there, and that accounts for a good deal that has happened. If I catch you again with that man I will make a public scandal in a way you little dream of; it is already a suppressed one. I prefer an open one, and at any rate I shall not be blamed for allowing such a state of things to go on. Unless this acquaintance ceases I shall carry out my threat and stop all supplies, and if you are not going to make any attempt to do something I shall certainly cut you down to a mere pittance, so you know what to expect.

In most of Queensberry's letters are to be found references to things he has heard or been told about his son and Wilde, and one can guess that he was fed on a good deal of malicious gossip, no doubt by the kind of troublemaker who enjoys watching a fight.

Even after those letters Wilde had no idea of his danger. He himself was a singularly unmalicious person who had never deliberately made an enemy. He could not see that there were many men who had watched his career with envious loathing, men to whom his very sleek overdressed person was an offence. His conceit was of a semi-humorous kind—among his friends he could laugh at his own self-importance, and he expected everyone else to join with him in smiling with friendly amusement at the spectacular figure of Oscar Wilde. He unwillingly recognized the hostility of a few men like Henley, but he put this down to literary rivalry and could not believe that anyone seriously wished him ill, so that when Queensberry began to attack him in letters to Bosie, he spoke of the Marquess as a madman and at first did not take his antics seriously.

Then for the first time Queensberry struck. He called at Wilde's house in Tite Street, and an interview took place which Wilde described later in Court so glibly that without some account from Queensberry's side, which we shall never have, he cannot possibly be believed. This is what he said:

At the end of June, 1894, there was an interview between Lord Queensberry and myself in my house. He called upon me, not by appointment, about four o'clock in the afternoon, accompanied by a gentleman with whom I was not acquainted. The interview took place in my library. Lord Queensberry was standing by the window. I walked over to the fireplace, and he said to me, 'Sit down.' I said to him, 'I do not allow any one to talk like that to me in my house or anywhere else. I suppose you have come to apologise for the statement you made about my wife and myself in letters you wrote to your son. I should have the right any day I chose to prosecute you for writing such a letter.' He said, 'The letter was privileged, as it was written to my son.' I said, 'How dare you say such things to me about your son and me?' He said, 'You were both kicked out of the Savoy Hotel at a moment's notice for your disgusting conduct.' I said, 'That is a lie.' He said, 'You have taken furnished rooms for him in Piccadilly.' I said, 'Somebody has been telling you an absurd set of lies about your son and me. I have not done anything of the kind.' He said, 'I hear you were thoroughly blackmailed for a disgusting letter you wrote to my son.' I said, 'The letter was a beautiful letter, and I never write except for publication.' Then I asked: 'Lord Queensberry, do you seriously accuse your son and me of improper conduct?' He said, 'I do not say you are it, but you look it, and you pose as it, which is just as bad. If I catch you and my son together again in any public restaurant I will thrash you.' I said, 'I do not know what the Queensberry rules are, but the Oscar Wilde rule is to shoot at sight.' I then told Lord Queensberry to leave my house. He said he would not do so. I told him that I would have him put out by the police. He said, 'It is a disgusting scandal.' I said, 'If it be so, you are the author of the scandal, and no one else.' I then went into the hall and pointed him out to my servant. I said, 'This is the Marquess of Queensberry, the most infamous brute in London. You are never to allow him to enter my house again.'

It must be conceded that some interview, probably a very unpleasant one, took place. Two further references to it, one from each protagonist, confirm this. Queensberry in a letter said that Wilde plainly showed the white feather on this occasion, and Wilde in *De Profundis* spoke of 'the gentleman with whom I was not acquainted' as Queensberry's 'bully' (from which comes the popular but unfounded story that Queensberry was accompanied by a prize-fighter). The exact terms in which the interview was conducted will never be known and perhaps do not greatly matter. What is astonishing is that Wilde did not realize what he was up against.

Bosie could have given him some account of Queensberry's past if Wilde had been interested. Queensberry's whole life had been given to the sports he loved—hunting, steeplechasing and boxing. He was small and sinewy as a young man, barely five foot eight, hirsute and horsy, reckless in the saddle and not yet given to the excesses and vices of his later years. At Cambridge he became friends with a man named John Graham Chambers, who had come from Eton to Trinity College. Chambers was a fine all-round athlete and oarsman who joined young Queensberry in his interest in boxing. In 1866 when they were twenty-two and twenty-three respectively, they founded the Amateur Athletic Club to combat the brutality and unfair practices of the professional bruisers which had caused the laws against prize-fighting to be more rigidly enforced. They also drew up fourteen

rules of the sport of boxing which are still known as the
Queensberry Rules. In 1867 young Queensberry presented cups
for the British amateur championships at all weights.

He was still only twenty-one when in 1865 he married Sybil,
one of the two beautiful daughters of Alfred Montgomery. The
marriage was in some ways a challenge to fate. Sybil was not only
a famous beauty but highly talented and perhaps over-educated.
She gave Queensberry five children in the first eight years of their
marriage, and when he neglected them and her for his own
friends and amusements, the marriage began to break up. Queensberry put up for sale the family place, Kinmount in Dumfries-
shire, because he was jealous of his wife and children who, he
said, were banded against him. His behaviour came into unfortunate public notice in the early '80s when he attempted to emulate
Charles Bradlaugh the atheist, who had caused scenes in the
House of Commons by refusing to take the oath. The press was
full of this in 1880 and 1881, and Queensberry's combative
atheism and love of publicity were aroused. A Scottish peer did
not sit in the House of Lords as a natural right, but Queensberry
had been elected one of the sixteen representative peers of Scotland. In 1881, while Bradlaugh was being ejected from the
Commons, Queensberry made a scene in the Lords, called the
oath of allegiance to the Crown 'Christian tomfoolery', and was
described by the *Annual Register* as 'a supporter of Bradlaugh'.
He thus became violently unpopular, not only with his fellow
peers who had elected him, but with the whole Establishment
and with the middle classes, who could not forgive atheism and
an 'insult to the Queen', as it was called, even in the inventor of
the Queensberry Rules.

Public opprobrium went to his head and he set out to invite it
in various ways. In 1882 Tennyson's unsuccessful play, *The
Promise of May*, was produced at a London theatre, and Queensberry, told that an agnostic would be unfavourably presented on
the stage by an actor called Herman Vezin, went to the theatre
with a bouquet of vegetables, and not only flung this at the cast,
but made a rather vulgar speech in defence of atheism. He made
no secret of what was considered at the time a highly scandalous

life—rather, he advertised himself as above the law and above convention.

How much of this, one wonders today, did Wilde know about Queensberry, and if he knew all, why did he not at least take his enemy's measure and not lounge complacently about calling him a madman and underrating him as a potential adversary for the curious reason that he was *déclassé* and something of a joke to Wilde's fashionable friends? Wilde seems to have thought that at any time, all he had to do to check Queensberry was to 'have him bound over to keep the peace', as he wrote to Bosie. He had no sense of reality in this and no vision of the kind of sympathy which would be given to Queensberry by those members of the public who saw Wilde as a fat successful seducer of virtue. In fact he had little sense of reality of any kind during this, his last complete year of freedom.

2

But there was some misunderstanding on the other side, too. The truth is that, like others at that time, Queensberry simply could not believe that two men would actually go to bed together, even though one of them was his own son of whom he was prepared to credit anything. Wilde was posing as a 'somdomite' (Queensberry's own spelling) in order to be 'smart' and in the fashion of these bloody long-haired aesthetes. That *must* be what it was, and right up to the time when his private detectives began to bring him evidence he thought that all he would have to answer was a charge of libelling Wilde as a mere poseur. The rest meant a bonus when the time came and he found that he had collected proof of far more than Wilde's posing—there was material on which he could be, and eventually was, sent to prison. That was a great moment for the Scarlet Marquis.

Meanwhile during the early months of 1894 he took no further steps perhaps because he was preparing for a divorce from a Miss Ethel Weedon whom he had married a few months before and who had left him after a fortnight.

Perhaps he did not know that Oscar was already suggesting that he should join Bosie in Florence where he had been sent by Lady Queensberry in order to separate him from Wilde. Oscar wrote of how he missed Bosie—'the gilt and gracious lad' having gone away, and he hates everyone else. He is in 'purple valleys' of despair and envies Bosie under Giotto's tower who must write poems like apple-blossoms. A second letter tells Bosie that he is always remembered at a barber's shop in Air Street where there are references to his gilt silk hair. Less exuberantly he says that he had had a telegram and call from Edward Shelley, who is in trouble for money.

Soon afterwards Wilde wrote another letter which seemed to presage what happened a week after it was sent—Wilde's sudden flight to Florence to join Bosie. It is really absurd, he says. He cannot live without Bosie, who is so dear, so wonderful. He thinks of him all day long and misses his grace, his boyish beauty, the bright swordplay of his wit and above all Bosie himself. London is a desert without his 'dainty feet'. He has no words for how he loves him.

No account survives of their stay in Florence, though Bosie afterwards claimed that Wilde wrote most of *A Florentine Tragedy* there. They probably saw a good deal of Lord Henry Somerset, a kindly song-writer who was exiled there through a homosexual scandal raised against him by his wife and mother-in-law, and they probably looked at pictures and architecture— like other visitors. All that is known is that in June they were back in London, still hard up, with Oscar under the pressing necessity of writing another play.

Then, as soon as Wilde and Bosie reached London, the Scarlet Marquis was roused again. Bosie went to stay with his mother, and Wilde was left in London. "Your father is on the rampage again," he wrote to Bosie, "been to Café Royal to enquire for us, with threats, etc. I think now it would have been better for me to have had him bound over to keep the peace, but what a scandal! Still, it is intolerable to be dogged by a maniac."

3

This did not at first cause Oscar to make himself scarce, rather he remained in London and continued to see Atkins and Parker and must have heard that Wood was back from America and sharing rooms with Parker, now staying at 72 Regent Street, Chelsea. What he did not know was that the two had joined forces with Cliburn and Allen and were engaged in blackmail, specialising as before in stealing compromising letters. During the spring Charlie Parker had gone home with Ernest Macklin, that old friend of Taylor's, and stolen from his pocket some letters from a silver broker named Clarke who lived at 3 Northumberland Mansions. Parker, by now if not before a hardened blackmailer, went to Clarke and demanded £10 for these, at the same time getting possession of his gold watch and chain. Clarke threatened to charge him with the theft of this and at last summoned the courage to send for a policeman.

The man on the beat in general seems to have been uninquisitive in cases like this, and simply told Charlie Parker to hand the watch back. But Parker still had letters written by Clarke to a man named Durnbach and tried to extort money for these.

He was given notice to quit his rooms at 50 Park Walk by the landlady, Lucy Rumsby, after complaints by another lodger, Mrs Bancroft, that he was being visited late at night by Wilde who kept his cab waiting outside the house. Moreover he met Alfred Taylor again though he knew that Taylor was being watched by the police. A plain-clothes man had been to the house in Little College Street and on the pretext of being a friend of Taylor's examined his rooms. Becoming aware of this, Taylor moved out during the following weekend without telling his landlady where he was going. He found rooms in Chelsea, at 3 Chapel Street.

4

At length Wilde decided to leave London and to forget such irritations as his impecuniosity, letters and telegrams from Edward

Shelley demanding money, letters from Ernest Scarfe and doubt-less others demanding the same, disquiet about Taylor and his trouble with the police, the return of Wood from America and a great number of pressing bills. He took rooms at Worthing for himself and his family, in order to write a new play, and it is noteworthy that in this chaos of anxieties and threats he wrote the most supremely carefree comedy of his life and one of the lightest, gayest, most scintillating plays in English—*The Importance of Being Earnest*. To his other difficulties may be added some strained relations—surely?—with his wife, since Bosie Douglas came to stay with the family in the small crowded seaside house. Also the fact that Alfred Taylor and Charlie Parker were arrested together at one of John Watson Preston's drag parties and Charles Mason, Taylor's friend, wrote to Wilde for money for his defence, which had to be refused.

Since an attempt was later made by Carson to introduce Preston's name in cross-examination, the occasion may be examined. Preston gave parties of this disreputable kind for profit, at which Arthur Marling, who had introduced Scarfe to Taylor, was a star transvestist. What happened can best be told by Christopher Millard (who anonymously edited *Oscar Wilde Three Times Tried*) from contemporary newspaper reports.

Eighteen men were taken into custody by the police in a midnight raid in Fitzroy Street on Sunday, August 12, 1894, two of them being men in feminine clothing. The prisoners were taken to Tottenham Court Road Police Station, and were brought up at Marlborough Street before Mr Hannay, the magistrate, on the following morning. Amongst them were Charles Parker, 19, of no occupation, 72 Regent Street, Chelsea; Alfred Taylor, 32, no occupation, of 7 Camera Square, Chelsea; John Watson Preston, 34, general dealer, 46 Fitzroy Street, W., the proprietor of the raided premises; and Arthur Marling, 26, of 8 Crawford Street. The last named was described as a female impersonator, and was charged with being an idle and disorderly person. He appeared in court dressed in a fantastic female garb of black and gold.

Detective-Sergeant Kane told how, with Superintendent Sheppard, he proceeded to 46 Fitzroy Street, on the previous night between eleven and twelve o'clock, and saw cabs drive up with men. Two of the prisoners (Marling being one) were in a hansom, dressed as women, one with a fan. A man in ordinary clothes sat on their laps. Mr Hannay asked Superintendent Kane if he had any idea of the object of the masquerade. Kane replied, 'I have, sir.' Marling said his business was to impersonate women at the halls, and the proprietor of the club at 46 Fitzroy Street, Mr Preston, asked him to go and sing at his house in feminine attire, and he agreed. Mr Hannay granted a remand for a week. He said there seemed to be something more than suspicion against five of the men found in the basement, but for the rest he would like to have something more definite in the charge when the accused next came before him. Superintendent Sheppard, in reply, said 'They are most of them known, your worship.' Some of the accused were then released on their own recognisances; others had to find sureties in the sum of £5.

On the hearing of the case being resumed on Monday, August 20th, Marling and another were bound over to keep the peace for three months. Taylor and Parker were amongst those who were discharged unconditionally. Five men were ordered to find sureties in the sum of forty shillings each to be of good behaviour for one month. The magistrate said that whatever suspicion there might be, there was no evidence against the majority of the prisoners. He had had a number of letters informing him that many of the men were of the vilest possible character, but no one had come forward to give evidence to that effect.

From his letter in reply to Mason's appeal, Wilde, who spoke of 'a dreadful piece of bad luck' for 'poor Alfred', does not seem to have been unduly worried—he was probably more so by the repeated quarrels with Bosie that went on that year—but what with one thing and another, it seems a miracle that *The Importance of Being Earnest* got itself written at all.

5

Long before it was finished Oscar began to enjoy himself with a number of boys whom he and Bosie picked up in Worthing. He had chosen the town because he foresaw little distraction from his work but a letter after Bosie's first stay there shows that Wilde had not been altogether confined to his writing-room.

My own dearest Boy, How sweet of you to send me that charming poem. I can't tell you how it touches me, and it is full of that light lyrical grace that you always have—a quality that seems so easy, to those who don't understand how difficult it is to make the white feet of poetry dance lightly among flowers without crushing them, and to those 'who know' is so rare and so distinguished. I have been doing nothing here but bathing and play-writing. My play is really very funny: I am quite delighted with it. But it is not shaped yet. It lies in Sibylline leaves about the room, and Arthur has twice made a chaos of it by 'tidying up'. The result, however, was rather dramatic. I am inclined to think that Chaos is a stronger evidence for an Intelligent Creator than Kosmos is: the view might be expanded.

Percy left the day after you did. He spoke much of you. Alphonso is still in favour. He is my only companion, along with Stephen. Alphonso always alludes to you as 'the Lord', which however gives you, I think, a Biblical Hebraic dignity that gracious Greek boys should *not* have. He also says, from time to time, 'Percy was the Lord's favourite', which makes me think of Percy as the infant Samuel—an inaccurate reminiscence, as Percy was Hellenic.

Yesterday (Sunday) Alphonso, Stephen, and I sailed to Little-hampton in the morning, bathing on the way.

Of the boys mentioned, Alphonse Conway was later discovered by Queensberry's agents and brought to London for the hearing though for some reason he was not a witness for the prosecution in the trials. The Hellenic Percy was never identified and Stephen may have been a friend of Conway's. Under cross-examination about Conway Wilde said:

When Lord Alfred Douglas and I were at Worthing we were accustomed to go out in a boat. One day when the fishermen were launching a boat on the high beach, Conway with another lad assisted in getting the craft down to the water. I said to Lord Alfred Douglas, 'Shall we ask them to come out for a sail?' He assented, and we took them. After that Alphonse and I became great friends, and it is true that I asked him to lunch with me.

Perhaps 'another lad' was Stephen.

The events of that warm and pleasant summer, the best-recorded of all periods the two friends spent together, were mercilessly dragged into evidence. They are so human and cheerful that now, eighty years later, they become vividly real from the few details given of them in Court, from Wilde's letters and from a pathetic passage of *De Profundis*.

Although, as Wilde wrote to Bosie, 'children at meals are tedious', the cramped quarters in the apartment house—appropriately '5 Esplanade'—meant that Wilde and his wife ate with the two small boys, now aged ten and eight, and their 'horrid ugly Swiss governess', all of them, one supposes, red and sandy from the beach. The scene must be vivid to most of us of the middle classes old enough to remember such holidays, but a touch of the outré is added, not so much by the presence of Bosie, who was fond of Wilde's children and got on well with Constance Wilde, as by Oscar himself with his thick curled hair and flashy summer clothes and by the occasional presence of Alphonse Conway. When Oscar was not writing, he, Bosie, Alphonse, Oscar's two boys Cyril and Vyvyan, and the unknown Stephen and Percy of the letter, played in the sunshine and went on the sea in accord and contentment for six weeks. Oscar in many things had the nature of a boy, as Hesketh Pearson so perceptively shows, and between Bosie and Alphonse there were only six years and between Alphonse and Wilde's sons only eight. The weather was kind, Wilde had a new play coming on in January (*An Ideal Husband*) and was finishing another with which he was mightily pleased. What Constance Wilde thought about it all we cannot guess, but the holiday, in spite of disagreeable worries left behind in London, was a success.

Alphonse Conway leaves one with a happier impression than most of the young blackguards with whom Wilde associated. Wilde's affair with him seems to have been a light-hearted seaside summery one, and Wilde said in evidence that Conway had become a great friend of his sons. Wilde bought him clothes and took him to Brighton for the week-end, then tried to get him a job on a ship. Great play was made by Carson of the fact that Conway sold newspapers at a kiosk on the pier. It was incredible to Carson, and later to most of the jurymen, that Wilde should have found this 'happy bright boy' a fit companion for his family, when his occupation was selling newspapers. But although Queensberry's solicitors had Conway in court during the trial of Queensberry, the Prosecution did not produce him at Wilde's trials. He may, like Mavor, have refused to testify about the statement he had been induced to make. It would be pleasant to think so. A more cynical view is that Queensberry could bribe him whereas the Public Prosecutor could not.

6

When Bosie made his third visit to Worthing, late in September, Constance Wilde and her small sons had left, and the two friends grew bored. Early in October they decided to have a few days in Brighton, where Oscar was to revise his play. Here they quarrelled with the usual bitterness.

At first they had between them enough money for their customary extravagance, and went to the Grand Hotel. After a week, Bosie fell ill with influenza, and with all the resources of a good hotel to call on, Oscar looked after him. "My friend is not allowed to go out today: I sit by his side and read him passages from his own life. They fill him with surprise," Wilde wrote to Ada Leverson, and on the next day wired to her: "Much better, temperature gone down, is to be allowed chicken to the sound of flutes at 7.30. Many thanks for kind enquiries." In four days Bosie recovered, and as their money had begun to run out they moved into inexpensive lodgings at 20 King's Road. Here Oscar had influenza, or believed he had, and care and attention were not so easily obtained or so necessary. Like most people who 'never have a day's illness', Wilde was a difficult invalid, petulant and exacting, and after a ferocious argument Bosie left him to his landlady and doctor. Wilde soon recovered and the quarrel was quickly ended by a letter from Bosie.

It was not the worst of their quarrels, and both of them had (Bosie supposed) 'forgotten all about [it] a week after it happened', but it took on monstrous proportions when Wilde came to write *De Profundis*.

The two friends did something that summer which had the gravest consequences for Wilde when he was on trial and for Bosie for twenty-five years afterwards. A handsome and homosexual undergraduate of Exeter College named John Francis Bloxam, whom Bosie had known at Winchester and Oxford, asked Bosie for a contribution to a periodical he was starting, and hoped that Wilde might be persuaded to write something for it also.

The paper was to be called *The Chameleon* and to bear as its subtitle Stevenson's line—'A Bazar of Dangerous and Smiling Chances'. Bosie agreed to contribute two poems and Wilde had ready some *Phrases and Philosophies for the Use of the Young*, intended for the *Fortnightly* which he now preferred to give to the beautiful Mr Bloxam. Only three numbers a year were to be issued of *The Chameleon* and each edition was to be limited to a hundred copies. The subscription was to be 15s. It was the sort of thing that appealed to Wilde whose obsession with Youth, in literature as in life, was growing. At the time he enjoyed the thing in all its indiscretion. When *The Chameleon* was published

Ada Leverson read a rather disgusting and blasphemous story in it called *The Priest and the Acolyte* which Bloxam had written himself, but published anonymously. Ada Leverson thought she recognized the style as that of John Gray (whom Oscar called 'Dorian') and wrote to tell Oscar this. " 'The Priest and the Acolyte' is not by Dorian," he wrote to her, "though you were right in discerning by internal evidence that the author has a profile. He is an undergraduate of strange beauty."

7

On 3 January 1895, *An Ideal Husband* was produced at the Haymarket during Tree's absence in America. It repeated the huge success of the other comedies. The Prince of Wales was in a box and congratulated Wilde, telling him not to alter a line of the dialogue, and even the press was more kindly disposed than after the previous productions. As soon as the play had commenced a successful run, the two friends made true the prediction of 'the Sybil of Mortimer Street (whom Mortals term Mrs Robinson)'. She had foretold that early in January they would go away together for a long voyage. They left for Algiers.

In Blidah they chanced to be staying in the same hotel as André Gide, and he wrote a picturesque but highly mendacious account of them and their behaviour.

All that we can trust of it is something we should in any case have deduced without the aid of Gide—that both Wilde and Douglas enjoyed themselves with the young Algerians to be found in great numbers, then as now, wherever tourists might appear. Algeria was just the place for a Lord of Life even on a short holiday, and although the maudlin reflections of Gide do nothing to interpret Wilde's mood, it can be assumed that, just like the parties of queers who visit North Africa in summer today, he had, as they proudly claim, 'a lovely time', and there is no need to doubt Gide's quoting him as wanting to see Arab boys 'as beautiful as bronze statues', a phrase typical of Wilde in his playful-romantic manner.

But the holiday was short, for Wilde had to hurry back to London for the production of *The Importance of Being Earnest* on 14 February, and left Bosie in pursuit of a young *caouadji* whom he wanted to take to Biskra.

It was as though Queensberry was lying in wait for Wilde's return. He had read in some newspaper of the visit together of Wilde and Bosie to Algiers, and it had awakened all the fury which had laid dormant since last July. He had not been able to object to his son staying with Wilde and his family in Worthing, the very name of which sounded respectable, but he had doubtless heard from his friends what kind of reputation the resorts of North Africa possessed.

His latest attack was described by Oscar in a letter to Bosie written three days after the first night of *The Importance of Being Earnest*.

The Scarlet Marquis made a plot to address the audience on the first night of my play! Algy Bourke revealed it, and he was not allowed to enter.

He left a grotesque bouquet of vegetables for me! This of course makes his conduct idiotic, robs it of dignity.

He arrived with a prize-fighter!! I had all Scotland Yard—twenty police—to guard the theatre. He prowled about for three hours, then left chattering like a monstrous ape.

This was all very well, and the simile was extremely apt and funny, but it was scarcely likely that Queensberry would see the joke. That he was very far from doing so was proved by his next move—the most unpardonable and fateful of them all. Four days after he had been refused entry to Wilde's play, he wrote on the back of a visiting card the words that with their misspelling have become famous—"To Oscar Wilde posing as somdomite", and left it with the hall-porter of Wilde's club, the Albemarle.

A good deal of speculation about Queensberry's state of mind at the time has been inevitable. He was not mentally deranged, though plenty of derangement among the rich and powerful in those days was accepted as eccentricity. He was humourless, spiteful and above all determined to avenge himself for having been made to look ridiculous. He acted, almost certainly, with a kind of lonely desperation and he acted knowing the consequences. His mind, if not unbalanced, was obsessed with his enmity for Wilde and he was moved by a great determination—to get at that beast Wilde at all costs. It is safe to say that if Oscar had ignored the visiting card—as so many of his well-wishers at the time and since have wished he had done—Queensberry would have found some other way to humiliate him, and if that failed, yet another.

TEN

Card with Hideous Words

At this juncture it will be as well to examine as best we may the person and personality of Oscar himself, and of those who surrounded him, before we see him overcome by the disasters that were awaiting him.

And first of all, since to so many who know his life it seems the most important aspect of it, let us consider him as a talker.

A part of the defence mechanism of the homosexual, particularly during the period that we have agreed to call Between the Acts, but probably throughout history, is a kind of inspired backchat or camp humour which in him takes the place of the heavier armour of true wit. It consists partly in a reversal of the sexes in conversation, using 'she' for 'he', particularly when speaking about someone of unquestioned virility, someone wholly alien to queers and queerness, like for instance a policeman, known as Miss Law, or a taximan—'she won't stop here'—or even, as a consolation for the contrariness of fate, 'Never mind. Trust in God. She'll help you.'

But this idiom of camp humour is far more than a reversal of the sexes—it embraces the whole once-secret vocabulary of a persecuted minority living among the hostile forces of normality, it prattles on with a never-ceasing improvisation and artificial gaiety. Many queers have become so accustomed to it that they can talk in no other way, and bring in every day with a rattle of paradoxes, forever laughing at the solemnly righteous world of normal desires and commonplace relationships. Camp humour is often funny when it comes from those who understand its application, or who are natural comedians, but much of it

G

depends for its success on an appeal to the bizarre and outrageous and it cannot be said to be funny so much as rebellious and malicious.

Wilde used it in a highly developed form with those who understood it, and he adapted it to his own gift of wittiness; so much is plain from his letters, particularly those to Ross and—later—Reggie Turner, and like other homosexuals who had learnt this turn of speech, he became famous for it among more serious and sincere hearers, who did not altogether approve of it but found it funnier than he did himself. It was not the only basis for the wit of his plays or the grace of his conversation—to which even his enemies testify—but it accounts for a large part of them. His trick of turning plain statements, particularly generalizations, into paradoxes became a habit, and he could depend on a delighted chuckle from any of those who listened. That he was a great conversationalist I cannot altogether believe, for he lacked so many gifts, mimicry, appeal to the deeper emotions and outright hilarity which are in the equipment of the few immortal talkers of the past whom we know by repute—there is no other way of knowing them. But he had a tremendous talent for entertainment, and certainly enchanted a great number of listeners from many spheres.

It would not be true to say that he was never better as a conversationalist than at this time, for it was only after prison and suffering that he attained to the full flower of his gifts both of humour and narrative, but he was certainly more assured and creative than ever before. He was, as he attended dress rehearsals of the two plays of his which would run at the same time, as he arranged little dinner parties at Kettner's for which he signed the bill, being pressed for money, as he justified himself to his wife and managed to placate the great actor-managers who were putting on his plays, as he talked and laughed and led the Cockney boys of his choice past the saluting staff of the Savoy, he was, it must be conceded, a very remarkable man.

Then we find in Wilde an extraordinary mixture of theoretical conceit and personal modesty. He believed himself to have genius, and in a well-known passage of the *De Profundis* letter, though written with abnormal paranoiac illusions, he showed some of what he had long felt about himself:

I was a man who stood in symbolic relation to the art and culture of my age. I had realised this for myself at the very dawn of my manhood, and had forced my age to realise it afterwards. Few men hold such a position in their own lifetime and have it so acknowledged. It is usually discerned, if discerned at all, by the historian, or the critic, long after both the man and his age have passed away. With me it was different. I felt it myself, and made others feel it. Byron was a symbolic figure, but his relations were to the passion of his age and its weariness of passion. Mine were to something more noble, more permanent, of more vital issue, of larger scope.

The gods had given me almost everything. I had genius, a distinguished name, high social position, brilliancy, intellectual daring: I made art a philosophy, and philosophy an art: I altered the minds of men and the colours of things: there was nothing I said or did that did not make people wonder: I took the drama, the most objective form known to art, and made it as personal a mode of expression as the lyric or the sonnet, at the same time that I widened its range and enriched its characterisation: drama, novel, poem in rhyme, poem in prose, subtle or fantastic dialogue, whatever I touched I made beautiful in a new mode of beauty: to truth itself I gave what is false no less than what is true as its rightful province, and showed that the false and true are merely forms of intellectual existence. I treated Art as the supreme reality, and life as a mere mode of fiction: I awoke the imagination of my century so that it created myth and legend around me: I summed up all systems in a phrase, and all existence in an epigram.

With this went the kind of modesty which made him smile at his own pretensions—however fondly he may have nurtured them in secret—and endear himself to those of his acquaintance who appreciated his good-natured wit. He was not an arrogant man, though his tall presence and lofty manner, especially with uninteresting strangers, made him seem so. He was generous, not merely with material things, but in praise and appreciation of others. He was rarely angry, preferring to dismiss causes for anger with an offhand 'How absurd!' to joining issue. He was not popular. Wise old G. B. Shaw said of him: "The vulgar hated him for snubbing them; and the valiant men damned his impudence and cut him. Thus he was left with a band of devoted satellites on the one hand, and a dining-out connection on the other, with here and there a man of talent and personality enough to command his respect, but utterly without that fortifying body of acquaintance among plain men in which a man must move as himself a plain man, and be Smith and Jones and Wilde and Shaw and Harris instead of Bosie and Robbie and Oscar and Mister. This is the sort of folly that does not last forever in a man of Wilde's ability; but it lasted long enough to prevent Oscar any solid social foundation."

In fact, as Shaw implies, he had no workaday friends, none left from Oxford, Fleet Street or literature, none met with his wife in London or Torquay; no male friends but Bosie, Robbie Ross, Arthur Clifton, Reggie Turner (whom he had met more recently) and Ricketts and Shannon. Of these, all six were queer, and although one might as a contrast add Frank Harris and Robert Sherard to the list, it is doubtful whether at that time Wilde would have done so.

He was not an unhappy man, then or ever. In prison he was to luxuriate in misery but even there his natural gaiety and friendliness broke through and communicated itself to warders and fellow prisoners. To his wife and children he rarely showed impatience, and although he did not spend much time with them they looked forward to his presence as something radiant and delightful. Oddly enough, Oscar was fond of his home, and would have been happy in more home life had it not been for the restless urges of his voluptuous nature and the boundless sexual curiosity which drove him out into the streets, the bars, Taylor's home or any other place that might provide one of those exciting, gradually revealing contacts which he loved to effect.

His home had an air of permanence about it which, perhaps, he only appreciated when he lost it and knew in prison that its contents had been sold. In spite of his lectures on the 'house beautiful', he had no sense of décor; he was no collector of pictures, and he only took conscious pleasure in the ownership of his books when he knew they were under the hammer. He wrote in *De Profundis* of "my library with its collection of presentation volumes from almost every poet of my time, from Hugo to Whitman, from Swinburne to Mallarmé, from Morris to Verlaine; with its beautifully bound editions of my father's and mother's works; its wonderful array of college and school prizes, its *editions de luxe*, and the like", and one may imagine him, before the crash came, sitting among his possessions, arranged carefully by Constance, with a sigh of satisfaction that his home was always there, always ready to receive him, after profligate nights in hotels or one of his trips abroad.

What, one cannot help wondering, did Constance feel about her husband before the whole truth was rudely revealed to her, after ten years of married life, four of which had been coloured by the anomalous presence of Bosie Douglas? To imagine that she was unaware, at least in some sense, of Wilde's nature, is absurd; the only question of interest is how much did she know? Was she able to blind herself to what would have seemed to her the hideous truth about Oscar's activities away from home by repeating one of the traditional calmatives—'Oscar is so fond of youth', or 'Oscar is an artist and has a strange temperament'? Did she accept Bosie as a charming young friend or see him as a rival? Perhaps somewhere in the later years she had been made forcibly aware of what went on—a story from the servants, it could be, or something she had unwittingly seen herself. Educated by Oscar to think of him as *different*, highly unconventional, a great artist with a touch of the madness of genius, she may have accepted the situation and even been thankful, as other women married to homosexuals have been, that his form of infidelity, however bizarre in her eyes, was not recognised by her women friends.

If this was so, if however dimly Constance knew the truth and had realised the reason for yet another of Oscar's young friends, when for instance he had brought Alphonse Conway home for lunch at the Worthing house, she showed a good deal of loyalty and courage even before these were tested by the case itself and her husband's conviction. One would need to know much more about their relationship and how far Constance studied Oscar's books as they were published to judge whether *Oscariana*, an anthology of quotations from his work, nominally chosen by Constance Wilde, in fact owed itself entirely or partially to her, or whether Oscar did the work and attributed it to her. But at least she gave her name to it and continued to live with Oscar in outward amity. Nor did she ever quite abandon him when the crunch came. Perhaps the truth is that Constance was first dazzled by Oscar and truly in love with him, and that disillusionment, when it came, as for other romantic-minded wives, was with inevitable everydayness of life and Oscar as a workaday husband rather than with anything abnormal.

As for Oscar's mother, in the last years she had kept entirely to her small house in Oakley Street where her days were passed in an alcoholic haze. The At Homes had been given up, since they no longer attracted even the raffish guests of Speranza's first years in London, and her only pleasure was to see Oscar when occasionally he came to sit with her. Her elder son Willie had not a very consoling effect on Speranza. The best contemporary description of him was left by Max Beerbohm: "*Quel monstre!* Dark, oily, suspect, yet awfully like Oscar: he has Oscar's coy carnal smile and fatuous giggle and not a little of Oscar's esprit. But he is awful—a veritable tragedy of family likeness." Willie was on the bottle, like his mother, and had been so ever since returning from America where his marriage to a rich widow had been a humiliating failure. He lived with Lady Wilde in the house in Oakley Street and even visits from Oscar could do very little to lighten the boozy gloom of the place.

It was not part of Oscar's casual nature to keep in touch with the many young friends he had cultivated in the past either through circumstances or from sexual motives, as we have seen from his loss of Kitten and Bouncer and many others along the way. He may by design have re-met from time to time in London such as Lord Ronald Gower, Norman Forbes-Robertson or Graham Robertson, but for the most part he depended on chance meetings, was friendly and charming for five minutes and then saw no more of his old friends till another coincidence brought them together. It was always for the other to cultivate his friendship, and when this happened Oscar responded. But he had no constancy. Robert Ross, however, who did not mean to be brushed off because of the glamorous Bosie, continued to be an intimate if somewhat patronised friend, and it is notable that on the very day of receiving Queensberry's card Wilde got in touch with him. Robbie, who was a busy little queen, forever obliging writers like Gosse or artists like Beardsley by doing favours for them, had made himself useful to Wilde ever since he had suggested the idea for *The Portrait of Mr W.H.* He was often seen with Oscar and Bosie, and appeared to be quite as fond of one as the other. Oscar wrote that January to Ada Leverson, 'Bosie sends sweet words, and so does our Scotch friend Ross.' Then there was Reggie Turner, a friend of Ross and perhaps the only intimate friend of Max Beerbohm, a good-natured waggish fellow who without making any song and dance about his 'loyalty' or about 'standing by Oscar in trouble', as poor Sherard was to do, would prove himself one of the best friends Oscar had. At this time Oscar thought him a comically ugly young man, and sent him up mercilessly, calling him the 'boy-snatcher of Clements Inn' and taking delight in his company. 'Can you come and dine with Bosie and me tonight? At Kettner's eight o'clock,' he wrote to Reggie, just after he and Douglas had returned from Florence, and one cannot help wondering who else was in the party. Certainly not Max, who tried to discourage Reggie from too much association with Ross and Wilde.

In addition to the steadies, like Ross, and the fly-by-night Cockney lovers like Charlie Parker and Alfred Wood, there was a number of young men whose relationships with Wilde are not recorded in any known letters, like Ben Horniman, the brother of Roy Horniman the novelist. Oscar told him, and he proudly repeated the story fifty years later, that he had the most beautiful feet in Europe. Then there was the lady-like Digby La Motte, a master at St Paul's School. Compton Mackenzie, who was in his form while Wilde was in prison, writes of him in *My Life and Times*. Mackenzie realized that he was homosexual, but obviously of the passive type and not in the least interested in boys. Wilde must have remembered him fondly for he ordered copies of his post-prison books to be sent to him. He also remembered fondly, and enquired for repeatedly from Reggie Turner, a certain Charlie Hickie who left for America while Wilde was in prison.

There seemed no reason, in that spring of 1895 why Oscar's pleasant life should ever have been interrupted. The police had not yet learned to use the Law Amendment Act, Section II, for the purposes of personal vendettas and prejudices, and although such as Taylor were occasionally run in, no one thought of interfering with well-off, well-connected or even well-dressed homosexuals until after Wilde's own prosecution opened the Law's eyes to its possibilities. Oscar would have added success to success, probably, and since Constance had remained with him till now, she would almost certainly have remained with him for her lifetime. Oscar might even have written something of real importance or of classic beauty, and not been satisfied with the exquisite comedy of *Earnest*. He might have realised all his ambitions and become solidly rich, sent his sons to Eton, been knighted by the Queen— about whom he had a 'thing'—in which case he would probably be remembered today as a minor playwright of the last century whose life, as a happily married man living in London, was of no particular interest. Instead he took Queensberry's offensive card away with him and that evening consulted Robert Ross.

2

The events which took Wilde to the Old Bailey, first to bring his action for libel against Queensberry and then to defend himself, are too well-known and have been too often gone over, to need repetition here. There are, however, a few bizarre aspects of the three cases before and during their trial which have not been noticed, or have been insufficiently exposed.

The main story goes like this. On receiving Queensberry's card Wilde, who was staying at a hotel called the Avondale, seems to have knocked back a few stiff drinks and written to Ross: "Bosie's father has left a card at my club with hideous words on it. I don't see anything now but a criminal prosecution. My whole life seems ruined by this man. The tower of ivory is assailed by the foul thing. On the sand is my life spilt. I don't know what to do. If you could come here at 11.30 please do so tonight." He sent the note by hand; Ross joined him at 11.30 that night and on the next morning Wilde went with Ross to Ross's solicitors, C.O. Humphreys, Son and Kershaw, and assured them that there was no truth in Queensberry's suggestion, after which they agreed to apply for a warrant. On 2 March Queensberry was arrested and remanded for a week. It was not until 3 April that the case against him finally came up for hearing and then the Scarlet Marquis scarcely had to appear in the witness box. After Carson's examination of Wilde and promise to produce a number of youths who had been mentioned, Wilde's counsel deemed it best to withdraw from the prosecution, so that Queensberry was found Not Guilty and discharged.

This made Wilde liable to prosecution for offences of which he had been made to appear guilty by Carson's examination, and on the same day as Queensberry was released, Wilde was arrested. All this is *vieux jeu*, and Sir John Betjeman has gone so far as to celebrate the arrest of Wilde in the Cadogan Hotel with an amusing poem. Wilde was refused bail and kept in Holloway Prison until 26 April, when he faced his first trial. The jury disagreed and he was at last given bail pending a second hearing which began on 20 May, when he was found Guilty and sentenced to two years imprisonment with hard labour.

So much is known or can be studied in detail in Millard's *Oscar Wilde Three Times Tried* or Montgomery Hyde's *Oscar Wilde* in the *Famous Trials* series. What can be added at this point by way of illumination or even sidelight on this story of Victorian cruelty and hypocrisy?

First there was Wilde's extraordinary conduct during his last month or two before the case. He arrived from Algeria alone and although he was hard up, instead of going to his home (where Constance was) he took a room at the Avondale Hotel in Picca-dilly, the proprietor of the Albemarle Hotel (where Wilde usually stayed during the production of his plays) having served him with a writ. At the Avondale until he received Queensberry's insulting card, his conduct was crazy. He picked up a young man called Tom Kennion and took him to dinner at Ada Leverson's. This, one gathers from his letter to the Sphinx, had nothing unusual about it. "You were kind enough to say I might bring someone to dinner tonight, so, after carefully going over the list, I have selected a young man, tall as a young palm tree (I mean 'tall as two young palm trees'). His Christian name is 'Tom'—a very rare name in an age of Algies and Berties—and he is the son of Colonel Kennion, and lives at Oxford in the hopes of escaping the taint of modern education. I met him on Tuesday, so he is quite an old friend." Nor was Kennion the only friend to visit Wilde at the Avondale—Ernest Scarfe came there, a fact after-wards elicited in cross-examination of Wilde.

This same Tom Kennion became a 'character' in London up to his death at eighty several years after the Second World War. He was nineteen when Oscar met him and entertained him for those few days at the time of the opening of *The Importance of Being Earnest*, and he seems to have lived on the memory. He became an antique dealer in partnership with Courtney Thorpe, an ex-actor to whom Wilde wrote from Berneval and the two kept, in common with all the old stagers who had known Wilde as boys, a repertory of unreliable stories of the '90s and of Oscar.

In Bosie's absence Wilde took Kennion to the first night of *Earnest* but let him return to Oxford when Bosie arrived from Algiers. Bosie had hurried home because he had received a cable from his brother Percy describing their father's behaviour at the theatre on the first night. 'I am greatly touched at your rushing over Europe,' Oscar wrote, and sent telegrams to both Calais and Dover to welcome him. Soon after his arrival, Bosie heard the dramatic and unpleasant news of Queensberry's card left at the Albemarle Club.

Almost the first thing Oscar and Bosie did was to consult a

fortune-teller. Wilde was an intensely superstitious man, a natural victim of fortune-tellers, palmists and the like, but because he always spoke and wrote flippantly about such things, their influence in his life has not been fully realised. He could not refer to his favourite prophetess, the fashionable Mrs Robinson, as anything but 'the Sybil of Mortimer Street', one of his nicknames which gives a false impression of levity to his respect for her, yet at every crisis, and particularly at the great crisis of his life, he consulted her, predictably only to be misled. "We have been to the Sybil Robinson," he wrote to the Sphinx a few days before his action against Queensberry. "She prophesied complete triumph and was most wonderful." It does not seem impossible that Mrs Robinson's rosy predictions had a real and fatal effect on Wilde's conduct at this time. When he was committed to prison, he asked, with pathetically failing faith, 'Why did the Sybil say fair things?' and thereafter for the rest of his life he does not seem to have consulted such high-class charlatans as Mrs Robinson, though Bosie had a story about him in the villa near Naples when they were besieged by a plague of rats.

After a time, however, we got rid of the rats, partly by means of a professional and orthodox rat-catcher, but also (and chiefly, according to Oscar's opinion) owing to the ministrations, hired for a small fee, of a potent witch who was recommended as infallible by Michele, and who came and "burned odours" and muttered incantations, which she assured us no rats could resist. She also told both our fortunes, and Oscar professed to regard her as a wonderful and powerful sorceress. In appearance she was quite the witch of literature and drama. She had a distinct beard and "with age and envy was grown into a hoop". Anyhow the rats disappeared.

But after receiving the encouragement of the Sybil, on 9 March, Wilde drove to the court in a carriage-and-pair with Bosie and his brother Percy (Lord Douglas of Hawick), who was now

Queensberry's heir. The magistrate ordered Bosie to leave the court at once. From the evidence given, it was clear that Queensberry had as yet nothing with which to justify his action, except two letters Wilde had written to Bosie and a lawyer's interpretation of some of Wilde's writing. Relieved, perhaps, to think that Queensberry had been bluffing, Wilde and Douglas went off to Monte Carlo while Queensberry was released on bail. How Wilde raised the money to pay for this was revealed, like so many other things, by Sir Rupert Hart-Davis's publication of his letters. He had just borrowed £500 from Ernest Leverson, and Bosie had scraped together £360, all he could raise from his family, for the costs of the action.

Perhaps of all their follies this rush to Monte Carlo was the greatest. The money they had raised should have been spent in suborning witnesses as unscrupulously as Queensberry was about to do. As it was, they left the field clear and Queensberry, of course, took full advantage of this, employing a pair of unprincipled private detectives who deserved a term of imprisonment for bribing and putting pressure on witnesses on Queensberry's behalf. The solicitors, too, behaved in the most disgraceful way in encouraging or at least turning a blind eye to this. The full story of how all the young blackguards were brought into court ready to swear Wilde's life away, and to admit to being not only male prostitutes but blackmailers, will never be known, but it seems likely that they were threatened with prosecution and prison themselves if they did not play.

The two men, Kearley and Littlechild, had been detectives in the Metropolitan Police and had recently retired to work privately. Whether or not they received any direct assistance from serving policemen, they had, or had recently had, access to information which was valuable to them. Moreover, so far as Parker, Wood and the rest of them were concerned, they were 'the Police' and could hector and persuade and threaten with police prestige behind them. They also had Queensberry's money to dispense when necessary.

After his return from Monte Carlo, Wilde made some feeble efforts to see some of the boys and win them over, a fact which became known to Carson, who taunted him with it. He and Bosie had stopped on their way through Calais to talk to a Savoy page-boy named Tankard and Wilde asked Shelley and Scarfe to dinner at the Avondale on separate nights. He tried to get in touch with Mavor, and consulted with Taylor. He even saw Atkins. But he could offer neither fear of punishment nor hope of reward on the Queensberry scale, and failed dismally to gain any support but Jenny Mavor's and perhaps that of Scarfe, who was not called to give evidence.

Kearley and Littlechild found Charles Parker in the Army (the Royal Artillery) and soon roped him in. His brother Bill, who disappeared from the London scene soon after meeting Wilde, was found in the country, and proved a no less eager witness. Charlie had joined up after receiving a small share of £300 which Wood and Allen had obtained by blackmail from a man who had taken him home. Cliburn and Allen were in hiding in Bournemouth but Kearley and Littlechild winkled them out, and they were kept at the court on subpoena. Harry Barford, a friend of Atkins who had been to St James's Place, was not found, apparently, but Wood and Atkins were bribed—Queensberry is said to have given his agents £500 for use if necessary.

Kearley admitted to entering Taylor's rooms by a subterfuge and stealing (though he did not call it that) papers belonging to Taylor. No criticism was made of this conduct by anyone in court and the Press ignored it, though Kearley was acting as a private individual. Another small mystery was Charles Parker's leave of absence from the Army. It lasted, he admitted, three months, from the time he was first brought up to London for the Queensberry trial. This was highly convenient to the Prosecution.

But the most incredible thing, and the proof that Wilde and Douglas were behaving like imbeciles in their eagerness to prosecute the Scarlet Marquis and—as Bosie certainly hoped—send him to prison, was the fact that after returning from their wasted visit to Monte Carlo, they went to the office of Wilde's solicitors and were able to examine at leisure and with all its fearful implications the plea of justification which Queensberry had put in.

From this document they should have seen that Queensberry's agents had secured so much evidence that it was wholly impossible for Wilde to get a verdict. There were *The Chameleon* and *Dorian Gray*, but these constituted only the 'literary side of the case' on which Wilde was quite prepared to be cross-examined, though even on these the issue might be doubtful. There were also mentioned Alfred Wood, Edward Shelley, Alphonse Conway, Sidney Mavor, Fred Atkins, Maurice Schwabe, Charles Parker, Ernest Scarfe, Walter Grainger, even the page-boy Tankard.

To anyone but a man deliberately walking to his own doom, these names would have been sufficient. There was only one thing for Wilde to do—drop his action and go abroad. Frank Harris told him this with brutal frankness and sincerity at an interview at the Café Royal at which Bosie and Shaw were present. "It was no use," said Shaw afterwards. "Wilde was in a curious double temper. He made no pretence either of innocence or of questioning the folly of his proceedings against Queensberry. But he had an infatuate haughtiness as to the impossibility of his retreating." He was, in other words 'acting almost automatically, the slave of his own imagination'.

To suggest, as many writers have done, and as Wilde himself did in *De Profundis*, that Bosie was responsible for the actions of a man in this condition is either to misunderstand or deliberately to distort the truth. Bosie was capable of realizing neither the impossibility of victory nor the consequences of defeat. He certainly encouraged Wilde to fight, he certainly wanted to see his father punished; but Wilde needed nothing of this, for he was already mesmerized by the bright eyes of danger. Bosie believed afterwards that he had screwed Oscar up to the 'sticking place' because of his own faith in Oscar's victory, which was to be brought about through Bosie being put in the box to give revelations of his father's behaviour and character. This was sheer delusion. Wilde needed no screwing up, for he was already walking blindfold to the scaffold, and Bosie's evidence might easily have been disallowed and was in any case not very relevant to the main issue. Certainly if it had depended on Bosie whether

Wilde should fight or not (even after seeing Queensberry's plea of justification), Bosie would have urged him to fight. But it did not depend on Bosie. From the moment Wilde failed to laugh at Queensberry's card, he walked in a straight line to destruction. Or, some may think, to destruction and immortality.

ELEVEN

The Trials

The events leading to Oscar Wilde's imprisonment under an iniquitous law which had been passed only ten years earlier and lasted until 1967 when its injustice was at last recognized, have been many times recounted, but for the sake of reference may be shortly recapitulated here.

On 28 February 1895, Wilde, who had recently returned from Algeria, where he had been staying with Lord Alfred Douglas, called at his club, the Albemarle, at about five in the afternoon, to be handed by the hall porter a card left for him by the Marquess of Queensberry. It had been put in an envelope by the hall porter and had been seen by no one else. The words on it—even the mis-spelling has become famous—were "To Oscar Wilde posing as somdomite." Wilde sent hurriedly for Robert Ross and on the following morning went with him to consult his (Ross's) solicitor, C. O. Humphreys. On 1 March Wilde applied for a warrant against Queensberry and on 2 March the Marquess was arrested and charged. On 9 March Queensberry was committed for trial on a charge of libelling Wilde and released on bail. Wilde and Douglas left for a holiday in Monte Carlo believing (at that time justifiably) that there was nothing against him but some suggestive writings and letters on which he could easily defend himself with the aid of the eminent counsel Sir Edward Clarke.

On his return from the South of France he learned from the summary of evidence for Queensberry's plea of justification that Queensberry's agents had been able to bribe, blackmail, menace or otherwise persuade to give evidence a number of the male prostitutes with whom he had associated. Nevertheless instead of dropping his *prosecution of Queensberry and disappearing abroad, he appeared against him and fell a victim to the clever advocacy of Sir Edward Carson, Queensberry's counsel. Sir Edward Clarke had to withdraw from the prosecution, thus admitting Queensberry's plea of justification and so making Wilde liable to arrest.*

This followed immediately, and on 6 April Wilde was charged with offences under the Criminal Law Amendment Act of 1885. His first trial began at the Old Bailey on 26 April and on 1 May the jury disagreed. There was a new trial starting on 20 May and on 25 May Wilde was found guilty and sentenced to two years' imprisonment with hard labour.

When Christopher Millard, who wrote the first account of the trials, called his book, which was published anonymously, *Oscar Wilde Three Times Tried*, he wanted to show that the trial of the Marquess of Queensberry became an ordeal not for the defendant but for Wilde himself. This he did, and the title was effective, but it has led to some misunderstanding. It cannot be sufficiently emphasized that Wilde might never have been tried at all if he had not provoked the prosecution of himself by prosecuting Queensberry for libel. He invoked the law which turned and slew him, and he afterwards saw the folly and cowardice of such a course. He should have been aware that he himself was living outside the law—unjust though it was—and not have cried to it for protection against Queensberry. Even poor Sherard, with his French clichés, recognized this. "For a man so versed in Parisianism," he quaintly wrote in *The Real Oscar Wilde*, "to run to the police for protection against another gentleman! *ça ne se fait pas.*"

There is no doubt that Wilde went to court armoured by the most dangerous illusions. He foresaw Queensberry 'in the dock', as both he and Bosie imagined it, reproved for his disgraceful behaviour and receiving a term of imprisonment for his criminal libelling of Wilde—or at the very least being effectively silenced for years to come. He saw himself as the Prosecutor, protected by one of the ablest of Q.C.s, Sir Edward Clarke, already famous for his defence in the Adelaide Bartlett and Tranby Croft cases, being perhaps a little embarrassed by questions about *The Picture of*

Dorian Gray but answering these with as much verve as he had shown to the newspaper critics on publication. As for the youths whom Queensberry's agents had apparently collected, surely a man of his presence would be able to dismiss all reference to these as mere nasty-mindedness on the part of Queensberry and his counsel? He was aware that he would be cross-examined by Sir Edward Carson, whom he had known at Trinity College, Dublin, but he probably thought this would be a gentlemanly affair which politely stressed Queensberry's misguided zeal on his son's behalf. Nothing else but such a rosy view of the prospects that awaited him could have persuaded Wilde, after seeing Queensberry's plea of justification, to continue to prosecute instead of dropping everything at whatever cost and going abroad for a year or two.

His conduct in the initial stages of the case supports this. He drove up to the Old Bailey in a carriage and pair, smartly dressed in a frock coat and wearing a flower in his button-hole, and chatted with his counsel, while Queensberry stood hat in hand and with drooping lower lip, quite alone. The course of things thereafter is known to everyone—Clarke's opening speech for the prosecution, and immediately afterwards Wilde's going into the witness-box to answer first Clarke's brief examination-in-chief and then his long cross-examination by Carson for Queensberry which lasted two days and is considered one of the most remarkable achievements by a famous barrister in the legal history of the last century. Wilde faced it at first with ease and good humour, but towards the end of the second day, when Carson had turned his line of cross-examination to questions about Taylor, Wood and Allen the blackmailer, and made it clear that he intended to produce other boys with whom Wilde had associated, Wilde's confidence visibly flagged. Yet at the end of the first day, when Carson had already pulled to pieces two of Oscar's love-letters to Bosie and questioned him about Wood, Shelley and Alphonse Conway, Oscar sent a telegram jointly with Bosie to Ada Leverson—"Pray excuse us from dining tonight as we have a lot of very important business to do. Everything is very satisfactory." What was satisfactory? Did Wilde think that the tide had been turned by his snappy answer to Carson in the last few minutes of the hearing? "I believe you have written an article to show that Shakespeare's Sonnets were suggestive of unnatural vice?" "On the contrary I have written an article to show that they are not."

Carson, of course, succeeded in getting the case against Queensberry dismissed, with credit and applause for his client and the prospect of an arrest for Wilde, which was duly made. Yet it is difficult to see how he could have done what he was paid to do without subjecting Wilde to that most gruelling cross-examination and promising to put into the witness-box the young blackguards whom the detectives employed had collected. Queensberry's action in leaving the insulting card at Wilde's club was, as Mr Justice Wills was to say, 'one which no gentleman would have taken'. It was a deliberate and cowardly libel, and the only way of saving Queensberry from its consequences was to make the case black against Wilde, to leave no doubt in the jury's mind that Queensberry was justified in calling Wilde a sodomite. No other way was open to Carson. An unjust law produces unjust advocates at the best of times, but in a case like this, it forces those who follow it to act in a cruel and degrading manner in order to preserve their own reputations. Only Wilde's lack of realism in worldly affairs could have made him imagine it otherwise. His counsel, to whom he had sworn on his honour as a gentleman that there was no truth in Queensberry's accusations, appears to have been too trusting of his client. How, it may be wondered now, could Clarke possibly have believed that *all* the accusations in the plea of justification were unfounded, *all* the youths who would testify were inventing evidence that would tell against themselves as well as Wilde, *all* that the defendant's lawyers and their spies had been able to produce against Wilde was so much slanderous nonsense? The answer, of course, is that Clarke did not believe it, or very quickly ceased to do so, but having undertaken to represent Wilde, he soldiered on nobly, in the last two cases without a fee.

It is sad now to read again the story of that cross-examination by Carson which has been described as a 'battle of wits', an 'encounter between two formidable adversaries' and so on, and recall all the smart answers of Wilde which may have raised a laugh in court but alienated the sympathy of the press and public when they were reported, for Oscar simply did not realize where he was being led. In biographies, in plays, in 'stage impersonations', in films, he stands there hitting back at a frequently discomforted Carson, but none of these show that at the same time he was throwing away any chance he might have had of freedom. Indeed those filmic and dramatic portraits of Wilde imply that he was sent to prison by an unappreciative court of law far more for his witty answers than for anything criminal which was proved against him. They do not remember that, according to the law at the time and for nearly seventy years afterwards, his actions were criminal, and the fact that on several occasions he made Carson look a fool is entirely irrelevant.

All the old Wildean gags have been repeated again and again— "I think it is quite unpardonable that better care was not taken of this original manuscript of mine," to a blackmailer who had given back a compromising letter. "It was worse—it was badly written," on being asked whether *The Priest and the Acolyte* was not an immoral story. "It is the first I have heard of his connection with literature," of Conway when told that he sold newspapers on the pier at Worthing. "Iced champagne is a favourite drink of mine— strongly against my doctor's orders"—"Never mind your doctor's orders, sir".—"I never do."

They still raise the faint echo of a nineteenth-century laugh which serves only to heighten the one moment of tragedy, in the dramatic sense, of the whole sorry pantomime—the arrest of Wilde, bewildered but chattering squiffily with the police, from the unlikely surroundings of a room booked by Bosie in the Cadogan Hotel, Sloane Square. He could have left that morning for the Continent and been on board one of the ferry boats before Clarke had finished making his announcement in court. In fact it might be argued that Carson—who later appealed to Lockwood, prosecuting in the third case, to 'let up on the fellow. He has suffered a great deal'—deliberately prolonged his address to the jury before calling his witnesses, to give Clarke time to intervene and Wilde to go abroad, since once Wood and the rest had appeared, Wilde would have no chance of either acquittal or escape. As a lawyer, Carson was relentless; as a man, he may not have been vindictive.

If Wilde had followed these unspoken invitations to decamp, he might have suffered no permanently damaging effects. There would have been an outbreak of what we later learned to call 'bad publicity' maintained by some sections of the press, like W. T. Stead's vendetta against Sir Charles Dilke. There would have been, perhaps, an everlasting debate on whether Wilde was guilty or not. It is doubtful whether even his two plays would have had to come off. But, until the very moment when the police arrived, Oscar could not make up his mind. He would not admit that such an idol as he considered himself to be had really fallen, and if he was capable of any fully coherent thought about it, he believed that the charges against him would be dismissed and in his struggle against Queensberry he would somehow be proved triumphant. Even when he had faced his first trial and heard the skilfully rehearsed accusations of Charles Parker, Alfred Wood, Frederick Atkins and Edward Shelley, he still believed, when the jury had disagreed, that he would have freedom after a new trial. Not until he was at last irrevocably in his cell at Pentonville did he admit to himself that all was lost.

This late realization was disastrous. For several months he was stupefied, and although he recovered after being given more humane treatment at Reading, that period in which he did not fully understand his surroundings or their significance remained dark and soundless at the back of his mind long after he was himself again.

But before speaking of his imprisonment proper, there are two very interesting periods which must be examined if we are to know Wilde at all, that when he was in Holloway Prison before his first trial, and that when he was on bail before the second.

To use an apt metaphor, all the stuffing had been knocked out of Wilde by the failure of his action against Queensberry. In two days of cross-examination by Carson and the strain of an interview with Clarke, when he had learned that his only hope was in withdrawal, he had been reduced to the dithering state of semi-drunkenness in which the police found him. He was refused bail and taken to Holloway, not then a women's prison, and until the next afternoon, when Bosie Douglas was permitted the first of his daily visits, he was left entirely to his own black thoughts. Ross, who felt himself too closely involved for safety, and had his mother to consider, fled across the Channel. Reggie Turner dared not visit him, because of both his family and his job. Arthur Clifton would come later but at present was suffering from distress and alarm about Oscar's arrest. Sherard remained in Paris, trying to appeal to the sympathies of French writers and Sarah Bernhardt. Wilde's brother, Willie, wrote him 'monstrous' letters, as Wilde reported to the Sphinx, and his mother had become almost inarticulate from alcohol and shock. Constance Wilde had gone to Babbacombe and would soon take the two boys abroad. Harris came to see him, but not till a month later, after the first trial. From 5 April when he was arrested till 25 April when he was put on trial, Bosie Douglas was the only person to visit him, and he did so every day.

This was deeply and tearfully appreciated by Wilde. To the Sphinx, who seems to have been the only woman friend who remained in touch with Oscar, he wrote: "Not that I am really alone. A slim thing, gold-haired like an angel, stands always at my side. His presence overshadows me. He moves in the gloom like a white flower." To More Adey and Robert Ross: "Bosie is wonderful. I think of nothing else." To Sherard: "Nothing but Alfred Douglas's daily visits quicken me into life." And to Bosie himself, a number of letters which are perhaps the most revealing that Wilde wrote in a lifetime of correspondence, and which by a singular irony are lost to us in any trustworthy version.

Sir Rupert Hart-Davis has done the best thing possible in the circumstances and produced three of them in English, translated back from much-corrected French versions made a year after they were written. The originals were destroyed during one of his later crises by Alfred Douglas.[1] These English versions, translators unknown, were brought to light by Christopher Millard, and as Hart-Davis says, 'their substance need not be doubted',

[1] There are explanations for this action in my book *Bosie: The Story of Lord Alfred Douglas.*

particularly as Wilde himself referred to them in *De Profundis*: "The letters I had written to you from Holloway Prison! The letters that should have been to you things sacred and secret beyond anything in the whole world!"

But the phraseology is often foreign to Wilde, even at his most repetitive and elaborate; and though some parts of them ring true enough, there are lapses into silly ecstasy which cannot be excused even by the circumstances in which they were written.

The first of the surviving three was written from Holloway on the day before the trial and the day after Bosie had left for the Continent, at Clarke's insistence; the others were sent a week or two later when Wilde had been given bail. It will be sufficient here to indicate the drift of them.

My dearest boy, This is to assure you of my immortal, my eternal love for you. Tomorrow all will be over. If prison and dishonour be my destiny, think that my love for you and this idea, this still more divine belief, that you love me in return will sustain me in my unhappiness and will make me capable, I hope, of bearing my grief most patiently. Since the hope, nay rather the certainty, of meeting you again in some world is the goal and the encouragement of my present life, ah! I must continue to live in this world because of that . . . As for you (graceful boy with a Christ-like heart), as for you, I beg you, as soon as you have done all that you can, leave for Italy and regain your calm, and write those lovely poems which you do with such a strange grace. Do not expose yourself to England for any reason whatsoever. If one day, at Corfu or in some enchanted isle, there were a little house where we could live together, oh! life would be sweeter than it has ever been. . . . Those who know not what love is will write, I know, if fate is against us, that I have had a bad influence upon your life. If they do that, you shall write, you shall say in your turn, that it is not so. Our love was always beautiful and noble, and if I have been the butt of a terrible tragedy, it is because the nature of that love has not been understood . . . Try to let me hear from you soon. I am writing you this letter in the midst of great suffering;

this long day in court has exhausted me. Dearest boy, sweetest of all young men, most loved and most lovable. Oh! wait for me! wait for me! I am now, as ever since the day we met, yours devoutly and with an immortal love   Oscar.

Every great love has its tragedy, and now ours has too, but to have known and loved you with such profound devotion, to have had you for a part of my life, the only part I now consider beautiful, is enough for me . . . Now I think of you as a golden-haired boy with Christ's own heart in you. I know now how much greater love is than everything else. You have taught me the divine secret . . .

Love me always, love me always. You have been the supreme, the perfect love of my life; there can be no other.

I decided that it was nobler and more beautiful to stay. We could not have been together. I did not want to be called a coward or a deserter. A false name, a disguise, a hunted life, all that is not for me, to whom you have been revealed on that high hill where beautiful things are transfigured.

During the last ten years of Bosie's life, when he spoke of Wilde with affection if not always with reverence, I tried to persuade him to talk about these letters, for although I had not seen the Millard versions and knew of them only from Bosie's *Autobiography*, I felt instinctively that they were of immense importance.

I do not think that Bosie had seen the Millard versions either; he certainly could remember almost nothing of the actual wording of the letters, but was tormented by the thought that he had destroyed them. "They were the most beautiful and sincere letters that Oscar ever wrote," he said. "Of course they were love letters—you could not call them anything else. I suppose that was why I destroyed them when I had been turned against Oscar's memory by *De Profundis*. There were many of them, I think about twenty, and in them Oscar said just exactly what he denied in *De Profundis*. I have cried over the memory of them many times since then. I do not think that at any time before or after we loved each other as much as we did during those weeks when I went to see Oscar in Holloway."

In his *Autobiography* Bosie remembered and painted a very moving picture of the scene:

I used to see Oscar every day at Holloway in the ghastly way that "visits" are arranged in prisons. The visitor goes into a box rather like the box in a pawnshop (if my gentle readers will forgive an allusion to such a low place). There is a whole row of these boxes, each occupied by a visitor, and opposite, facing each visitor, is the prisoner whom he is visiting. The two sides of visitors and prisoners are separated by a corridor about a yard in width, and a warder paces up and down the corridor. The 'visit' lasts, as far as I remember, a quarter of an hour. The visitor and the prisoner have to shout to make their voices heard above the voices of the other prisoners and visitors. Nothing more revolting and cruel and deliberately malignant could be devised by human ingenuity. And it is to be remembered that I am speaking of a remand prison, where the prisoners are waiting trial, and possibly quite innocent of any offence whatever. Poor Oscar was rather deaf. He could hardly hear what I said in the babel. He looked at me with tears running down his cheeks and I looked at him. Such as it was, as he told me in nearly every letter he wrote (and he wrote every day with clockwork regularity), this interview was the only bright spot in the day. He looked forward to it with pathetic eagerness. There was literally nothing else I could do for him. The world outside the prison, as represented by the newspapers, was howling for his blood like a pack of wolves.

2

The other short period of interest is that during which Wilde was out on bail after the jury in his first trial had disagreed and

before the case was heard again. Each of his two early biographers claim to have seen him and made propositions to him
at this time, Sherard more credibly than Harris.

Sherard had been invited to stay with the Wildes for the previous Christmas or perhaps, we are justified in guessing, had
invited himself. It cannot have been much of a success since
Sherard admits that during the last years there was a feeling on
his side of having been 'cast off'. Stories of Wilde's luxurious
living had reached Sherard and he reproduces them, always using
the plural—'the villas at Goring, the fashionable hotels, the butlers
and under-butlers'. "At this dinner, at Christmas 1894, he was not
himself at all. He exuded unctuous prosperity and reminded me
of a Roman emperor of the decadence." "There is no doubt that
at this time Oscar Wilde was 'doing himself' far too well. It
occurred to me, more than once during dinner, that he was *en
route* for a stroke of apoplexy. The veins in his forehead were
swollen and pigmented, his breathing was oppressed and his
adiposity had enormously increased."[1]

A Christmas guest with thoughts of that kind about his host,
however well-deserved they were, cannot have been a very
welcome addition to the family party, and Sherard probably went
back to Paris without regret. He heard nothing from Wilde and
only read in the Paris newspapers the accounts of the first two
cases, but when Wilde was released on bail, he received a telegram
—sent by whom he does not say—asking him to come to London
'to take Wilde into the country'. As unfortunately was not unusual with him, he was completely broke at the moment, so one
supposes that his fare was telegraphed at the same time. When he
came, eager to enter into the conspiracy and supposing that 'into
the country' implied a journey at least to South America, to
which Jabez Balfour had decamped on bail, he was disappointed
to find that the telegram meant exactly what it said. "It was
thought that it would be a good thing for Wilde to go into the
country or up the river, or somewhere, while awaiting his second
trial, and I had been selected to accompany him." Moreover his

[1] I shall have failed in my delineation of Sherard if the reader does not
recognize his touch in the phrase '*en route* for a stroke of apoplexy'.

reception from Oscar, who was lying in bed at his mother's house in Oakley Street ('a nervous wreck', Sherard says) was by no means hearty. The first thing Oscar seemed to consider—though Sherard did not give it this explanation in the account he wrote of it—was how to get Bob back to Paris, since everything possible had been pawned and there was not money in the house to pay his fare. "Your chivalrous friendship—your fine chivalrous friendship—is worth more than all the money in the world," Wilde had written from Holloway when Sherard had tried in vain to touch Sarah Bernhardt on his behalf, but to have him arriving here in Oakley Street making the prediction that Wilde would get two years hard labour, telling him how to make prussic acid in order to call his bluff about suicide and generally cheering him up by his presence, was too much to bear, and when the Sphinx called and insisted that Oscar should stay at her house for the rest of his time on bail, Wilde gladly accepted it and left Sherard with Willie and his mother. After that Wilde recovered his spirits and was ready to face the last trial with some calm and poise.

Harris says that he came to Oakley Street, and in spite of Willie Wilde's opposition, took Oscar out to lunch and arranged to meet him at Ada Leverson's house a few days later. There he told him that he had a brougham 'with a pair of fast horses' waiting at the door which would take them to Erith, where a steam yacht was anchored ready to take Oscar abroad. "There's a little library on board of French books and English; I've ordered supper in the cabin—lobster à l'Américaine and a bottle of Pommery." Harris, who never owned a yacht and just then, as he had to admit later, was particularly hard-up, may have come once to see Wilde at Oakley Street, may even have taken him out to lunch, but when nineteen years later he invented this story, he intended it to show, like the rest of his ridiculous book, what a splendid, resourceful, courageous friend Frank Harris was, and what a poor weak fool ('Oh Frank, I can't go. I should be seized by the police!') was Oscar Wilde. I do not know whether either of the films about Wilde add the picturesque touch of 'a yacht with steam up at Erith', but if not I recommend it to other film-makers and stage impersonators and romancers in the future who are not bothered by such limitations as accuracy, or even probability.

Wilde remained quietly at the Leversons who treated him with kindness and understanding, as another Jewess, Adela Schuster, blessed by all who care for the memory of Wilde, treated him with great generosity.

3

As for the two trials themselves, they were the first under Section II of the Criminal Law Amendment Act, the Black-mailer's Charter as it has been called, and they set the pattern for all other prosecutions of the same kind right through the nine decades during which this abomination lasted. The prosecution of Wilde was different from others in only two respects; it had been invited by the victim himself, and the defendant was a famous man. In other cases, where men of title and distinction or relationship with the Royal Family were concerned, matters were successfully hushed up. Both Lord Henry and Lord Arthur Somerset had been allowed to go and reside abroad, as later Lord Beauchamp was, while there are others whose scandals were so promptly and effectively suppressed that their names never reached even the most keenly eavesdropping of the public. But Wilde had asked for it.

Otherwise the case went like all its successors: the wretched boys, bullied, cajoled, bribed or tricked into making statements, told that they too could be charged and imprisoned if they did not give the evidence required of them; the witnesses among persons of reputedly good character who were not involved in the actual charges—landladies, hotel servants and the rest—speaking their pieces with unction; counsel determined to get the verdict they demanded at all costs; everyone so keen to show that he was guiltless even of *thoughts* of the kind being mentioned that proceedings became a sanctimonious imposture; the defendant assumed from the first to be guilty, though on any other charge,

even murder, a decent allowance of credit would be given to his
word: we have seen the whole thing again and again in Britain in
the period between the Acts. The prosecution of Wilde seems
more tragic only because his fall was steeper and provided more
dramatic contrasts.

One of those contrasts was noticed by Max Beerbohm who
was present in court. No film or play, I feel sure, could show the
scene so clearly and brilliantly as Max does in his letter to Reggie
Turner.

I have been all day at the Old Bailey and dining out in the evening—and coming home very tired. Please forgive me—Oscar has
been quite superb. His speech about the Love that dares not tell
its name was simply wonderful—and carried the whole court
right away—quite a tremendous burst of applause. Here was this
man—who had been for a month in prison and loaded with insults and crushed and buffeted, perfectly self-possessed, dominating the Old Bailey with his fine presence and musical voice. He
has never had so great a triumph, I am sure, as when the gallery
burst into applause—I am sure it affected the gallery. . . . Hoscar
(sic) stood very upright when he was brought up to hear the
verdict and looked most leonine and sphinx-like. . . . Hoscar is
thinner and consequently fine to look at. It was horrible leaving
the court day after day and having to pass through a knot of
renters (the younger Parker wearing Her Majesty's uniform—
another form of female attire) who were allowed to hang around
after giving their evidence and to wink at likely persons.

4

The appalling snobbery evident in cases of this kind was
demonstrated again and again, and while it may be admitted
that Wilde's 'socialism' was pretentious and designed to conceal
chiefly his taste for working-class boys, we can still marvel that
counsel should have allowed themselves to voice sentiments

which today would choke anyone with any pretension to sociological decency. "Who was Wood?" asked Carson, leaving no doubt about the implications of the question which were perfectly understood by Wilde, who replied, "So far as I could make out he had no occupation but was looking for a situation. He told me he had had a clerkship. I don't care about different social positions." Or again, "Did you become fond of their office boy?" "I deny that was the position held by Mr Edward Shelley." Or, "Did you become intimate with a young lad named Alphonse Conway at Worthing? He sold newspapers at the kiosk on the pier?"—"No I never heard that his only occupation was selling newspapers."—"What was he?" "He told me his father had been an electrical engineer and died young. He led a happy, idle life."—"He was a loafer in fact? You dressed this newsboy up to take him to Brighton? In order that he might look more like an equal?"—"Oh no. He could not look like that." Later, "Did you know that Parker was a gentleman's servant out of employment?"—"No."—"But if he were, you would still have become friendly with him? What enjoyment was it to you to entertain grooms and coachmen?" Later still, "Were they persons of that class?" "They did not seem to have the manners of that class. They spoke of a father at Datchet as a person of wealth—well, not wealth but of some fortune."—"You did the honours to the valet and groom?" And again, "Did you consider Atkins respectable?" "Respectable? Yes. I thought him pleasant and young." "Did you know Ernest Scarfe was a valet and is a valet still?"—and so on.

Carson was not the only barrister to exploit this line of questioning, for to a jury nothing could more certainly damn a man than his having ignored class distinctions. What explanation could there be except an immoral one when a 'gentleman' associated with 'grooms and valets'? Frank Lockwood, the Solicitor-General, knew this very well. "What pleasure could you find in the society of boys much beneath you in social position?" he asked, and Wilde's answer sounds rather forlorn. "I make no social distinctions," he said. "You have no sense at all of social differences?" further asked Lockwood incredulously, and coming back to Alphonse Conway, "Of what station in life is he?" "Of no particular station," replied Wilde, only to be asked inevitably if he sold papers on the pier.

This does not reflect so much on the barristers as on the times they lived in. It is noted that in spite of his frequent disclaimers, Wilde was very much conscious of class, his own as he saw it and that of other people. It would be an exaggeration to say that the naming of the Parkers as groom and valet respectively, of Shelley as an office boy, Atkins as a bookmaker's hanger-on and Wood as unemployed was the cause of Wilde's downfall, but it would not be remote from the truth.

It was of considerable assistance to Frank Lockwood in the third case, in his final speech for the prosecution, when he made a vicious personal attack so deadly that it destroyed the slim chance of acquittal that Clarke had been at great pains to create. Wilde called it "that appalling denunciation of me, like a thing out of Tacitus, like a passage in Dante, like one of Savonarola's indictments". It was none of these. It had not the honest conviction or the dignity of a great speech. It was a mean and cowardly condemnation, carefully planned to obtain a verdict of Guilty from the jury. Lockwood, after the previous jury had disagreed, had been briefed to make sure that Wilde went to prison. He was a bloated bottle-nosed character, a comedian in his private life and a determined careerist who saw that a successful prosecution of Wilde in this much-publicized case would assist his reputation. (His careerism, like his career, ended with his death two years later.)

So Mr Justice Wills was able to pronounce sentence with words that have been handed down to us as an example of British injustice in the '90s but which in fact are no more full of bias and spleen than the words of any judge or Recorder or magistrate trying cases like Wilde's in the decades since then. "I shall, under such circumstances, be expected to pass the severest sentence that the law allows. In my judgment it is totally inadequate for such a case as this. The sentence of the Court is that each of you be imprisoned and kept to hard labour for two years."

TWELVE

Prison

Generalizations about prison and the endurance of prison conditions are dangerous, for no one can foresee how the individual will come through his experiences following conviction under an abominable law. Who would have anticipated in similarly rigged prosecutions in the 1950s of this century (under the orders of the Home Secretary, that dirty-minded puritan Maxwell Fyfe), that it would be the old Etonian peer who, among those who suffered, would saunter through his sentence most courageously and live to look back with most amused contempt on its initiators? Who would have imagined that Oscar Wilde, who started by losing twenty-two pounds in weight and much of his intelligent awareness of life about him, would spend his last nine months in prison writing letters to his friends and notes to be pushed under the doors of good-looking prisoners and finally have gone out in a mood of cheerful triumph, making jokes about his 'stay in the country'?

At first, of course, it was hell. 'I am sorry for you; it is harder for the likes of you than it is for the likes of us,' whispered a fellow-prisoner to Wilde at Pentonville, to which Wilde replied, 'No my friend, we all suffer alike.' This may have been true; certainly no one knows what mental agonies torment the most brutal-seeming of prisoners behind cell doors at night, or the most sensitive. But for the 'respectable' prisoner, the man who has known and taken pride in the good opinion of his neighbours and built a position which is now destroyed, above all for the man of fame or eminence, the sufferings of imprisonment have an extra dimension. He has not only lost, at least for as long as he can foresee, his freedom, the companionship of his family, his prosperity and his pleasures, he has lost everything that gave meaning to his life. His memories of the past are fouled, and he has no future.

Moreover, for the homosexual, sentenced with pharisaical words by some paid mouthpiece of society, it is all to no avail. For the criminal, prison is an occupational hazard, and though for him too the punishment may seem unjust and vindictive, he knows that he has done something to deserve it, and can take comfort, perhaps, in seeing others more severely punished for the same offence. For the sexual antimonian (as Wilde himself called him) there is no such consolation. He cannot find encouragement in making resolutions for the future or blaming himself for his actions in the past. He knows that he will not change, for change in his case would be against nature. He may be angry, frustrated, rebellious about the conditions of prison and humiliated by the petty tyrants given authority over him. But unlike those who find solace in repentance, he has nothing to repent.

This state of mind will pass. He will learn cynicism or humility, humour or fellow-feeling, with which to combat the black devils that infest his dreary cell. But for his first few weeks or months the very sky of his existence is blotted out.

Wilde knew all the horrors of prison, which have scarcely changed from his day to ours: the callous, incompetent doctors, the revolting system of sanitation, the repulsive food, but above all the sense of utter loss, of having been dropped into limbo, without hope, from the smiling contentment of a former life. Two daily newspapers[1] reported that he had become insane. This was not true; but he had become insensate, numb and utterly listless.

The commonest remedy for one in his condition, the remedy sought by almost every prisoner who has ever eaten porridge, is to find someone or something to blame for his misfortune, since it is rarely that a convicted man blames himself. The thief blames his bad luck, and resolves that next time he will take more care with his preparations; the wife-murderer blames the wretched woman he has killed—'she egged me on to do it'; the swindler

---

[1] According to H. Montgomery Hyde's account in *Oscar Wilde: The Aftermath*, the *Pall Mall Gazette* (June 4/5) and the *Daily Chronicle* (June 5).

blames an extravagant mistress for whom he had to raise more money; and Oscar Wilde, having exhausted the idea that Queensberry was solely to blame, since he felt that Queensberry as an enemy was scarcely worth the attention of a man like himself, chose a scapegoat as a victim for his wild recriminations, his savage nocturnal ravings, someone who had been above all others dear to him, who barely two months earlier had been 'dearest of all created things', 'golden-haired boy with Christ's own heart in you', that is—Bosie Douglas. In one month of the blackest despair of which Wilde was capable, he turned his 'immortal', his 'eternal' love for Bosie to distrust first, and then to a violent if passing hatred.

In this he followed all the precedents and a kind of distorted logic. There was really no one else to blame. Constance had not deserted him—indeed she was coming to see him soon. Sherard might be gauche in his devotion but had also applied for permission to visit him and show his embarrassing loyalty. The young men 'of his own class' who had surrounded him had faded out of sight and hearing, but that was to be expected. It was the lover who had shared his life who was to blame for it. Bosie's only offence was to follow too literally Wilde's instructions to leave for Italy, and write lovely poetry. But Oscar had converted himself to a fierce contradiction of all he had felt.

It had to be either Constance or Bosie against whom he turned —that was, either against heterosexuality, which was to him abnormal but had the approval of the Philistines, or against homosexuality, natural to him with only Bosie's understanding and support. He chose the second of these as a scapegoat and pleased his first two visitors, Constance and Sherard. Constance had the guardianship of his boys, and controlled his only means of living in the future. He did not in so many words realize this, or revile Bosie because it was prudent to do so. To a nature like his in circumstances like these it was inevitable. 'He (Oscar) has been mad these last three years and says if he saw Alfred Douglas he would kill him,' Constance told Sherard after her first visit to Oscar, and no doubt Oscar had conforted her with some such words.

Sherard realized that Wilde had contrived a complete volte-face since the occasion on which he had written that nothing but Alfred Douglas's daily visits quickened him into life, so Robert accommodated himself to it, earning the encomium in *De Profundis*, 'bravest and most chivalrous of all brilliant beings', which would one day, after Bosie was long forgiven, turn back to reality and Wilde's bare endurance of poor Robert. "I saw Robert Sherard last night. He was very insane, and sentimental: wept over a friendship of seventeen years; upon the other hand abused all my friends in the foulest way." "Robert has almost lost all his good looks. He was dreadful of aspect last night: quite dreadful."

For his second visit, Sherard found he had some excellent material for the support of Wilde's new anti-Bosie bias, which to the man in prison was fast becoming an obsession. Having ranged himself on the side of Constance and Sherard in his view of his own life, Wilde did not want to be reminded of the 'love that dared not speak its name' or his defiant indulgence in 'strange sins'. His sense of humour, not unnaturally in the circumstances, failed him, and he deliberately forgot how he had once derided sexual conventionality. When he heard of Bosie's attempt to defend him, his spirited letters to Labouchere of *Truth* and W. T. Stead which made no secret of the young man's loyalty, Wilde claimed to be horrified, and the fact that, in standing beside Wilde, Bosie was offering himself to the world's opprobrium, left Oscar untouched.

Sherard wrote later:[1]

I think that Wilde would have had a better chance of some alleviation of his sentence if it had not been for the misguided championship not only of some of his friends, but of certain people who, believing him guilty, started an insane campaign to prove that what they called 'the Greek movement' had no essence of criminality in it, that it was pure Philistinism to object to it, and that, if guilty, Wilde should be considered a martyr to

[1] Robert Sherard, *The Real Oscar Wilde*.

Puritanical prejudice. For my part, I considered with the gravest apprehension any attempts to palliate his guilt, if indeed he were guilty, which I did not and could not believe. When I heard that Lord Alfred Douglas was projecting an article in *La Revue Blanche* which—as I understood—was to defend Wilde on aesthetic grounds, I was so seriously alarmed as to what the consequences might be to the prisoner that I telegraphed to the editor, whom I happened to know, following up my telegram with a long letter, in which I pointed out how ill Wilde's interest would be served by the publication of any such article.

Moreover he obtained special permission to see Wilde again. H. Montgomery Hyde, in *Oscar Wilde: The Aftermath*, writes: "The ostensible grounds were the conditions under which a reconciliation could be effected between Wilde and his wife, but the visit seems to have been prompted mainly by a piece of news about Alfred Douglas which had come to Sherard's knowledge. Sherard said he had heard that Douglas had written an article on Wilde which contained a number of Wilde's letters to Douglas." Oscar, wrote Sherard, was 'greatly taken back and much annoyed' and told Sherard to have the article stopped. For this proof that he was on the side of the angels, Wilde was in his turn rewarded. Sherard was warned that the interview must end, and to the warder's 'great horror', Sherard boasted, 'I put my arms round my friend and pressed him to my bosom and so departed.'

Sherard was then, and throughout his association with Wilde, a comedy figure, but it was not funny for the unfortunate Oscar, torn with obsessions and the need to create some image to take the place of his fallen self—a necessity with every man in prison who has once been generally respected. As the modish master of words and repartee, as the adventurer among exotic sins, as the Lord of Life, there could be no comeback. Perhaps as a devoted and industrious husband, forgiven for his wife's sake, and proving himself a serious writer after all? Perhaps as a penitent seeking a semi-monastic existence? Perhaps as a resident abroad with a changed name and a completely changed viewpoint? All these he considered and each had its appeal to the histrionic in Wilde, but he realized in the agony of his humiliation that all of them meant a complete break with Bosie, standing as Bosie did for 'the beauty and the loving in the world'. Finally he settled for a conception of himself as a Man of Noble Forbears and Literary Genius Who Had 'Played With that Tiger Life' Until Betrayed by an Unworthy Companion and Was Now Sunk in the Lowest Depths of Dante's Inferno, being Damned as Once he had been Exalted, to the Last Extreme.

During the first months of Wilde's imprisonment, after he had created in himself this violent revolt from his adoration of Bosie, he received a visit from a solicitor's clerk. The man brought him a message in terms which would have delighted him a little time earlier, but now he was able to build up a cause of angry rancour in this, and in Bosie's discreet use of one of Wilde's nicknames for him.

It all flashed across me, and I remember that, for the first and last time in my entire prison-life, I laughed. In that laugh was all the scorn of all the world. Prince Fleur-de-Lys! I saw—and subsequent events showed me that I rightly saw—that nothing that had happened had made you realise a single thing. You were in your own eyes still the graceful prince of a trivial comedy, not the sombre figure of a tragic show. All that had occurred was but as a feather for the cap that gilds a narrow head, a flower to pink the doublet that hides a heart that Hate, and Hate alone, can warm, that Love, and Love alone, finds cold. Prince Fleur-de-Lys! You were, no doubt, quite right to communicate with me under an assumed name. I myself, at that time, had no name at all.

This was in the *De Profundis* letter, written nearly a year later, but Wilde's resentment had if anything increased.

It was totally unreasonable, as we shall see from further examination of *De Profundis*, but it was totally understandable, too. It must be remembered that Wilde was tortured by mental distress far more than by any physical pain or deprivation. The conditions of prison were loathsome enough, but he was in such agony of mind that he scarcely noticed them, and his passing descriptions of them in *De Profundis* are oddly unconvincing and suggest a cultivated self-pity rather than any truly unbearable suffering. Harris, of course, has bloodcurdling accounts of prison conditions, but Harris (who thought of his own short term in Brixton Prison as a crucifixion) lies with even more exaggeration than usual, as Warder Martin proved later in his letters to Sherard. Harris wrote of his interview with Wilde as follows:

"You know how glad I am to see you, heart-glad to find you looking so well," I began, "but tell me quickly, for I may be able to help you, what have you to complain of; what do you want?"

For a long time he was too hopeless, too frightened to talk. "The list of my grievances", he said, "would be without end. The worst of it is I am perpetually being punished for nothing; this governor loves to punish, and he punishes by taking my books from me. It is perfectly awful to let the mind grind itself away between the upper and nether millstones of regret and remorse without respite; with books my life would be livable—any life," he added sadly.

"The life, then, is hard. Tell me about it."

"I don't like to," he said, "it is all so dreadful—and ugly and painful, I would rather not think of it," and he turned away despairingly.

"You must tell me, or I shall not be able to help you." Bit by bit I won the confession from him.

"At first it was a fiendish nightmare; more horrible than anything I had ever dreamt of; from the first evening when they made me undress before them and get into some filthy water they called a bath and dry myself with a damp, brown rag and put on this livery of shame. The cell was appalling: I could hardly breathe in it, and the food turned my stomach; the smell and sight of it were enough: I did not eat anything for days and days, I could not even swallow the bread; and the rest of the food was uneatable; I lay on the so-called bed and shivered all night long.

". . . Don't ask me to speak of it, please. Words cannot convey the cumulative effect of a myriad discomforts, brutal handling and slow starvation. Surely like Dante I have written on my face the fact that I have been in hell. Only Dante never imagined any hell like an English prison; in his lowest circle people could move about; could see each other, and hear each other groan: there was some change, some human companionship in misery. . . ."

"When did you begin to eat the food?" I asked.

"I can't tell, Frank," he replied. "After some days I got so hungry I had to eat a little, nibble at the outside of the bread, and drink some of the liquid; whether it was tea, coffee or gruel, I could not tell. As soon as I really ate anything it produced violent diarrhoea and I was ill all day and all night. From the beginning I could not sleep. I grew weak and had wild delusions. . . . You must not ask me to describe it. It is like asking a man who has gone through fever to describe one of the terrifying dreams. At Wandsworth I thought I should go mad: Wandsworth is the worst: no dungeon in hell can be worse; why is the food so bad? It even smelt bad. It was not fit for dogs."

"Was the food the worst of it?" I asked.

"The hunger made you weak, Frank; but the inhumanity was the worst of it; what devilish creatures men are. I had never known anything about them. I had never dreamt of such cruelties. A man spoke to me at exercise. You know you are not allowed to speak. He was in front of me, and he whispered, so that he could not be seen, how sorry he was for me, and how be hoped I would bear up. I stretched out my hands to him and cried, 'Oh, thank you, thank you.' The kindness of his voice brought tears into my eyes. Of course I was punished at once for speaking; a dreadful punishment. I won't think of it: I dare not. They are infinitely cunning in malice here, Frank; infinitely cunning in punishment. . . . Don't let us talk of it, it is too painful, too horrible that men should be so brutal."

This goes on for several pages more and is in contradiction to all we know of the prison system in the '90s and of all we have been told of Wilde in prison, particularly by H. Montgomery Hyde, who in his book *Oscar Wilde: the Aftermath* has made a minute and documented study of the subject. From this it appears that so far from Wilde's *physical* sufferings being worse than those of others, he was what Sherard of course calls a '*criminal de marque*', a prisoner privileged above any other, long before his last months at Reading Gaol under the humane governorship of Major Nelson. After his first fortnight in gaol he was examined by the medical officer by the direct order of the then Home Secretary, H. H. Asquith. It was probably Asquith who suggested that R. B. Haldane should visit Wilde, which he did, obtaining for him the use of books and writing materials and leaving him overcome with gratitude. Wilde had to wait three months, according to the rules of that time, before his first visit, which was from Sherard, but meanwhile, on his transfer to Wandsworth, he was put on extra diet and 'a further increase in diet', whatever that might mean. He was then examined, on orders from recently appointed Chairman of the Prison Commission, Sir Evelyn Ruggles-Brise, by the Superintending Medical Officer of Prisons, who reported as follows:

I have seen Oscar Wilde in consultation with Dr Quinton. He was cheerful and comfortable, and had just eaten a hearty dinner. As his appetite is exceedingly good, he thoroughly appreciates the very considerable increase that Dr Quinton has made in his diet.

I had a long conversation with him and found no evidence of despondency. On the contrary, the prisoner is adjusting himself in a sensible manner to his new environment, and seems to have no difficulty in reconciling himself to the inevitable. He did not manifest any want of nerve or courage, and I could find nothing in his demeanour, appearance or conversation to indicate that he is in the least degree 'crushed' or 'broken'. He does not appear to wish to be placed in association. In point of fact he stated to me that he had a dislike of seeing 'fresh faces'. I should imagine from what dropped from him that he would like to be left a little more to himself.

In cases of this kind it is sometimes advisable not to manifest great solicitude, and I think it would be desirable, for the present at least, to leave him where he is. At the same time he will be carefully watched, and the able medical officer Dr Quinton will do whatever is necessary.

Thereafter he was seen by two brain specialists sent from Broadmoor who found him amusing other prisoners in the infirmary, to which he had been moved, and found in his mental condition 'no indication of disease or derangement'.

Because of our knowledge of the men who are charged with the care of prisoners today, as in Wilde's time, we need not be too impressed by all these rosy reports, but it would seem that in Wilde's case, with the interest of the Home Secretary aroused, some particular attention was given, and this made Reading Gaol, during Oscar's last nine months there, what modern prisoners would consider in their own term a 'holiday camp'.

But no amount of attention could relieve one of Wilde's greatest anxieties. He could not bear ridicule, and he had a horror of being seen by anyone except the uniformed warders and the prisoners like himself in broad-arrow slops and with roughly sheared hair.

"As I sit here in this dark cell in convict clothes," he begins one of the paragraphs of De Profundis. "Even the spectacle of me behind the bars of a wooden cage . . ." he says later. "After my terrible sentence, when the prison-dress was on me . . ." he goes on, and "Twice have I been shown under conditions of unspeakable humiliation to the gaze and mockery of men," he cries pitifully, and finally gives the details, often repeated, of the scene on Clapham Junction station:

Everything about my tragedy has been hideous, mean, repellent, lacking in style. Our very dress makes us grotesques. We are the zanies of sorrow. We are clowns whose hearts are broken. We are specially designed to appeal to the sense of humour. On

November 13th, 1895, I was brought down here from London. From two o'clock till half-past two on that day I had to stand on the centre platform of Clapham Junction in convict dress and handcuffed, for the world to look at. I had been taken out of the Hospital Ward without a moment's notice being given to me. Of all possible objects I was the most grotesque. When people saw me they laughed. Each train as it came up swelled the audience. Nothing could exceed their amusement. That was of course before they knew who I was. As soon as they had been informed, they laughed still more. For half an hour I stood there in the grey November rain surrounded by a jeering mob. For a year after that was done to me I wept every day at the same hour and for the same space of time.

This incident seems to have pained Wilde more deeply than anything else which he suffered in prison. He tells the story in *De Profundis* a year after it happened and when he was about to be released he petitioned the Home Secretary to arrange that it should not be repeated.

The petitioner, however, is most anxious that he should not under any circumstances be transferred to another prison from the one in which he is at present confined. The ordeal he underwent in being brought in convict dress and handcuffed by a mid-day train from Clapham Junction to Reading was so utterly distressing, from the mental no less than the emotional point of view, that he feels quite unable to undergo any similar exhibition to public gaze, and he feels it his duty to say that he was assured by the former Governor of Reading Prison that he would not under any circumstances be again submitted to so terrible an experience.

Robert Sherard goes even further: "I had heard of this outrage shortly after it happened and was informed indeed that the occurrence was even worse than what Wilde relates. I was told that the man who first recognized the prisoner shouted: 'By God, that is Oscar Wilde,' and spat on him. I published the story in the hopes that some of those who were present might read my comments. The fact was denied then, but *De Profundis* confirmed it." It did nothing of the sort.

Common sense suggests that Wilde greatly exaggerated the incident. He was so extremely sensitive about appearing in public that he may have imagined people on the platform noticed and recognized him. Even if they did that, the probable reaction of the English public would be to turn away in embarrassment as we do from the outwardly diseased or crippled.

This horror and detestation of being looked at by people from the world outside prison is one which Wilde shared with other convicted men, particularly those of some education and previous standing in the community. Governors who bring their private guests in to 'have a look' at the gaol risk causing dissatisfaction and even an outbreak of violence by doing so. Perhaps Wilde carried it to a morbid extreme; if so, he was deserving of sympathy.

In this sensitiveness Wilde shows a touch of the paranoia which was so evident in D. H. Lawrence when he was called before a medical board during the First World War. Lawrence, however, maintained an attitude of defiance impossible in the circumstances to Wilde. "He stood there with his ridiculous thin legs, in his ridiculous thin jacket but he did not feel a fool." "Because they [the examining doctors] had handled his private parts and looked into them, their eyes should burst and their hands should wither and their hearts should rot." This is no more silly than Wilde's writing to More Adey: "They brought me down here handcuffed and in convict dress by a mid-day train, mobbed and hooted at every station."

2

By the time Wilde had been moved down to Reading, certain changes were notable in his thoughts about himself. He realized that there were not only the two extremes, the forces of Constance, Sherard and conventional morality on the one hand, and his professed love for Bosie and the old life on the other. A third, a compromise between the two, as though by a law of nature, had appeared in the person of Robert Ross. It was necessary for Wilde to hate Bosie—his reason at that time depended on it. He must show that his friendship with Bosie was to blame for his attacking Queensberry, 'a course of conduct that from the outside seems a combination of absolute idiocy and vulgar bravado'. But he was not willing to range himself entirely on the side of the Philistines and deny his own supremacy, both in the past and possibly in the future, as a Lord of Life, a genius able to appreciate the beauty and splendour of his own sex. There *was* another way. Ross and his friends More Adey and Arthur Clifton were queer and could enjoy the humour of queerness, but they were ready to listen sympathetically to abuse of Bosie and to struggle with Constance and her lawyers for a share of the marriage settlement for Wilde. They were not committed to one side or the other, and they did not wish to commit Oscar.

When Ross returned from abroad towards the end of the year, he went with Ernest Leverson to visit Wilde at Reading, and three months later returned with Sherard. Wilde said very little at that time but wrote to Ross on the following day a letter which showed his state of mind about Douglas. Bosie is not to dedicate a book of poems to Wilde, 'the proposal is revolting and grotesque'; he is to hand over to Ross all the letters which Wilde wrote him. "The thought that they are in his hands is horrible to me, and though my unfortunate children will never of course bear my name, still they know whose sons they are and I must try and shield them from the possibility of any further revolting disclosure or scandal." Also Ross is to possess himself of all the books and jewellery Oscar gave Douglas. "The idea that he is wearing or in possession of anything I gave him is peculiarly repugnant to me." There is a note of hysteria in Wilde's further statement. "I will not have him in possession of my letters or gifts. Even if I get out of this loathsome place I know that there is nothing before me but a life of a pariah—of disgrace and penury and contempt—but at least I will have nothing to do with him nor allow him to come near me."

The truth is that, on the subject of Bosie at this time, Wilde was very nearly mad, and had he not found a safety-valve in writing the *De Profundis* letter, his obsession might have reached the point of certifiable insanity. It was as well for him that he did so.

Among the privileges accorded to Wilde by Major Nelson, the Governor who took charge of Reading Gaol some months after Wilde was transferred there, was the use of a pen and apparently limitless official lined paper. He used it to set down the many bitter and ugly thoughts, and some noble ones, which he had brought to coherence in his mind, regret for his past life, frustration and anger at finding himself in gaol and above all rancour against Bosie whom he loved. He had to prove that he was imprisoned not for any fault of his own but because in his relations with Bosie he had been half-simpleton half-saint, a genius and a nobleman betrayed by one unable to appreciate his heroic qualities. Only by showing that Bosie had never been worth the love (and money) he had squandered on him could he re-establish himself in his own estimation. He had to find faults in Bosie other than those he had heard from Sherard, in order to portray himself garbed in the splendid purple of a royal sinner. He had to remember, with a pettiness not in the least characteristic of him at any other time, all the wretched little quarrels which in nearly four years of a neurotic love-affair had caused them to separate and come together again, and all the expenses he had incurred in the course of keeping Bosie with him. He had to express the contempt and hatred he felt for Queensberry and for all the lawyers who had served him. And finally having reduced Bosie to tears of shame, he had to show his own generosity by forgiving him.

It was a scheme of both consolation and reprisal, and it might have worked if Oscar had been a meaner man. As it was, it broke down. Oscar started with a brilliantly contrived tirade, but long before he had reached the climax he discovered that, by putting his bitterness into words, he had lost it. He had in fact written his way out of his bad temper and regained most of his peace of mind. It makes grim but fascinating reading now, that long piece of special pleading, which starts with something like hatred and ends with instructions to Bosie on how they should meet again. It is written with all the consuming sincerity of an obsessed and deluded man. There is pathos in it, but mostly of an unconscious kind, for Wilde's attempts to be tragic are apt to end in self-pity. And what humour exists is also entirely unconscious for—again like other prisoners—Wilde had completely lost his sense of fun, and wrote at times with pomposity that is laughable, at times with exaggerations that approach fatuity. All the saving flippancy with which he had once voiced his pronouncements had left him, and a ponderous kind of over-writing had taken its place. "The morning dawn of boyhood with its delicate bloom, its clear pure light, its joy of innocence and expectation you had left far behind" is how he tells Bosie that he was no longer innocent when they met, and to say that uneducated people may be charming he needs an entire paragraph: "One who is entirely ignorant of the modes of Art in its revolution or the moods of thought in its progress, of the pomp of the Latin line or the richer music of the vowelled Greek, of Tuscan sculpture or Elizabethan song may yet be full of the very sweetest wisdom." His narrative is interspersed with phrases like: 'Your father attacking me with hideous cards left at my club', 'Blindly I staggered as an ox to the shambles', or his description of poor Speranza as 'My mother who intellectually ranks with Elizabeth Barrett Browning and historic-ally with Madame Roland.' One comes on whole passages which are incredible as the work of a sane man who could use the English language with effect.

And I remember that afternoon, as I was in the railway-carriage whirling up to Paris, thinking what an impossible, terrible, utterly wrong state my life had got into, when I, a man of world-wide reputation, was actually forced to run away from England, in order to try and get rid of a friendship that was entirely de-structive of everything fine in me either from the intellectual or ethical point of view: the person from whom I was flying being no terrible creature sprung from sewer or mire into modern life with whom I had entangled my days, but you yourself, a young man of my own social rank and position, who had been at my own college at Oxford, and was an incessant guest at my house.

Or this:

I need not remind you how I waited on you, and tended you, not merely with every luxury of fruit, flowers, presents, books, and the like that money can procure, but with that affection, tenderness and love that, whatever you may think, is not to be procured for money. Except for an hour's walk in the morning, an hour's drive in the afternoon, I never left the hotel. I got special grapes from London for you, as you did not care for those the hotel supplied, invented things to please you, remained either with you or in the room next to yours, sat with you every evening to quiet or amuse you.

Or other passages which become nothing but uncontrolled raving, or overwriting like this: "Of course I discern in all our relations, not Destiny merely, but Doom: Doom that walks always swiftly, because she goes to the shedding of blood." Can it be seriously doubted that Wilde, who had turned this kind of prose to good account in the fantasy of his fairy stories, was mentally a sick man when he wrote it now to the one young friend who had remained by his side in his first days of imprisonment when no one else could or would stand by him? The whole letter needs to be read, with its megalomania and self-delusion, its moments of uncontrolled spite and its attempts at semi-religious mysticism, in order that the reader may appreciate how near it comes to a kind of literary delirium. It goes on and *on* about Bosie and Queensberry and Wilde's previous eminence and noble descent and present disgrace, until it loses all the reader's

sympathy and arouses no more than pity, in spite of its occasionally splendid prose.

But it did him good. He wrote to Ross: "Of the many, many
things for which I have to thank the Governor there is none for
which I am more grateful than for his permission to write fully to
A.D. and at as great length as I desired. For nearly two years I
had within me a growing burden of bitterness, much of which I
have now got rid of." Even his style of writing seemed to lose its
tension, and in the same letter to Ross, in giving instructions
about that enormous letter to Douglas, he showed the first glint
of humour since he was sentenced: "I assure you that the type-
writing machine, when played with expression, is not more
annoying than the piano when played by a sister or near relation.
Indeed many, among those most devoted to domesticity, prefer
it." And again, "If the copying is done at Hornton Street the lady
type-writer might be fed through a lattice in the door like the
Cardinals when they elect a Pope, till she comes out on the bal-
cony and can say to the world 'Habet Mundus Epistolam'; for indeed it is an Encyclical Letter, and as the Bulls of the Holy Father
are named from their opening words, it may be spoken of as the
Epistola: In Carcere et Vinculis." Not very hilarious perhaps, but
proving that by writing Wilde had got rid of his spleen.

3

When he had completed the letter Wilde wanted the original
to be sent to Douglas, but the Commissioners ruled that although
he could take it out with him when he was released, it must be
kept with his property till then. He became then and thereafter
almost indifferent to the fate of the manuscript. The minute
instructions he had given to Ross could not be carried out, of
course, till Wilde had handed over the letter to Ross, meeting
him at Dieppe. Wilde had originally wanted two typewritten
copies made of it, one for him and one for Ross, while the original
went to Bosie, but if a typewritten copy was made during Wilde's
lifetime, he never saw or corrected it; witness the 'several hun-

dred' errors found by Hart-Davis when he examined the typescript with the original, including Ross's revisions of Wilde's
syntax and grammar and the shifting of passages from one
portion of the typescript to another.

There has been a lot of baloney and discussion about this. The
truth is very simple. Wilde handed the MS to Ross and thereafter
lost interest in it. It had no commercial value at the time and it
had served its purpose with Wilde. Re-united with his 'dearest
Bosie' before any typescript could in any case have been made,
Wilde did not want the thing shown to Bosie at all, and it remained, in manuscript, in Ross's possession till after Wilde's
death. It would be interesting to know—though now beyond
investigation—when Ross *did* have the typewritten copy made.
Possibly not till he wanted to make his extracts from the MS to
publish as *De Profundis* in 1909. Certainly not during Wilde's
lifetime.

If Oscar had been able to foresee the trouble his manuscript
would bring about in the future, he would certainly have destroyed it himself. It was the cause of the internecine war between
Ross and Douglas which killed the former and clouded Bosie's
life for years.[1]

4

The physical conditions of Wilde's first year in prison were
probably more degrading than anything the modern prisoner has
to endure, especially since Wilde was sensitive about his appearance. The ugly hair crop, the hideous clothes, the lack of shaving
facilities have all been to some extent improved, and the food is
less nauseating today than in the nineteenth century. But in his
last months at Reading, Wilde had privileges which no present-
day convicted man could dream of in any of our gaols, and before
his release he had recaptured much of his blithe spirit and good
health.

[1] See chapters 11 and 12 'The Night of Long Knives' in my book *Bosie:
The Story of Lord Alfred Douglas His Friends and Enemies.*

He was allowed to write twenty folio sheets, each of four pages, of *De Profundis* on blue-ruled official notepaper, whereas anything a modern prisoner writes that deals with his own case, as this did, would be instantly confiscated, even if it was possible today to obtain a proper supply of paper and ink and the use of a usable pen. Wilde was allowed to write and receive virtually what letters he liked and obtain what books he sent for. He had a daily newspaper, ginger biscuits and other forbidden articles brought to his cell by an obliging warder who passed his notes to other prisoners, chiefly—one finds from his instructions to Reggie Turner after release—the younger and more attractive males among them. He was allowed a light (gas) in his cell till late at night. The Governor, Major Nelson, himself posted and received letters for him outside the usual allowance. "If anybody posted letters for Oscar, it was Major Nelson himself. I am certain that he received letters, addressed to himself, for Oscar and these he would deliver personally and wait in the cell until they were read, then bring the letters away with him, but sometimes forgetting the envelope," wrote Warder Martin, a friendly screw who was dismissed the prison service for kindness to child prisoners at about the time when Wilde was released. "From six a.m. when I opened his cell door . . . until I went off duty in the evening he spent the day reading or writing in his cell."

That he formed illicit friendships with other prisoners is evident from Warder Martin's letters to Sherard, who many years after Wilde's death, having himself at last learned something of homosexuality—he was now seventy-seven years old and still writing about Wilde—asked him whether Wilde indulged in 'any such practices' in prison. Montgomery Hyde, quoting Martin writing to Sherard, reports this in *Oscar Wilde: The Aftermath*:

In regard to the other subject of your letter, I may say that I have no knowledge whatever of Oscar having indulged in any such (homosexual) practices as you mention.

I am well aware that in convict prisons especially this vice is prevalent. When I was at Dartmoor, I heard the warders speak about it. In fact these sexual problems presented a never-ceasing worry to the officials and necessitated constant vigilance. For instance, two prisoners were never allowed to be left alone together. It was a sure 'half-sheet' for the warder in charge and a subsequent heavy fine, if a principal warder made the discovery. The food restrictions, in a great measure, are due to reasons of sexual psychology.

In regard to Oscar, I never heard his name mentioned in connection with anything of the sort. And the subject never once entered my mind until I read your letter this morning. Of course, it would be absolutely impossible for me to state definitely and emphatically that he did not. I never did night-duty in the prison.

The note which he asked me to deliver to the young prisoner, who was located in another block, and which I tore up, was merely a request from him to call at the Post Office and ask for a letter, and he would find a little money in it which would help him. I told the youth verbally what Oscar had said in the note and several months afterwards I was glancing through the pages of a new penny weekly journal (I have forgotten its name) when I noticed a headline entitled: 'Curious Letters from Oscar Wilde'. On reading through I learned that the two letters quoted were written from Berneval to this youth, who wanted to sell them. The contents, though not compromising, were indiscreet, and I wrote to Oscar immediately and advised him to be more careful.

Perhaps they were written to the young prisoner about whom Sherard wrote in *Twenty Years in Paris*. "One of the youths to whom he thus showed kindness was a lad who acted as 'cleaner' to the corridor in which (Wilde's) cell was situated. It is to be noted that he might have taken advantage of the lad's services to empty his slops and fetch water for him, (but) he insisted on performing these menial offices himself. He was greatly interested in the little fellow."

There were several young men who might have been the recipients of the 'indiscreet' letters of Wilde. He wrote to Warder

Martin not long before his release "Please find out for me the name of A.2.11." Also "You must get A.S.2 to come out and clean on Saturday morning and I will give him my note then myself." Was he perhaps Sherard's 'little cleaner'?

After he was released, Wilde sent Ross from Berneval a list of nine prisoners and one warder to whom he wanted money sent. 'They are my debts of honour.' Ross must have been relieved to know that the total (£20 10s.) would leave only Jim Cuthbert, Jim Huggins and Harry Elvin, who would come out in October to December. "Please be careful not to mix the letters (sent with the money). They are all nuanced." He wants the *Daily Chronicle* containing his letter on prison reform to be sent to one of these, Arthur Cruttenden, with a note: "Dear Friend, The enclosed will interest you. There is also another letter waiting in the Post Office for you from me, with a little money. Ask for it, if you have not got it. Yours sincerely C.3.3." We learn through another letter to Ross that the unfortunate A.2.11, Wilde's friendship with whom had cost Warder Martin so much trouble, is to be flogged again: "I am very sorry, but you must put a £1 Postal Order or whatever it is called into enclosed letter, and send it. *Read the letter*, and you will see I must do it. It makes me sick to think that A.2.11 has been flogged again. It fills me with despair."

Less than three weeks after release he wrote to Reginald Turner, begging him to send £6 10s. to Arthur Cruttenden, a young American who had been in the British Army, as he intends to invite him to stay with him at Berneval. He warns Reggie Turner, "I had better say candidly that he is not 'a beautiful boy'. He is twenty-nine years of age, but looks a little older, as he inherits hair that catches silver lines early: he has also a slight, but still *real*, moustache. I am thankful and happy to be able to say that I have no feeling for him, nor could have, other than affection and friendship. He is simply a manly simple fellow, with the nicest smile and the pleasantest eyes, and I have no doubt a confirmed '*mulierast*', to use Robbie's immortal phrase." Reggie apparently obliged and Arthur Cruttenden duly arrived. "He is very nice and gentle but not very well." For another of his Reading acquaintances, Lawley or Langley, Wilde tried to arrange a job with Harris. "All soldiers are neat, and smart, and make capital servants. He would be a good *groom*; he is, I believe, a Third Hussars man. He was a quiet well-conducted chap in Reading always."

By October of that year there was only one of Wilde's friends still in prison, 'the one I liked best; a very handsome young soldier of twenty years of age—Harry Elvin', Wilde wrote to Turner, enjoining him to give the usual assistance. Thereafter Wilde's prison friends fade out of our knowledge. If he ever saw them, no mention of it is made in his letters to Ross and Turner. Most of his consideration for them certainly came from his own good nature, and it would be mean to remember that he helped them at the expense of Turner and Ross. There is not enough evidence to suggest that any relationship of his at Reading, prisoner or warder, was of a homosexual nature, though the urge to befriend young men, some doubtless of the type of his pre-conviction acquaintance, needs no explanation. Oscar's sexual character did not change with his tragedy and eclipse.

5

The *De Profundis* letter to Bosie Douglas was not the only bitter and malicious one which Wilde wrote in prison. He suffered, even in his last months, from that agonizing frustration, those unreasonable recriminative brainstorms familiar to psychiatrists who have studied the mental disturbances of prisoners, and known among the latter as gaol fever. Very few of those outside who still concerned themselves with him escaped violent abuse. The worst offenders in his eyes were Robbie Ross and More Adey, who had tried to make some arrangement in his favour with Constance's lawyers. Adey was 'utterly incompetent and had repeated down to the smallest detail the whole of the Queensberry episode'. To Ross there is an enormous letter, which recalls the most bitter passages of *De Profundis*, and in fact tells Ross that Bosie stands up well in comparison with him. The letters comprise thousands of words written to Ross and More Adey which show Wilde's morbid condition. "You see the state I am in," he wrote to Adey, "I am wrecked with the recurring tides of hysteria." Only a few months earlier Constance's proposal had been 'a cruel and heartless one'; while "when I reflect that the only two people who have, since my imprisonment, tried to distress me by terrible letters are my wife and Lord Queensberry, I feel fixed on some shrill pinnacle of horror." As for the solicitors —all three of them, Humphreys, Hansell and Holman, make Wilde rave with anger and frustration, and the opinions of one are 'worthless and pernicious'.

'The distressing thing to me is the uncertainty,' cried Wilde in words familiar to everyone who enters a prison where small worries which will soon be resolved on release, and do not matter anyway, can reduce a man to frenzy. Concern with trivial possessions becomes an obsession and anyone who has had experience like Wilde's will recognize the tone of his letters. "The people who disposed of my fur coat," wrote Wilde, referring to his brother and sister-in-law, "have also, or should have, my two rugs, one a fur rug, the other a travelling rug; two portmanteaus, one brown leather with my initials, the other black: my large double hat-box. Would you write to them to ask them for these things, or to know what has become of them. I simply want to know. If they have pawned them, very well, I shall know that. If not I can get them. I also want to know where and when my fur coat was pawned. These people will probably try to annoy me: they have already tried to do so lately: I want their letters kept, for my protection."

Frank Harris is given his share of blame: "He said he . . . would send me a cheque for £500 before my release. I admit that, in my unnerved state, I was very deeply moved at his generous present, and made no attempt to conceal my feelings, which were indeed beyond my control. I now learn that he has sent a verbal message through you to say he is very sorry but cannot do it . . . The Frank Harrises of life are a dreadful type. I hope to see no more of them." Of Ernest Leverson, who had been ex- tremely kind to Wilde, he wrote: "For Leverson to come now and claim alone of all my creditors to be paid 100 per cent and have his pound of flesh is simple fraud and dishonesty." Even poor Charles Ricketts, who had made great efforts to accompany Ross to Reading, gets it in the neck. "I was wrong to have Ricketts present: he meant to be cheering, but I thought him trivial: everything he said, including his remark that he supposed time went very fast in prison (a singularly unimaginative opinion, and one showing an entirely inartistic lack of sympathetic instinct), annoyed me extremely."

Within a few hours of Wilde's release, all these annoyances, great and small, had vanished. He forgot the letter to Bosie and the mistakes of Ross and More Adey, even the fur coat, in the ecstasy of freedom. But they were real and racking enough while he was still in prison.

THIRTEEN

Freedom

There remain to be recalled two periods of Wilde's life between his coming out of prison on 19 May 1897, and his death on 30 November 1900. The first is of his stay at Berneval culminating in his reunion with Bosie, when the two lived and worked together and found a brief, peaceful fulfilment for their troubled love until they were separated by their respective families and well-wishers. Wilde had voiced the hope during his days in Holloway before he was sentenced—'If one day, at Corfu or in some enchanted isle, there were a little house where we could live together oh! life would be sweeter than it has ever been' and for several months it was.

In his last three years, when his headquarters were in Paris, Wilde found fulfilment of another kind. There were no more attempts to write, or even think about writing; friendship with Bosie was without passion or strain, and he lounged about the boulevards and amused himself with young male prostitutes and wrote supremely entertaining letters about them to Ross and Reggie Turner.

When he was first released, he became a centre of intrigue which involved nearly all his acquaintances, his wife and her family, as well as Bosie and his family. Wilde was by no means a passive figure; he showed in his genial way as much cunning as most of the others. But he was conditioned by penury, which he made no serious attempt to relieve by writing. He may have realized—and it may have amused him—that the intrigue came from the jealousy between two young men who had been his lovers, Ross and Bosie. Their warfare was not yet lethal, but Ross had powerful weapons, the control of nearly all Wilde's financial resources, the ear of Wilde's wife, the assistance of More Adey, and his own industry and perseverance. Bosie had one great advantage, Wilde's help-less love for him, but he was restrained by his family, by his blind failure to realize that he had determined and crafty enemies and by the fact that he was not prepared to dedicate his whole life to this warfare.

At first Ross was in undisputed possession. Wilde's letters during his last months in prison had been largely concerned with money, and Ross held a sum which had been variously calculated, but was probably about £200, for his immediate needs. Wilde had signed an agreement with his wife by which she had control of his children but would give him an income of £150 a year so long as he did not associate with 'disreputable persons', and this was paid through Ross.

2

Wilde crossed the Channel with More Adey on the day of his release, and travelling on the night boat, reached Dieppe, where Ross and Reggie Turner awaited him. The four went to the Hotel Sandwich but during the first week Reggie Turner re-turned to London and More Adey went to Paris, where he met Bosie and gave him the news of Wilde. Ross stayed with Wilde for another week, settled him at a small hotel in Berneval, a village three miles from Dieppe, then he too returned to London. When Bosie heard from More Adey of Wilde's whereabouts, he wrote to him, and Wilde replied. By 2 June, that is within a fortnight of Wilde's release, Wilde was writing to 'My dear boy' and two days later had become, 'ever, dear boy, with fondest love'. At first he tried to reassure Ross about Bosie—he was never going to see him again. But during June, when Wilde and Bosie were planning to meet, all mention of Bosie ceased in Wilde's almost daily letters to Ross.

Thus on 28 May, the day following Ross's departure from Berneval, Wilde wrote to him of Bosie's 'revolting' letter and said he had a real terror of 'that unfortunate ungrateful young man with his unimaginative selfishness'. To be with him again, he assured Ross, would be to return to the hell from which he had been released. Wilde felt Bosie as 'an evil influence'.

Next day he reverted to this *De Profundis* attitude in a shorter letter to Ross. He is terrified about Bosie, who can almost ruin him. Bosie's letters to him are 'infamous'.

But three days later, on 2 June, he wrote a long, affectionate, though not yet loving, letter to Bosie, whom he addressed as 'my dear boy', signing himself 'ever affectionately yours'. On the same day he told Ross that Bosie had written, 'for him nicely'.

Next morning he wrote to Bosie again, having seen in *Le Jour* an interview about him which Bosie was supposed to have given. It was quite harmless, he said, and he was sorry Bosie had taken any notice of it. On the same day he wrote to Ross, mildly ridiculing Bosie for threatening to fight a duel over the interview.

On 4 June, that is barely two months after the completion of *De Profundis*, Wilde wrote to Bosie: 'Don't think I don't love you. I love you more than anyone else.' But their lives are severed so far as meeting goes. He is 'ever dear boy with fondest love'. On the next day he wrote to Ross, perhaps in answer to a query, that Bosie telegraphs every day. 'This is an exaggeration but I made him wire about the duel.' The duel never took place.

On 6 June Wilde wrote to Bosie that he (Wilde) must give up the *absurd* habit of writing to him every day. It comes from the strange joy of talking to Bosie daily. He is glad Bosie went to bed at seven. Modern life is terrible to vibrating delicate frames like Bosie's.

Wilde was visited by Rothenstein and others, and for some days had little time for letter-writing. But by 15 June he was arranging for Bosie, 'dear honey-sweet boy', to visit him under the name of Jonquil de Vallon. On the following day he wrote again, underlining 'I have asked you to come here on Saturday.' He has a bathing-costume for Bosie but wants him to bring lots of cigarettes and books. The weather is very hot, so Bosie will want a straw hat and flannels. Wilde hopes to be in his chalet by Saturday, so Bosie will stay with him there.

This proposed meeting was reported to Ross, who immediately went to Wilde's solicitor, and Wilde was warned that if Bosie came down to see him, Queensberry would cross to Boulogne and make a scene. This reduced poor Oscar to a condition of panic. He wired to Bosie to put him off, and on June 17 he wrote to Bosie that he had had to send his friends away because he was so 'distressed in nerve' by his solicitor's letter. It was impossible for them to meet. 'I think of you always and love you always, but chasms of moonless night divide us.'

Ross was reassured by a letter from Wilde. 'A.D. is not here, nor is he to come,' and another sent on the following day, 19 June, saying: 'I have now put off Bosie indefinitely. I have been so harassed, and indeed frightened, at the thought of a possible scandal or trouble." But Wilde continued to write to Bosie as 'my own darling boy' while he told Ross of a long indictment of him which Bosie had sent. 'You can understand in what tone I shall answer him.'

But on 7 July Wilde wrote to Bosie as 'My darling boy', ending his letter 'with my love, dearest boy, ever your Oscar', and on 28 August Wilde went to Rouen to meet Bosie. They stayed at the Hotel de la Poste, from which Bosie had written his letters to Clarke and W. T. Stead two years earlier. This made it impossible for Bosie to use an assumed name, which disappointed Wilde who loved such things and spoke of himself as 'that strange purple shadow who is known as Sebastian Melmoth'. Wilde went by train.

The meeting was a great success (wrote Bosie in his *Autobiography*). I have often thought since that if he or I had died directly after that, our friendship would have ended in a beautiful and romantic way. Poor Oscar cried when I met him at the station. We walked about all day arm in arm, or hand in hand, and were perfectly happy. Next day he went back to Berneval and I returned to Paris, but we had settled that when I went to Naples about six weeks later he was to join me there.

This left both of them with some difficult explanations to make. Wilde had to break the news to Ross, who was, says Hesketh Pearson, 'extremely angry', as well he might be. Bosie wrote to his mother, whose reply was to hurry over to France and take him to Aix-les-Bains for some weeks in the hope of persuading him not to see more of Wilde.

After Wilde's return to Berneval, the three-cornered correspondence continued. On 31 August Wilde sent Bosie what was perhaps the most sincere and significant letter he had written since he came out of prison. Addressing him as 'My own Darling Boy', he assured him that his only hope of doing beautiful work in art was being with him, for Bosie could really recreate in him that energy and sense of joyous power on which art depended. Everyone, he said, was furious with him for going back to Bosie, but they did not understand. 'Do remake my ruined life for me,' he wrote, and wished that when they had met at Rouen they had not parted at all.

Finally he closed this episode of attempted equilibrium between himself, Bosie and Ross by a letter to Ross which must have curdled in its recipient's mind. "Yes, I saw Bosie," he said, "and of course I love him as I always did."

3

Overshadowed by all that tense intrigue, the other events of Wilde's life during his four months at Berneval seem scarcely worth recounting, but there was one episode of interest and some entertainment—his sudden and passionate friendship with the poet Ernest Dowson. To dismiss this as something extraneous to the sensual or even to the sexual life of Wilde suggests that baleful habit of absolute categorization of people which confuses so many issues. 'Dowson was not homosexual', so runs the argument, 'his taste was for very young girls and his life was dominated by his love of one of these. *Therefore* there could not have been "anything between" him and Wilde.' It may well be that there was not; we shall certainly not discover now, but there are certain aspects of the affair which are difficult to explain if the two men remained emotionally indifferent to one another, in spite of the decaying teeth from which both suffered, the small moustache which Dowson had grown to hide this ailment, Dowson's generally neglected appearance and Alfred Taylor's warning of long ago—'Mr Wilde likes nice clean boys.'

They met[1] at a momentous time in the lives of both of them. Wilde had just come out of prison, and Dowson had left London where he had stayed in rooms above the restaurant kept by the parents of Adelaide Foltinowicz, and knew that she was shortly to marry Augustus Noelte. Desmond Flower and Henry Maas, the editors of *The Letters of Ernest Dowson*, say 'the friendship between them, two lonely people, had deepened suddenly', and we soon find Wilde writing letters of the kind he had addressed to young men in the days of his splendour, while he wrote to Ross and Bosie about his new friend. 'Ernest Dowson, Conder, and Dal Young come out here this afternoon to dine and sleep—at least I know they dine, but I believe they never sleep,' he told Ross. 'Ernest has a most interesting nature,' he wrote to Bosie on the following day. To Dowson himself he wrote asking to be introduced to a certain Jean, who 'has the boats or knows about them'. Ten days later Dowson arrived to stay with Wilde at Berneval for three days and Wilde had a carriage to drive him back to Arques-la-Bataille where he was staying. 'I like him immensely,' he told Bosie. To Dowson—"I arrived safe, under a cold white moon, at one o'clock in the morning. My servant was asleep, so I woke him up and enquired about his early life, which, as I expected, was quite uninteresting. There is a fatality about our being together that is astounding—or rather quite probable. Had I stayed at Arques I should have given up all hopes of ever separating from you. Why are you so persistently and perversely wonderful? . . . I suppose I shall see you in ten minutes from this. I am looking out for the green costume that goes so well with your dark hyacinth locks." Was that, one cannot help asking, as

[1] Not for the first time. Sherard had brought Dowson to Oakley Street while Wilde was on bail, and they had seen each other before that at the Rhymers Club.

Carson did in his cross-examination of Wilde, 'the kind of letter a man writes to another'? Wilde was enthusiastic, even when he wrote to Will Rothenstein, not the most sympathetic receiver of confidences: "Ernest Dowson has been most charming, and stayed three days here with me. He and I dine with Thaulow the Swedish painter in Dieppe on Wednesday."

Wilde and Dowson went to and fro between Berneval and Arque-la-Bataille to visit one another, and Wilde arrived home 'not safe, but very unsafe, at Berneval in pouring rain at 10.30. There was only one lantern to the *voiture* so one wheel of the carriage was always in the air.'

On my arrival I found André Gide, who had come from Paris to see me [he continues to Dowson]. Madame Bonnet made me drink *two* hot grogs, so I came to life at 11.15 and had a wonderful evening. André left yesterday at eleven o'clock. He was most charming, and had heard of you and your work.

All my invitations to my Jubilee Garden Party were issued yesterday through Marcel, the little grandson of Madame Darcy of the Café de la Paix, Berneval-le-Grand. He supervised the invitations, and struck off several names on the perfectly right grounds that he did not like them. The list was strictly limited to twelve: as the garden only holds *six* at the most, I felt that *twelve* would be sufficient: I hate crowds. Today I go in to order straw-berries. I still hope you may come. A green coat always lights up a garden so well. I intend to wear my turquoise-coloured shirt.

Finally I have found my overcoat! A dear woman at Belleville picked it up on the road. So I now 'know *Joseph*' again.

Two days later Wilde sent a note by hand to Dowson: "Do come here at once: Monsieur Meyer is presiding over a morning meal of absinthe, and we want you. I am a wreck of course, but *la belle sœur* is like the moon. You were wonderful and charming all last night." A few days later, and : "I write a little line, whose only excuse is its entire illegibility, to tell you how charming you are (at Berneval) and how much I like *your* friend, *and mine*, the dear Achille. He is a most noble and splendid fellow, and I feel happy to have his esteem and friendship. Tonight I am going to read your poems—your lovely lyrics—words with wings *you* write always. It is an exquisite gift, and fortunately rare in an age whose prose is more poetic than its poetry. Do come soon and see me. . . . Give to Achille my sincere friendship: you have it, and other things."

In August, Dowson returned to London, Wilde having lent him money for the fare. Wilde wrote asking for the return of this: "I hope you will be able to send me what you owe me in a few days, as I have no money. Your bill with Monsieur Bonnet was £11, and then in Dieppe of course there were huge expenses, and I also lent you money. It comes to £19, which I hope to receive within a week, as I cannot pay Monsieur Bonnet and he is getting offensively tedious. I have lost many pleasures in life. One is the pleasure of playing a host's part. I have not the means: nor do I know how to live at all." A few days later, having in the meantime had his necessities relieved, he wrote more lightly: "As for the cheque: I know, dear Ernest, you will send it as soon as you can. I scramble on somehow, and hope to survive the season. After that, Tunis, rags, and hashish." The money was not paid until the following October, but Wilde's letters in the meantime are not impatient or unfriendly. In October he wrote from Posilippo: "I hope you will be able to find time to come to Naples, which I know you would like. The museum is full, as you know, of lovely Greek bronzes. The only bother is that they all walk about the town at night. However, one gets delicately accustomed to that—and there are compensations."

Dowson on his side, during his intimate friendship with Wilde spoke enthusiastically about him. To Conal O'Riordan he wrote: "The other day I met Oscar & dined with him at his seaside retreat; I had some difficulty in suppressing my own sourness & attuning myself to his enormous joy in life just at this moment—but I hope I left him with the impression that I had not a care in the world. He was in wonderful form, but has changed a good deal—he seems of much broader sympathies, much more human &

simple. And his delight in the country, in walking, in the simplici-
ties of life is enchanting." Again to O'Riordan: "Oscar came
over & lunched with me the other day & carried me back with
him to Berneval. His gorgeous spirits cheered me mightily. I was
amused by the unconscious contrast between his present talk
about his changed position & his notions of economy & his
practice, which is perversely extravagant. He does not realize in
the least that nobody except himself *could* manage to spend the
money he does in a *petit trou de campagne*. He is a wonderful man."

It was altogether a happy and mutually beneficial friendship
and quite unclouded, though both would die within the next three
years.

4

The letters in which Wilde and Bosie planned their flight
together to Naples have not come to light. Wilde wrote to a
number of people to say that he was going to Italy or to Naples,
but gave no hint of who his companion would be. As the date
planned for his departure approached, Wilde wrote to Bosie to
say his money was exhausted, and Bosie sent him his fare. It was,
unfortunately, characteristic of the post-prison Wilde that on his
way through Paris he lunched with Vincent O'Sullivan, and said
he would start for Naples tonight if he had the money. O'Sullivan
drew sufficient from his bank and gave it to him, afterwards
reflecting, "It is one of the few things I look back on with satisfaction. It is not every day that one has the chance of relieving
the anxiety of a genius and a hero."

Bosie came straight from Aix-les-Bains, and they met on the
train between Paris and Italy. They had scarcely any money
between them, so, being Oscar and Bosie, they went straight to
the Hotel Royal in Naples and in two weeks ran up a bill of £60,
at the time a vast amount to spend in a Neapolitan hotel. This
bill remained unpaid until Bosie obtained the money from his
mother several months later.

Their staying together in Naples had at first the added delight of being clandestine. Bosie had not told his mother at Aix-les-Bains exactly what he intended to do. Wilde had not told his wife or her solicitors, or, so far as is known, Robert Ross. But very soon their flight and whereabouts were known to everyone, to Ross and his friends, to Constance Wilde and her family, to Bosie's mother and brother. All hell, as they say, broke loose.

Wilde's first letter of explanation was to Ross (21 September): 'My going back to Bosie was psychologically inevitable.' He went on to explain in conciliatory terms that he could not live without an atmosphere of love, and though he could have lived his whole life with Ross, Ross had other claims on him and could only give him a week of companionship. He begged Ross that when people spoke against him for going back to Bosie, Ross would explain that Bosie offered him love and that after three months struggle with a hideous Philistine world, he had turned naturally to him.

To Reggie Turner he wrote in less pompous terms. He loved Bosie and had always loved him. Bosie was the first of all the young poets of England. 'So stick up for us, Reggie, and be nice.'

Ross's expostulations must have been violent, judging from Wilde's reply on 1 October: 'I have not answered your letters, because they distressed me and angered me.'

To Leonard Smithers, the publisher who was issuing his *Ballad of Reading Gaol*, Wilde wrote even more irritably on the same day: "How *can* you keep on asking is Lord Alfred Douglas in Naples? You know quite well he is—we are together. He understands me and my art, and loves both. I hope never to be separated from him."

After this they were left in peace for six weeks and began to create a way of living together. In appearance Wilde had changed greatly since their first meeting six years earlier. He had come out of prison with rather short hair, and he never again attempted the elaborate Neronian hair-do of his London days, for he was growing somewhat bald. His features were not marked by suffering in the way one might have expected, his expression was not tragic, but almost commonplace. Contemporary photographs show him looking like a Dublin businessman on holiday. His height and weight and his rich speaking voice gave him some distinction but the arrogant and dressy figure of Tite Street was no more. His teeth, which had given him much concern when he took great trouble over his appearance, were now badly decayed. He was also increasingly deaf.

They found a villa at Posilippo and moved into it at once. 'We have a lovely villa over the sea', wrote Oscar, 'and a nice piano.' Servants were cheap and they had a cook called Carmine, a maid Maria and two boys who waited on them—Peppino and Michele. The villa had a terrace and marble steps leading down to the sea, but as they discovered at once, it was overrun with rats. Bosie had a horror of rats and mice, and to Oscar's amusement took a bedroom in the house opposite till their own was cleared. His description of this trivial incident seems to carry the memory of cordial humour between the two friends, for one of the very foundations of their friendship was that they laughed together and at one another.

"The solitude of our life here is wonderful," Wilde wrote to Ross, "no one writes to either of us. It is lucky that we love each other." "Of the worldly-success point of view," he told Reggie Turner, "I really cannot say: it may be so: but I myself feel that I am happier with Bosie than I could be if all my laurels were given back to me . . . If we had money, we would be all right." To More Adey: "Is there any chance of your coming to Naples? Bosie and I would like immensely to see you again. I am getting rather astonishing in my Italian conversation. I believe I talk a mixture of Dante and the worst modern slang."

They were both working. "Bosie has written three lovely sonnets, which I have called 'The Triad of the Moon'—they are quite wonderful. He has sent them to Henley. I have also got him to send his sonnet on Mozart to the *Musician*." Although no progress was made with any of the projected plays, Wilde completed, and sent to Leonard Smithers for publication, *The Ballad of Reading Gaol*, a remarkable piece of versification which Wilde had hammered out stanza by stanza, as long ago he had done with his poems *The Sphinx* and *The Harlot's House*. He had great plans for work. Dalhousie Young, a well-to-do composer who had written a pamphlet *Apologia pro Oscar Wilde*, published in the first month of Wilde's imprisonment, had now commissioned him to write a libretto for *Daphnis and Chloë*, advancing him £100 for the work, though, as Wilde said afterwards, he accepted it knowing in his heart that it was meant half as a gift, half as an encouragement. Whether any of the libretto was completed is unknown. (Bosie was supposed to have written some of the lyrics.) Eight months after he had received the money Oscar admitted, 'I have not done it yet. I may never do it.'

It was drama which chiefly attracted him, though never to the point of actually writing scenes. To Stanley Makower he wrote of the *Ballad of Reading Gaol*: 'It must be finished. Then I turn to the Drama,' and to Ross: 'Tomorrow I begin the *Florentine Tragedy*. After that I must tackle *Pharaoh*.'

He wrote to Ernest Dowson: "I have begun today the tragedy in one act I told you about at Berneval, with the passages about clothes in it. I find the architecture of art difficult now. It requires sustained effort, but I must do it."

"I now think", he wrote to Reginald Turner, "of beginning my play for George Alexander, but I cannot see myself writing comedy. I suppose it is all in me somewhere, but I don't seem to feel it. My sense of humour is now concentrated on the grotesqueness of tragedy." In reply to a suggestion from Augustin Daly, conveyed to him through Smithers, he wrote: "With regard to Daly, it would be very kind of you if you would write to him and say that I will begin a comedy for him for £100 down, and £100 for each completed act, the royalties to be such as I received for my last American play."

But nothing more was heard of any of these projects. It may be thought that this is tragic, that Wilde ought to have buckled to and produced something in his years of freedom, if it was no more than enlargement into a book of his letters to the *Daily Chronicle* on penal reform, something which the public would take from him. But readers of Wilde take an almost proprietary interest in his work, and there are many, I believe, who would not wish to have another (perhaps mediocre) play in exchange for the letters he wrote in his last two years.

Oscar and Bosie went over to Capri together and lunched with

Axel Munthe at San Michele—'a great connoisseur of Greek things. He is a wonderful personality,' said Wilde in a letter to Ross.

In his novel *L'Exile de Capri*, Roger Peyrefitte gives a picture of them at the Hotel Quisisana, where an Englishman, he says, threatened to leave if they were served. But as he portrays Wilde with 'long grey hair' and his fingers 'loaded with rings', and says that Bosie had again rented the Villa Federico which he had occupied two years earlier, the whole scene must be taken for what it was—a piece of fiction. (They stayed only a day or two in Capri, and Bosie's home on his previous visit was the Villa Caso.) But I like the description of Bosie, who 'carried himself insolently' and, when refused service, tapped the *maître d'hôtel* on the shoulder with his cane, saying 'In England's name, friend, my congratulations.'

It is pleasant to think of Oscar and Bosie after all their tribulations together and apart, and after all Oscar's grandiloquent accusations in *De Profundis*, having that last belated honeymoon in Posilippo and pleasant to think, after Wilde's hysterical claim that Bosie was the ruin of his art, that the months they spent there were not unproductive.

But those determined to separate them were busy. Oscar and Bosie were first made to realize this by a visit from one of the *attachés* from the British Embassy whom Bosie had met in the previous year when he had been in Rome with his mother. This was Beauchamp Denis Browne, an acquaintance of Reggie Turner's. He came ostensibly to make a friendly call, and was 'very witty and talkative'. However he told Bosie privately that the *ménage* at the Villa Giudice was *mal vu* at the Embassy and a cause of great embarrassment to them all.

The intrigue between the various parties determined to part the friends then grew intense. At least five principals were directly involved in this, and several more played minor parts, adding their advice or criticism or threats as occasion demanded. First of all was Ross, who was outraged at Wilde's return to the man he regarded as his rival. Next Constance Wilde, who had been pumped full of anti-Bosie propaganda by Ross and others and invariably spoke of 'that *beast* A.D.' and threatened to cut off Wilde's small allowance. The two solicitors—Hargrove, who acted for Constance Wilde, and Hansell, who was supposed to be protecting Wilde's interests—agreed in their determination to break up the friendship, though Queensberry, inexplicably, seems to have taken no part in the affair. More Adey supported Ross; Robert Sherard added his indiscretions, and Leonard Smithers his advice. It was a full-scale conspiracy.

Oscar at first did not realize the scope of it, and thought he had no one but Constance to contend with. He even wrote to Ross for sympathy and support, asking him how Constance could really imagine she could influence or control his life. He supposed she would now try to deprive him of his 'wretched £3 a week'. Women were so petty and Constance had no imagination. If for revenge she managed to bring Wilde to trial again, she would be able to claim that for the first time in her life she had influenced him. Things were dark with storm.

Then Oscar heard that Sherard had been abusing him in the Authors' Club for returning to Bosie. Sherard received a stiff letter from Wilde and dropped out of the running for a time.

Ross now had a major success. Wilde heard from his solicitor that he was to be deprived of his allowance since he was living with Bosie, who was, Hansell agreed with Hargrove, a 'disreputable person'. Wilde had caused a 'public scandal' by returning to him.

Still Wilde failed to see Ross's hand in this, and wrote in fairly dignified distress to Ross to tell him what had happened, not to worry him about the prejudged matter but 'because I tell you everything'. It was unfair to say that he had created a 'public scandal' by returning to Bosie—his very existence was a scandal, but he did not think he should be blamed for continuing to live. He could not live alone and Bosie was the only one of his friends who was able or willing to give him his companionship.

"If I were living with a Naples renter," he said bitterly, "I suppose I would be all right."

A few days later he wrote to Ross again and said he was writing to More Adey and Adrian Hope about 'this monstrous attempt to

I*

leave me to starve because I live with the only human being—amongst gentlemen—who will live with me'. His solicitor had apparently told him that he held 'any member of the Queensberry family' as being in the category of 'a disreputable person'. He had always distrusted Hansell but had not thought he would strain the meaning of a legal document to ruin his own client.

He was still under the impression that Ross, though he might resent his return to Bosie, would not join Wilde's enemies to gain his ends. But the letter he received from More Adey disillusioned him and revealed the whole mean little conspiracy, for Adey, a franker man than Ross, admitted that when he and Ross had been asked whether Bosie was a 'disreputable person', they had felt bound to answer yes, and had agreed that Constance was 'strictly within her rights' in cutting off Wilde's allowances.

This roused all the anger of which Wilde was capable, and it seems probable that if it had not been for Ross's hold on his resources, his quarrel with both Adey and Ross might have been permanent. In what way, he thundered, was Bosie more disreputable than they were? Constance herself had expressed her horror when she heard that Adey had been to see him in prison and had required that he would have nothing more to do with such 'infamous companions'. This had been on information about Adey and Ross supplied to her by George Lewis. She knew what Ross's life was and had been. Wilde simply did not know how to describe his feelings of utter amazement and indignation.

He wrote to Reggie Turner, not wanting, as he said, to mix him up in the matter but to say that Ross and Adey had done a most unjust and illegal thing. What they had done was 'unfair, stupid and utterly unjust'.

Constance Wilde, in a letter to her brother, confirmed that the betrayal had taken place. Wilde's 'legal friends' in London made no defence and no opposition to her stopping Wilde's allowance. She, poor woman, was in a difficult position, being pressed by members of her own family. Harris was later to publish the fact that her father, Horatio Lloyd, Q.C., had himself been in trouble for a sexual offence, and in his Notes to Harris's book, Ross was to say that the charge against Horatio Lloyd was of a 'normal' kind. "It was for exposing himself to nursemaids in the gardens of the Temple." With her father and husband both involved in scandals, and with two small sons to look after while she herself was in failing health, she relied on others to advise her.

But Oscar could not afford to maintain this attitude of indignation towards those on whom he depended for a livelihood, and by 23 November he was writing to Ross miserably to know whether, if he agreed not to *live* with Bosie, in the same house, it would be regarded as a concession. To say that he would not speak to him again would be childish and out of the question, but he was quite ready, as Bosie was, to agree that they would not live under the same roof. He wrote with this suggestion to Adey, but the poor little olive branch was ignored.

Meanwhile Lady Queensberry joined her efforts to the others', and got in touch with Adrian Hope and perhaps with Constance Wilde. She was as anxious as everyone else that the 'scandalous Naples *ménage*' should be broken up.

All through November and early December the acrimonious correspondence continued. Then a heavier blow fell. Lady Queensberry wrote to Bosie, saying categorically that if he did not leave Wilde, his own allowance would be stopped.

Both friends recognized this as final. Bosie wrote to his mother, saying in effect that if she would send him enough money to settle up matters in Naples, pay a quarter's rent on the villa in advance so that Wilde could remain there, and give Wilde £200 for his immediate living expenses, Bosie would agree not to live with Wilde again. His mother accepted these terms readily. She sent Bosie what he required in Naples, and paid the £200 in two instalments to More Adey for Wilde.

With his first £100, Wilde went to Sicily with someone referred to by Adey as 'The Russian Elder' and made the acquaintance of an amusing and notorious old homosexual called Baron von Gloeden who, according to Rupert Hart-Davis, 'acquired some reputation for his photographs of Sicilian youths posed "noble and nude and antique" in the guise of Theocritan goatherds or shepherds'. On his return to Posilippo he wrote to Smithers: "I have had many misfortunes since I wrote to you—influenza, the robbery during my absence in Sicily, of *all* my clothes etc. by a servant whom I left at the villa, ill-health, loneliness, and general *ennui* with a tragi-comedy of an existence, but I want to see my poem out before I take steps." Then rather than 'take steps', with the remainder of the first or the second hundred pounds he decided to leave for Paris, and reached there on Sunday, 13 February 1898.

FOURTEEN

Frivolous Last Years

When Wilde reached Paris he was scarcely on speaking terms with Ross, whom he blamed for allowing that clause in the agreement with his wife by which she could stop his allowance if he lived with Bosie.

The character of Ross has puzzled most of the biographers of Wilde, and Wilde himself changed his attitude to him several times after he came out of prison. He had been a cheerful and resourceful little queen when Wilde first knew him, but he was scared by Wilde's arrest, believing that it was the beginning of an immense witch-hunt in London. Although he quickly recovered his confidence, he was inwardly soured, and showed it later.

In the Paris years he was helpful and loyal to Wilde and on quite good terms with Bosie, whom he continued to meet in London after Wilde's death. But a vindictive jealousy of Bosie broke out in the years just before the last war and caused the terrible struggle between them. In 1918, prematurely old and bald and growing stout, Ross died before he was fifty.

The state of things between Wilde and Ross when Wilde first came to Paris could not continue. In spite of £200 paid him by Lady Queensberry, Wilde soon needed his allowance, and Constance would not pay it to him unless he not only abjured the company of Bosie but abused him roundly in letters to Ross. He started by discussing his time with Bosie without rancour. "Who *are* the people", he asked Ross, "who object to my having been with Bosie at Naples, and spent my days with Heliogabalus, and my nights with Antinous? I mean are these people who were *ever* my friends? Or are they simply those to whom Uranian love is horrible? If the latter, I cannot care. If the former, I do." But this solved nothing. Ross was not placated and the allowance was not renewed, and Wilde had to produce something which would satisfy both Ross and Constance. He did so on 2 March 1898:

The facts of Naples are very bald and brief.

Bosie, for four months, by endless letters, offered me a *home*. He offered me love, affection, and care, and promised that I should never want for anything. After four months I accepted his offer, but when we met at Aix on our way to Naples I found that he had no money, no plans, and had forgotten all his promises. His own idea was that I should raise money for us both. I did so, to the extent of £120. On this Bosie lived, quite happy. When it came to his having, of course, to repay his own *share*, he became terrible, unkind, mean, and penurious, except where his own pleasures were concerned, and when my allowance ceased, he left.

It is, of course, the most bitter experience of a bitter life; it is a blow quite awful and paralysing, but it had to come, and I know it is better that I should never see him again.

It was in fact just a fortnight after writing this letter of 'the most bitter experience of a bitter life . . . a blow quite awful and paralysing' that Wilde met Bosie again, but in the meantime Constance had sent him £40. On 18 March he wrote to Ross: "What do you think of his [Bosie's] going to London? *He tells me* he returns there with his mother in May." Thereafter Oscar and Bosie met often; turning their once passionate friendship to a humorous and easy one, they moved into the laughing, mischievous relationship of the last three years, teasing one another about their acquaintance among the boulevard boys, dining sumptuously when Bosie had any money, appreciating one another's conviviality as never before. Wilde had said his final word on Bosie in a letter to Reggie Turner from Posilippo: "Somehow he is my life: of course, he is unchanged: he is just what he was: kinder and more considerate in a thousand ways: but still the same wilful, fascinating, irritating, destructive, delightful personality." It was perhaps a prosaic epilogue to the great romance which had caused them both so much torment and rapture in the past, but it was a happy one.

2

Life in Paris suited Wilde. He had always regarded the city as a refuge and a playground, and had for it the sentimental affection common to most Englishmen in the nineteenth century and the first half of the twentieth. Until the de Gaulle family with their morbid Puritanism had applied the process called—in relation to cities—cleaning up, it had been the home of amusing and harmless, because hygienic, night life. Englishmen read *La Vie Parisienne* and packed the Folies Bergère, while for the less Philistine visitors there was the tradition of the starving Parisian poets and painters who lived in garrets and showed themselves in eccentric clothes on the boulevards. It was not any of these secondhand notions that brought Wilde to Paris, but the heavenly tolerance, the unsuspicious liberalism, the feeling that here at least the dirty narrow-mindedness from which he had been made to suffer in England would be at a discount.

He became the most regular and devoted among the boulevardiers, scarcely failing for an evening to come out and sip his cognac and talk in the cafés of his choice. He was known to the bad boys; loved them all with little discrimination, and not only took them home but listened to their gossip and reported it to Robbie Ross, Reggie Turner and Bosie Douglas, who knew the boys as Wilde did, rejoiced in any good fortune that came to them, and sympathized with their frequent arrests and imprisonments. Wilde and his friends gave nicknames to many of them—'Edmond de Goncourt' for Edmond, the 'Florifer' for Bosie's little friend who sold violets, 'Casquette' and 'Le Premier Consul'. They wrote to one another about them, Wilde particularly giving the Londoners the latest news. What Mr Justice Wills, who once told Wilde he had been the centre of a circle of extensive corruption of the most hideous kind, would have said to Oscar,

Reggie, Robbie and Bosie about their goings-on it is difficult to imagine, but much of it was comedy rather than vice, and to talk of 'corrupting' the male whores of Paris would have been then, as today, ludicrous.

Wilde had at last an uninhibited, aimless and contented life. He did not romanticize his relationships as feasting with panthers or see himself as a Roman emperor at play. There was no furtiveness as there had of necessity been in London—though it must be admitted Wilde had shown little discretion in the old days. He no longer showed off either his vices or his determination to be democratic. He talked of his favourites and laughed at them and himself. He was, for much of the time, almost as hard-up as the boys were, but he managed to keep them round him.

This meant friction with Robert Sherard, who was living in Paris. He had stayed with Wilde at Berneval ('in his grenadine all the time') and had boasted that he could arrange 'for a lot of money' the publication of Wilde's *Ballad*, at that time not yet written, in the *New York World*. While Wilde was at Posilippo with Bosie, Sherard was 'playing Tartuffe as if it was Termagant' at the Authors' Club, and censuring Wilde's life so loudly that he could be heard from Naples.

In Paris: "Robert Sherard is here. On Wednesday he created a horrible scene in Campbell's Bar by bawling out '*A bas les juifs*,' and insulting and assaulting someone whom he said was a Jew. The fight continued in the street, and Robert tried to create an anti-Semite, anti-Dreyfusard demonstration. He succeeded, and was ultimately felled to the ground by the Jew! Bosie and I met him at Campbell's by chance on the next day. Campbell told him that the only reason he would consent to serve him was that Bosie and I had shaken hands with him! This rather amused me, when I remember Robert's monstrous moralizing about us, and how nobody should know us . . . Yesterday he turned up again, and had to receive a rather insolent lecture from Campbell, who told him he preferred Jews to drunkards in his bar. He was much depressed, so of course I gave him drinks and cigarettes and all he wanted. To show his gratitude he insisted on reciting *The Ballad of Reading Gaol*, at the top of his voice, and assuring me that I was '*le plus grand mâitre de la littérature moderne, et le plus grand homme du monde*'. At the end he got very tedious, and lest I might love my poem less than I wish to, I went away. Poor Robert, he really is quite insane, and unbearable, except to very old friends who bear much." Ernest Dowson, who was to die under Sherard's roof, wrote to Smithers even more strongly about him in Paris. "Sherard as I believe is now in London, probably maligning me— you will do me a favour by contradicting him. I have lent him money, borne with his temper, stood him and his wretched little whore of a mistress innumerable meals and been rewarded with nothing but insolence and abuse." Small wonder that when Sherard met Wilde after his return to Paris from Naples "he was no longer as friendly as he had been formerly, for he seemed to bear some sort of resentment against me, because I had blamed him for going to Naples, which I considered an impolitic act of public defiance. But that he was embittered one could not but see. There was the continual irritation of impecuniosity, for in despite of the fixed income, and Douglas's boundless charities, there were many occasions on which, as he told Gide one night in a café, he was *absolument sans ressources*." "I think that the only occasion on which he ever spoke with real irritation to me was in Paris shortly after his brother's death. I had condoled with him, and I had added: 'I hope something will come to you from his affairs.' I used the word 'affairs' in the French sense, and referred to the small entailed estate which Willie Wilde had held, and which I supposed had reverted to his brother on his death. He snapped up the word 'affairs'. 'What do you mean by "affairs"?' he asked, quite angrily, and though I could see that he was offended I could not for the world imagine why."

Sherard went to call on Oscar during his last illness, and had to insist in order to reach him. " 'I will send up and see if Monsieur Melmoss receives,' said the landlord, and a waiter was despatched. When the man returned and, with a 'thousand regrets', informed me that Monsieur was *très fatigué*, far too tired to receive anybody, I wrote a message on a card and sent it up. I was then asked to *monter*. When I reached Oscar's door I found him waiting for me. He caught hold of my two hands and drew

K

me into his room. 'I really *am* too tired to speak to anybody to-day,' he said: 'but I don't like to send *you* away.' " The rest of their conversation was like one of those reported by Frank Harris:

He answered: 'one has to do something. I have no taste for it now. It is a penance to me, but, as was said of torture, it always helps one to pass an hour or two.' I then said: 'If you never wrote another line, Oscar, you have done enough to ensure your immortality.' He seemed really pleased, and brightened. But then his face went all grey again, and I saw him glance towards the stimulant and I was reminded of poor Alphonse Daudet, in the moments just before the morphine syringe was produced and the injection taken. He went and threw himself on the bed, exhausted it seemed, and I rose. 'Come and see me again,' he said, 'though I hardly like to ask people to see me in this room.' He was referring to the poverty of our surroundings. 'Why, I had never noticed it,' I said.

Sherard philosophizes further in his account of that interview but not surprisingly the two never met again, and it was not until seven years later that Sherard printed privately his *Oscar Wilde: The Story of an Unhappy Friendship* which began his series of books about his rehabilitated hero. Even when he published in 1905 *Twenty Years in Paris*, it was found to be largely about Wilde, and the manuscript (unpublished) is in existence of a last argument on Wilde's behalf, *Ultima Verba*.[1]

3

The first young Parisian friend of Wilde's of whom we have any record, and also the last, since he attended Wilde's funeral, was named Maurice Gilbert, and Wilde seems to have met him, oddly enough, through Leonard Smithers, the publisher. Smithers

[1] See H. Montgomery Hyde, *Oscar Wilde the Aftermath*.

was what Ross called a 'mulierast', a humorously coined word, denoting the heterosexual version of a pederast. To say that Smithers liked young girls was an understatement. With alcohol and drugs and limited editions, they made up his whole existence, but he was, for Wilde at least, a likeable and entertaining fellow, and he encouraged Wilde's most perverse confidences. In Wilde's letters to Smithers in London, after Smithers had been across to Paris, there are frequent messages from Maurice and fragments of news of him. "Maurice sends his kindest regards", "Maurice has won twenty-five games of bezique and I twenty-four: however, as he has youth, and I have only genius, it is only natural that he should beat me." "Maurice says he is too old to play marbles, and I am too young to begin, so we bezique our youthful lives away." "Maurice took it to the bank, so I dare say it was on account of his *beaux yeux*. He grows dearer to me daily, and we now dine at a restaurant for two francs." "Maurice is sweeter than ever."

But it is when Maurice has been introduced to Ross and Turner that we really begin to learn something about him, and he leaves the impression of a charming and generous character, perhaps the kindest and gentlest boy in Wilde's life. Hart-Davis says that he has failed to discover anything about him except that he was the son of an English father and French mother. He was brought up in France and was "all French lily and English rose, as I have mentioned to my publisher in a business-letter I was writing to him", said Wilde.

It seems that for a time Maurice actually lived with Wilde. "When I arrived the Mauritius was not here but has since turned up," Ross wrote to Smithers from Wilde's hotel. "Do you love Maurice?" Wilde asks Ross in one letter, and in the next, "Are you in love with Maurice?" Later Wilde seems to have sent Maurice on a visit to London, where he stayed with an amiable alcoholic named Ashton, known to Wilde and his friends as 'Sir John', and saw a great deal of Ross. "How is my golden Maurice? I suppose he is wildly loved. His upper lip is more like a rose-leaf than any rose-leaf I ever saw. I fear he would not be a good secretary; his writing is not clear enough, and his eyelashes are too long."

262 THE UNRECORDED LIFE OF OSCAR WILDE

On Maurice's return to Paris, Wilde wrote with a touch of satire to Smithers: "Maurice arrived this morning, looking tired and beautiful. He seems to have been a great success in London, and is full of pleasant reminiscences of the inhabitants. My friend Robert Ross especially seems to have taken quite an interest in him. He is so fond of children, and of people, like myself, who have childlike simple nature." To Ross: "No cheque this morning, but instead my sweet Maurice, *our* sweet Maurice, looking quite charming and as delightful as ever. He seemed a little *tired*, but of course that was the journey. He was full of affectionate memories of you and Reggie, and is quite devoted to you both. He also has lovely clothes, and looks as if he had fallen from Paradise." Reggie Turner gets a similar sly dig: "Just a line to inform you of the safe arrival of our dear Maurice. He appeared, jonquil-like in aspect, a sweet narcissus from an English meadow, at ten o'clock, and was sweet and loving and lovable as ever. He was quite cut up at his parting with you and Robbie. It is wonderful how well all flowers of the narcissus kind thrive in the old musty Law-Inns of London: there is something in the air that seems to suit them."

Soon Bosie Douglas is counted among Maurice's admirers, for there seemed to be no end to the young man's generosity and adaptability, as Wilde knew. "I wish", Wilde writes to Ross, "you would tell me how much you love Maurice. He is a great dear, and loves us all, a born Catholic in romance; he is always talking of you and Reggie. Yesterday he and I and Bosie went to the Salon. As modern art had a chastening effect on Maurice, and he seemed sad, we went afterwards to the *Foire aux Invalides*, where Maurice won a knife, by foolishly throwing a ring over something." Already "Bosie had great trouble because Maurice used to stay with him. The proprietor demanded Maurice's name, and said he was bound to take the names of people who passed the night in the house." But later: "Bosie is now inseparable from Maurice; they have gone again to Nogent." Even Sherard, it seems, is converted at least to tolerance of the all-charming Maurice. Sherard "begged me to lunch with him and to bring Maurice, but I declined, feigning temporary good health as my excuse! His asking me to bring Maurice was astounding, as when he was last in Paris he refused to call on me because M. was staying with me, and generally was offensive about a lovely and loveable friendship." Wilde's own devotion grew no less. "The curves of his mouth are more wonderful than ever. His mouth, when he talks, and he is never silent, is the most beautiful mouth I know. It has the curves of Greek art and English flowers." And he continued to razz Ross about Maurice. "Reggie wrote to me a fortnight ago that you were coming over to see Maurice, and would no doubt call on me and on Bosie."

Then Maurice got a job with Rowland Strong, the Paris correspondent of the *New York Times* and the *Observer*, a man secretive about his homosexuality but not about his anti-Semitism. "Maurice is looking very ill," Wilde wrote to Ross. "Bosie insists that he is consumptive, but I don't believe it. He works, or rather overworks, with Strong from 9 a.m. till 9.45 p.m. in a stuffy room. He is always sweet and nice. And the curves of his mouth are a source of endless wonder and admiration to me. Out of such a mouth I would drink Lethe in this world and in the next ambrosia." But Strong had an unfortunate influence on Maurice, not understanding his generosity towards his several friends. "Maurice never comes to see me. I asked him to breakfast last Sunday week and he never even answered my letter. I am sorry, for I used to like him very much." "I dined with Strong who has reduced Maurice to a state of silent frightened idiocy. Dogma without Literature is bad for boys." But there was an end to this. "I saw Strong last night at the Horse-Shoe: he has taken Grandcourt as his secretary: I did not discuss his treatment of Maurice at all. I thought it better not. Maurice, I hope, dines with me tonight."

In Wilde's last year: "Maurice—you remember Maurice?—has kindly come to see me and I've shared all my medicines with him, shown him what little hospitality I can." But Maurice wanted to go to London for the state drive of Queen Victoria. "Of course his place was by my side, as I am very ill, but he longed to see the Queen, so I gave in. He has been most sweet and kind to me, quite a darling boy, and looked after me in every way. When he is away from the chilling torpedo-touch of Strong he is quite as nice as he used to be." Later in the year:

I have seen Maurice lately; we spent two evenings at the Exhibition. He was pale, and sweet, and gentle. He now forms part of a *ménage à trois*: none of the members sleep: the girl—a rose-like thing I hope[1]—lies in the middle, and knows the pleasure and insecurity of the *Via Media*. Maurice won't tell me the name of the other partner, but admits he has a slight moustache. He does odd jobs for Strong, and quarrels with him incessantly. I find I am very fond of Maurice still. He is a dear fellow.

During Wilde's last illness Maurice visited him but, Reggie Turner said, did not like being in the room, and Wilde could scarcely recognize him. At Ross's request he tried to take a photograph of Wilde after his death, and he was among the few faithful friends who sent a wreath and followed the hearse.

The fragrant memory of Maurice, 'all French lily and English rose', compensates for that of some of the wretched little blackmailers who appeared at Wilde's trial. Wilde was not in the least possessive about his young friends, least of all about the versatile Maurice, which was just as well. He was rewarded by the selfless affection of this one of them who did not attempt to be faithful but gave himself readily, and in his own way was devoted to Wilde.

4

None of the others showed or was shown such constancy. During the last three years of his life Oscar in his letters (chiefly to Ross and Turner) mentioned by name no less than thirty-one boys with whom he or his friends had associated, and designated by description eight more. There was Reggie Turner's Eugene,

[1] Wilde's ideal women were all flower-like. See his description of his bride on p. 98.

for instance, who had been with him since Wilde was at Berneval, one of the few young Parisians, apparently, whose features Wilde does not admire. He reports him as quite devoted to Reggie and in excellent spirits, but calls him, rather ambiguously, a 'wonderful harvest moon',[1] though he sends his love to him and thinks it unkind of Eugene not to write. "That harvest-moon, Eugene, looked on me on the Boulevard the other day. He looked like a prize melon." In addition to this unfortunate resemblance Eugene seems to have put on weight, for when Wilde passed the Café de le Paix, Eugene 'seemed to fill up the *terrasse*'.

Bosie's particular favourite was younger, though there is no need to accept the estimate of his age given in a letter gently deriding Bosie for his pederasty.[2] "He is devoted to a dreadful little ruffian aged fourteen, whom he loves because at night, in the scanty intervals he can steal from an arduous criminal profession, he sells bunches of purple violets in front of the Café de la Paix. Also every time he goes home with Bosie he tries to rent him. This, of course, adds to his terrible fascination. We call him the 'Florifer', a lovely name. He also keeps another boy, aged twelve! whom Bosie wishes to know, but the wise 'Florifer' declines." But Bosie's 'devotion' does not last long. "Bosie has grown tired of the 'Florifer', but intends using the word in a sonnet. All romances should end in a sonnet. I suppose all romances do."

Robbie Ross seems to have been rather more secretive about his attachments in Paris, and Oscar's news to him chiefly concerns his own. However, Ross was no doubt grieved to hear that 'Marius' has a cold and later pleased that 'Casquette' is well and has a blue suit. But at Nice there is Ross's 'little friend' Henri who "plies up and down all day, and has the sweetest and most compromising smiles for me, especially when I am with friends".

[1] This epithet and others connected with the moon were in frequent use by Wilde and his friends, and have puzzled many biographers and critics. The terms were used exclusively by those round Oscar. A harvest moon referred to an uncircumcized penis, just as a 'gourmet', as applied to certain of the boys, designated one given to the practice of what Montgomery Hyde delicately calls *fellatio* or oral copulation.

[2] No one in his senses, and least of all Bosie himself in his last years, denied that at this period he pursued young boys.

The good-natured drunk, I.D.W. Ashton, nicknamed 'Sir John', quite 'wonderful and improbable', as Wilde says, was unfortunate. He was turned "out of his hotel by a *commissaire de police* because he was intoxicated. He was in bed at the time, and asleep, and Maurice and I had to dress him and take him out of the hotel at 10.15 at night." Nor does he seem to have been more lucky in his friendships. "Sir John was astonishing, went through a romance with an absurd Boulevard boy, who, of course, cheated him, and treated him badly. The reason was that Sir John had given him a suit of clothes—an admirable reason. To undress is romance, to dress, philanthropy." "He is the last great sentimentalist left to us, and clothes everybody except the naked." He was expected, Oscar tells Robbie Ross, with a boy from St Malo, and arrived long after midnight. He found his little friend Joseph with a black eye and a swollen nose, caused by intoxication and a political discussion. Joseph also left him on Sunday morning, and did not appear till the next day, having had vine-leaves in his hair. "He is a little Dionysiac, and the conversation of Sir John, which is chiefly composed of good advice, drives him to drink. Tonight I dine with Sir John at Bosie's flat: Joseph is to serve, if he is sober: if not, he is to dine with us, I suppose. I am glad to say Sir John is getting cured of his infatuation: and I have begged him never again to try to have a good influence: it simply drives happy bright-eyed lads to *delirium tremens*." Joseph later went to prison for attempted murder; the boy brought from St Malo, that 'snub-nosed little horror Walter', went back to England, and Sir John, 'in the best of spirits (and water)', left for America and was heard of no more.

Oscar was reminded of his former friends in London by an unaspirated youth who was brought to Paris by someone named Hylton. He, the Cockney youth, was called Herbert, and Wilde found him 'almost impossible'. "He is a sort of grown-up man with a hysterical womb, and makes scenes with Sir John like a woman with child. On the whole I don't think I can stand him much longer, though of course he professes lavish adoration of me and perhaps feels some too."

But Leonard Sarluis, a Dutch-Jewish painter "introduced a

wonderful boy with red hair like the hair of a Botticelli angel. His occupation by day is preparing the ingredients necessary for *vol-au-vents*, in a shop near the Halles. At night, attired in one of Sarluis's best suits, he looks wonderful."

Wilde himself had a somewhat disreputable friend named Gaston, and Bosie Douglas made a gaffe in his company. "Bosie is now furious with me, because when Davray, who is or wishes to be most respectable, invited me to a café to meet a poet who desired to know me Bosie turned up ten minutes after my arrival with *Gaston*! of all people, and placed him at Davray's table, where he gabbled about bicycles, and was generally offensive. Davray was much annoyed, and so was I. Bosie cannot understand the smallest iota of social tact, and does not see that to thrust 'Giton, the boy-paederast' into a literary reunion, without being invited, is vulgar. So life goes on." Léon, on the other hand, seems to have been a well-behaved boy for when Wilde pleaded with Ross to let him take unfurnished apartments, he said—"I have not been visited by a single boy since the day Edmond came—in the *daytime* I mean. Of course when the moon is full I often return with Léon, to smoke a cigarette or to weave words about Life, but no one comes to see me." A few nights later, "I went yesterday to the *Fête des Fous*—naturally—and saw the Miracle Play. I afterwards dined with Stuart Merrill who had asked most of the actors and actresses to meet me. We had a delightful evening, and the whole Quartier Latin was bright with beauty and wine, and the students in their mediaeval costumes picturesque and improbable and gay. A meeting with *Léon*, whom I found wandering in the moonlit chasm of my little street, ended an admirable Continental Sunday."

Reggie Turner received more intimate confidences. "Do you remember the young Corsican at the Restaurant Jouffroy? His position was menial, but eyes like the night and a scarlet flower of a mouth made one forget that: I am great friends with him. His name is Giorgio: he is a most passionate faun." But Reggie was given some bad news: "Your little friend Alphonse was arrested last night for *chantage*. He demanded fifteen francs, and was only given ten and a car-fare, so on being expelled from the house he made a scene and was taken up. There is much joy amongst his friends, as his general conduct did not meet with approval. It is a pity he always wanted to behave badly; it gave him a demoniac pleasure. He was quite an imp, though attractive in love-scenes."

Towards the end of 1898 Wilde went at Harris's suggestion to stay at Napoule outside Nice. He had difficulty in making Harris honour the invitation he had given, and suffered some days of anxiety with hotel keepers on that account, but he did not lack company, for Georges, whom he had known in Paris, 'one of the noble army of the Boulevard' was spending the season there. Wilde had met him at Kalisaya, an American bar which had become the literary resort of Oscar and his friends. "One beautiful boy of bad character—of the name of Georges—goes there too, but he is so like Antinous, and so smart, that he is allowed to talk to poets." Wilde reported him to Ross now as being eighteen, very elegant and apparently a leader of fashion at Nice. "At least he seemed to known everyone, and, on my leaving, accompanied me to the station, and borrowed five francs." Reggie Turner, as usual, heard more about the *rencontre*. "A great friend of mine, a Paris boy called *le petit Georges*, is now at Nice, and I have promised to run over and see him. He is like a very handsome Roman boy, dark, and bronze-like, with splendidly chiselled nose and mouth, and the tents of midnight are folded in his eyes; moons hide in their curtains. He is visiting Nice on speculative business. It is beautiful, and encouraging, to find people who can combine romance with business—blend them indeed, and make them one."

Ross wrote to suggest to Wilde quite seriously that he should consider marrying again, Constance having died eight months earlier. ('Of course Oscar did not feel it at all,' Ross wrote to Smithers.) But for the marriage suggestion Ross got *his* answer. "As regards my marrying again, I am quite sure that you will want me to marry this time some sensible, practical, plain, middle-aged boy, and I don't like the idea at all. Besides I am practically engaged to a fisherman of extraordinary beauty, age eighteen. So you see there are difficulties."

Wilde went over to Nice from Napoule and enjoyed it. "I met one beautiful person, called André, with wonderful eyes, and a little Italian, Pietro, like a young St John. One would have followed him into the desert." He also, he told More Adey, knew at Nice "three lads like bronzes, quite perfect in form. English lads are chryselephantine; Swiss people are carved out of wood with a rough knife, most of them. The others are carved out of turnips."

5

During his years of prosperity Wilde, as we have seen, made no friends in the everyday sense, and after he came out of prison he had only the trio Bosie, Robbie and Reggie, who in their various ways 'kept company' with him. These and the two biographers-to-be, Harris and Sherard, and a few *revenants* from his old life—and of course the boys—were the only human beings to show him warmth and companionship.

But he made friends by correspondence, and was always, as in the old days, ready to answer letters from fans, particularly if they were young men. A Radley schoolboy named Louis Wilkinson got into touch with him, inventing a dramatic society for which he wanted to make a play of the *Picture of Dorian Gray*. Wilde continued to exchange letters with him up to the time of his last illness, and Wilkinson sent him his photograph, which 'fascinated' Wilde, who invited the boy, then seventeen years old, to stay with him in Paris. Wilde had to put him off because of his illness, and it may have been just as well, for Wilkinson was not quite the schoolboy Wilde anticipated. In after years he wrote novels under the name of Louis Marlow and was married four times.

Another young enthusiast who exchanged photographs with Wilde was an amateur ballet-dancer named Herbert Charles Pollitt, who preferred to be called 'Jerome'. "I like your Christian name so much: I suppose you are your own lion?" The Sphinx, Wilde tells Pollitt, a recognized authority on the colour of young men's hair, had assured Wilde that Pollitt was quite golden, and Wilde had always thought of him as a sort of gilt sunbeam masquerading in clothes. When Jerome comes to Paris he must go to some purple place which will go with his hair.

Apparently the visit was never made, but Wilde took Pollitt's photograph with him to the Riviera. Of course Pollitt should have been there. Wilde searched for him daily. The inhabitants had beautiful eyes, crisp hair of a hyacinth colour and no morals—an ideal race. Wilde's last letter thanked Pollitt for another photograph. "It is not a bit like the others, so I feel sure a good likeness, and the Coan robe most becoming. Your personality becomes more and more mysterious, more and more wonderful, each portrait that I receive, but indeed all my life Sphinxes have crossed and recrossed my way."

But there was an actual meeting in the flesh with a young man, for in Nice Wilde came across one who tried in his neurotic way to befriend him. His name was Harold Mellor and he was a Lancashireman who had been left a large private fortune by his father, the owner of some cotton mills at Bolton. He was distantly related by marriage with John Bright. Harold would have been called a psychopath if he had been living today, and even in Wilde's time he was considered a very eccentric young man. He committed suicide in 1925, and at the time Wilde met him was thirty years old, homosexual and, according to Wilde's later estimate, avaricious.

At first the friendship promised to be a great success. "A nice fellow called Harold Mellor, who is staying at Cannes, comes over constantly to see me," Wilde told Ross. "He has a pretty Italian boy with him. They stayed last night at Napoule, and we had plum-pudding and Mellor ordered Pommery-Greno, so I kept Christmas pleasantly, and Christmas improves by being kept a day." A week later he repeated himself, forgetting that he had already confided in Ross. "There is a charming fellow called Harold Mellor (sent away from Harrow at the age of fourteen for being loved by the captain of the cricket eleven) who is staying with his mother near Cannes, and comes over on his bicycle to breakfast every morning. He is about twenty-six, but looks younger. Sometimes a very pretty, slim, fair-haired Italian boy bicycles over with him. His name is *Eolo*; his father, who sold him to Harold for 200 lire, having christened all his children—seventeen in number—out of the *Mythological Dictionary*. Harold is a nice fellow, but his boy bores him. It is dreadfully sad." After a month the friendship still flourished: "Harold Mellor will be in London at the end of the month. He is going there to get me some neckties. I have asked him to write and let you know. He is a charming fellow, very cultivated, though he finds that Literature is an inadequate expression of Life." "Occasionally my friend Harold Mellor orders a bottle of Pommery for dinner. Then the exquisite taste of ancient life comes back to me."

Then Ross learned that Mellor had invited Wilde to stay with him at Gland in Switzerland. "I hope to be happy there: at any rate there will be free meals, and champagne has been ordered."

Another month and still all was well. "This is a pretty house on the Lake. We look over to the snows and hills of Savoy. Geneva is half an hour by rail. You are to come whenever you like. April is lovely here, I believe, and flaunts in flowers. There is an Italian cook, also the lad Eolo, who waits at table. His father told Mellor at Spezia that he was christened Eolo because he was born on a night on which there was a dreadful wind! I think it is rather nice to have thought of such a name." But in the next letter, to More Adey, there was a remark which sounded an ominous note: "I don't like my host and the Swiss are so ugly to look at that it conveys melancholy into all my days." When another fortnight had passed, Wilde made no attempt to conceal his feelings, at least with Turner: "I don't like Mellor: he is a silent, dull person, cautious, and economical: revolting Swiss wines appear at meals: he is complex without being interesting: has Greek loves, and is rather ashamed of them: has heaps of money, and lives in terror of poverty: so I regard it as a sort of Swiss *pension*, where there is no weekly bill." Nor with Robbie Ross: "I dislike Mellor, because he is unsocial, taciturn, wretched company, and taking no pains to please or gratify his guest. He is very well off, but absurdly mean in everything. He gives me at dinner the most horrid Swiss *vin ordinaire*, though he has a capital cellar, and is quite amused by the fact that I don't like it. There is insanity in his family. His mother is under restraint, and his brother went mad and killed himself. His own insanity is misanthropy, and meanness. I am philosophic about it now; indeed we only meet at meals. In the evening he reads *The Times*, or sleeps—both audibly. But I should love to get away."

When he at last left Mellor, he wrote revealingly to Ross: "I could not stay any longer at Mellor's: he really is too insane and impossible. I never disliked anyone so thoroughly. My visit has taught me a curious and bitter lesson. I used to rely on my personality: now I know that my personality really rested on the fiction of *position*. Having lost position, I find my personality of no avail. Mellor has treated me as I would not have treated the most dull and unimportant of the lower middle-classes. I feel very humble, besides feeling very indignant: the former being my intellectual realisation of my position, the latter an emotion that is a 'survival' of old conditions."

Finally, to Ross: "Mellor is too repulsive for anything. When I got your fiver, I had no money at all, and asked him to lend me three francs to go into Geneva with. He declined, on the ground that he had made it a rule never *to lend money* to anyone! I had to get my railway-fare from the cook! On my return, to a dreary dinner with Swiss beer, he told me that he did not like people borrowing money from his servants! On the other hand when I told him I was going away, he went into floods of tears, and said that all his friends deserted him! Tartuffe and Harpagon sum him up, though on too grand a scale."

Wilde was probably not an ideal guest, and the episode might have been an ordinary enough coming-together and parting between two men with certain similarities of temperament, one of them suffering from Mellor's pathological avarice and the other being Oscar Wilde. But there was an incomprehensible sequel. Just a year later, from a letter to Ross we hear: "Mellor, with whom I am now friends (below zero of course) has invited me to go to Italy to the extent of £50! When that gives out I shall have to walk home, but as I want to see you, I have consented to go, and hope to be in Rome in about ten days." Mellor took Wilde to Rome and left him there for about a month, arranging to meet him afterwards at Chambéry and drive him in his motorcar to

Paris. "I suppose one of us will arrive safe; I hope it will be me."
After Paris the two stayed at Gland again. "'The Mellor cure' was
dull, but I got better. He is now in Paris with his slave Eolo, who
like all slaves is most tyrannical. He and I, however, are great
friends. I think Harold is on the verge of acute melancholia. At
present he has almost arrived at total abstinence—drinks and
talks mineral waters. I like people who talk wine." "My last
visit to Mellor had given me melancholia," Wilde told Harris.
"I must go no more." There was no need for that last resolution.
In two months Wilde was dead and Harold Mellor was one of
those who sent a wreath to his funeral.

6

But that stay of Wilde's in Rome in the last year of his life
was an eventful one. His expenses were all paid, Ross told Adela
Schuster, by Harold Mellor, and in a still existing photograph of
Wilde, well-dressed with a broad-brimmed hat and a neatly
rolled umbrella, he looks debonair if not actually swaggering.
"It will be delightful to be together again," he told Ross, "and
this time I really must become a Catholic, though I fear that if I
went before the Holy Father with a blossoming rod it would turn
at once into an umbrella or something dreadful of that kind."
About this, Ross wrote to Adela Schuster after Wilde's death:

He wanted me then to introduce him to a priest with a view to
being received into the Church, and I reproach myself deeply for
not having done so, but I really did not think he was quite serious.
Being a Catholic myself, I really rather dreaded a relapse, and
having known so many people under the influence of sudden
impulse, aesthetic or other emotion become converts, then cause
grave scandal by lapsing, that I told him I should never *attempt his
conversion* until I thought he was serious. You, who once knew
him so well, will appreciate the great difficulty. He was never
quite sure himself where and when he was serious.

Exactly. If ever the absurd phrase 'flirting with Catholicism' can be well used, it describes Wilde during the next few days in his enthusiasm for everything Papal. "Yesterday, to the terror of Grissell and all the Papal Court, I appeared in front rank of the pilgrims in the Vatican, and got the blessing of the Holy Father—a blessing they would have denied me."

He further described the incident to Robbie, wavering between flippancy and sincerity in an extraordinary passage:

He (the Pope) was wonderful as he was carried past me on his throne, not of flesh and blood, but a white soul robed in white, and an artist as well as a saint—the only instance in History, if the newspapers are to be believed.

I have seen nothing like the extraordinary grace of his gesture, as he rose, from moment to moment, to bless—possibly the pilgrims, but certainly me. Tree should see him. It is his only chance.

I was deeply impressed, and my walking-stick showed signs of budding; it would have budded indeed, only at the door of the chapel it was taken from me by the Knave of Spades. This strange prohibition is, of course, in honour of Tannhäuser.

How did I get the ticket? By a miracle, of course. I thought it was hopeless, and made no effort of any kind. On Saturday afternoon at five o'clock Harold and I went to have tea at the Hôtel de l'Europe. Suddenly, as I was eating buttered toast, a man, or what seemed to be one, dressed like a hotel porter, entered and asked me would I like to see the Pope on Easter Day. I bowed my head humbly and said 'Non sum dignus,' or words to that effect. He at once produced a ticket!

When I tell you that his countenance was of supernatural ugliness, and that the price of the ticket was thirty pieces of silver, I need say no more.

A few days later he wrote to Ross again. "By the way, did I tell you that on Easter Sunday I was completely cured of my mussel-poisoning? It is true, and I always knew I would be. Five months under a Jewish physician at Paris not merely did not heal me, but made me worse: the blessing of the Vicar of Christ made me whole." "Need I say that I see the Holy Father tomorrow? I am thrilled with the prospect of an old pleasure, and I am promised a seat for the canonisation, or beatification, on the 24th." He told More Adey: "I do nothing but see the Pope: I have already been blessed many times, once in the private Chapel of the Vatican. He, as I wrote to Robbie, is no longer of flesh and blood: he has no taint of mortality: he is like a white soul robed in white. I spend all my money in getting tickets: for, now, as in old days, men rob the pilgrims in Rome. The robbing is chiefly done by hotel porters, or rather by real robbers disguised as hotel porters, and it is perhaps right that heretics should be mulcted, for we are not of the fold. My position is curious: I am not a Catholic: I am simply a violent Papist."

What is one to make of such a letter as this to Ross?—"Today is wet and stormy, but I have again seen the Holy Father. Each time he dresses differently; it is most delightful. Today over his white and purple a velvet cap edged with ermine, and a huge scarlet and gold stole. I was deeply moved as usual." Probably he was moved in his fashion, and Ross may be trusted when he recalls to Adela Schuster: "Shortly after his release when Mr Adey and I left him at Berneval, he made friends with a French priest and was very nearly received then, he told me, and of course you know that as a young man he was only prevented from doing so by his father and Professor Mahaffy." But it is hard to believe that Wilde's wordy and exhibitionistic devotion to the Pope was not, like his similar devotion to Queen Victoria, more than half the most riotous camp.

7

Wilde's Papal enthusiasms did not deter him while in Italy from enjoying several gay little love-affairs—rather the contrary.

Already on his way to Gland he had passed through Genoa, where in his own words to Reggie Turner he "met a beautiful young actor, a Florentine, whom I wildly loved. He had the strange name of Didaco. He had the look of Romeo, without Romeo's sadness: a face chiselled for high romance. We spent three days together." When he came back through Genoa Wilde hoped to find waiting for him a "young lad, by name Edoardo Rolla, one of the sea-farers. He has fair hair, and is always in dark blue. I have written to him. After the chill virginity of Swiss Alps and snow, I long for the red flowers of life that stain the feet of summer in Italy."

Before Rome, Wilde went to Palermo, where the *cocchieri* were most 'dainty finely-carved boys'. "In them, not in the Sicilian horses, is race seen. The most favoured were Manuele, Francesco, and Salvatore. I loved them all, but only remember Manuele." He also made great friends with a young Seminarist who "lived *in* the Cathedral of Palermo, he and eleven others in little rooms beneath the roof, like birds. Every day he showed me all over the Cathedral."

At first, my young friend, Giuseppe Loverde by name, gave *me* information: but on the third day I gave information to him, and re-wrote History as usual, and told him all about the Supreme King and his Court of Poets, and the terrible book that he never wrote. Giuseppe was fifteen, and most sweet. His reason for entering the Church was singularly mediaeval. I asked him why he thought of becoming a *clerico*: and how.

He answered 'My father is a cook, and most poor, and we are many at home, so it seemed to me a good thing that there should be in so small a house as ours one mouth less to feed, for, though I am slim, I eat much: too much, alas! I fear.'

I told him to be comforted, because God used poverty often as a means of bringing people to Him, and used riches never, or but rarely. So Giuseppe was comforted, and I gave him a little book of devotion, very pretty, and with far more pictures than prayers in it; so of great service to Giuseppe, whose eyes are beautiful. I also gave him many *lire*, and prophesied for him a Cardinal's hat, if he remained very good, and never forgot me. He said he never would: and indeed I don't think he will, for every day I kissed him behind the high altar.

Wilde met Ross in Rome, but after some days Ross went back to London, leaving Wilde "a legacy of a youthful guide, who knows nothing about Rome. Omero is his name, and I am showing him Rome." Omero, or Homer as Wilde sometimes called him, talked much—a little too much—of Robbie, Oscar said, which is perhaps why Wilde added "one Pietro Branca-d'Oro to the group. He is dark, and gloomy, and I loved him very much."

He decided to give up Armando, a very smart elegant young Roman Sporus, because he cost too much in clothes. "He was beautiful, but his requests for raiment and neckties were incessant: he really bayed for boots, as a dog moonwards. I now like Arnaldo: he was Armando's greatest friend, but the friendship is over. Armando is *un individioso* apparently, and is suspected of having stolen a lovely covert-coat in which he patrols the Corso. The coat is so delightful, and he looks so handsome in it, that, although the coat wasn't mine, I have forgiven him the theft." But he does not forget Homer. "Omero was with me, and Armando, forgiven for the moment. He is so absurdly like the Apollo Belvedere that I feel always as if I was Winckelmann when I am with him. His lips are the same, his hair, his somewhat vulgar, because quite obvious, pride; and he also represents that decadence of the triumph of the face over the body, never seen in great Greek art. . . . His body is slim, dandy-like, elegant, and without a single great curve. He has not come out of the womb of giant circles."

Wilde found "the Vatican Gardens were open to the Bohemian and the Portuguese pilgrims. I at once spoke both languages fluently, explained that my English dress was a form of penance, and entered that waste, desolate park, with its faded Louis XIV gardens, its sombre avenue, its sad woodland. The peacocks screamed, and I understood why tragedy dogged the gilt feet of each pontiff. But I wandered in exquisite melancholy for an hour. One Philippo, a student, whom I culled in the Borgia room, was with me; not for many years has Love walked in the Pope's pleasaunce."

When he left Rome, he took leave of Homer: "Today I bade goodbye, with tears and one kiss, to the beautiful Greek boy who was found in my garden—I mean in Nero's garden. He is the nicest boy you ever introduced to me."

8

The inspired flippancy of Wilde's letters about boys, the mischievous humour with which he laughed at himself and those about him, is echoed clearly to us from those last three years, and shows Wilde as the happy jester which at his best he was. It is cheering to find a master of words, a student of Walter Pater who cared deeply for the purpose and nuances of his prose, devoting all his gifts to little anecdotes about Casquette and his new blue suit and Armando's stolen covert-coat, and giving them the capricious wit which he had once exploited in his plays. He had suffered for the right to indulge in that totally unpornographic freedom of speech which can be found in the writing of no one else for the next sixty years, and then without his grace and humour.

I for one feel a certain gratitude and sense of privilege in reading these letters, which brought Wilde no material reward but were penned for his own amusement and that of his friends. How much more worth while they are than the history-making communications of statesmen, or even the ponderously sincere love-letters of great writers. They are trivial but only as *The Importance of Being Earnest* is trivial—they represent the creation of comedy at its very best. For out of the pain and tragic confusion of Wilde's career they rise, exhalations of sheer happiness which enliven his last days.

In spite of the perpetual requests for money which the letters contain, for loans in sudden emergencies, for advances of his allowance, for sums he believes due to him, they are for the most part those of a cheerful man chuckling over the absurdities of life about him and his own misfortunes; they show a comic artist turning every grotesque or whimsical incident to a laugh, and one feels that half—no, almost the whole—of the pleasure Wilde had from his boys came from his writing of it later to Ross and Reggie. Not a chance for sly fun is missed, from Maurice returning from London 'a little *tired* but of course that was the journey', to the 'scanty intervals seized from an arduous criminal profession' by the Florifer.

But the letters were not all about boys, and Wilde throws off some delicious asides which help us to believe in the persistent stories of his skill as a talker. There is a touch of bitchiness about some of them, but even that is without real malice. Whether or not the laughter such asides may provoke is uproarious depends, I suppose, on the reader, but for many it makes the kind of nonsense Wilde liked to write supremely entertaining. He avenges himself on Whistler, for instance, for all the telegrams and anger, with a couple of lines: "Whistler and I met face to face the other night, as I was entering Pousset's to dine with Thaulows. How old and weird he looks! Like Meg Merrilies."

9

In the Wilde of the last period there was a singular combination of humour, good humour and wit, and it remained with him till he became unconscious. All the pomposity and paranoia had disappeared, and although he was irked by poverty and sometimes shamelessly demanded money from friends and acquaintances —and was cheerfully resigned to refusals—he was genial and generous-minded to the last. One may or may not believe in the authenticity of the remark supposed to have been made to his sister-in-law on 25 October, 'I am dying as I have lived, beyond my means'; but he certainly *could* have said that, and it suited his humour. 'Last words' are always pretty dubious, and of William

Pitt the Younger it is not known whether he made his exit to the noble sentiment of 'My country! Oh my country!' or the more credible remark, 'I think I could eat one of Bellamy's veal pies.'

Oscar was himself to within five days of the end, and as Shaw said, "Even on his deathbed he found in himself no pity for himself, playing for the laugh with his last breath and getting it with as sure a stroke as in his palmiest prime." He argued in letters with Harris over the rights of his play (which in Harris's hands became *Mr and Mrs Daventry*), and the only conclusion one can draw from their argument is that both of them behaved unscrupulously. "Though he assured me his sufferings were dreadful," wrote Ross afterwards of a period a month before Oscar's death, "at the same time he shouted with laughter and told many stories against the doctors and himself." But it was Reggie Turner and not Oscar who made the best quip during the last illness. Oscar said he had a dreadful nightmare, he dreamed he was supping with the dead. Characteristically, because he was a wag himself, Reggie said, "My dear Oscar, you were probably the life and soul of the party." This delighted Oscar who in Ross's words 'became high-spirited again, almost hysterical'. When a 'very nice letter', enclosing a cheque, arrived from Bosie Douglas (who was in Scotland), Oscar wept a little but soon recovered himself.[1]

For the last few days Oscar was only occasionally aware of his surroundings, but it was in one of his periods of consciousness that he was received into the Roman Catholic Church by Father Cuthbert Dunne of the Passionist Fathers, who gave written testimony afterwards. (A story persists that at some time after 1860 Lady Wilde had her two sons received into the Catholic Church by a Father Crideaux-Fox, who was the Director of the Glencree Reformatory near which the Wildes had a cottage, and that Sir

[1] During the time that Bosie was in Scotland, actually a few days before Ross wrote to Bosie to suggest sending some money with the result described, an Englishman got into trouble with a couple of *maquereaux* and was beaten up. In certain Paris newspapers he was referred to as Lord X, and there has recently been a childish attempt to identify him with Bosie, supposed to be visiting Paris, unknown to Wilde, 'for the sake of his lusts'. Anyone who believes that can believe anything in this old and boring game, now surely played out, of abusing the memory of Douglas.

William gave permission for this. No documentary proof exists of this and it seems most improbable. But what has been cleared up beyond all doubt is the fact that Wilde was received into the Catholic Church on his deathbed. The priest who officiated was Father Cuthbert Dunne who, like Wilde, was a Dubliner. He maintained complete silence on the subject, believing that what took place at the bedside of a dying man should not be disclosed, but a few years before his death in 1945 he broke his silence to Father Edmund Burke, handing to him all the written evidence which he had carefully kept for forty years, but stipulating that these should not be revealed till after his death. Father Burke, who is happily still living in Dublin, wrote a full account of this, which was published in *The London Magazine* for 1961. This disposes of the usual crop of Harris-based rumours which have followed poor Wilde's life and death through the mouth of ignorance and bigotry. No one could blame Ross for discouraging Oscar from being received while he spoke of the Church with the engaging flippancy of his letters from Rome, but when the end came in earnest, Ross was the first to ensure that Wilde was received and given the sacraments of Baptism and Extreme Unction, not being in a condition to have the Holy Viaticum administered to him.)

Wilde died at 1.50 p.m. on the afternoon of 30 November 1900. Bosie Douglas, summoned by telegram, arrived from Scotland in time to pay the funeral expenses but not to see the body, the coffin having already been screwed down. But the three men, Bosie, Reggie and Robbie, who had loved Wilde most (or four if one includes Maurice Gilbert), attended the funeral service at the Church of St Germain des Prés, to which they walked behind the hearse from the hotel, and afterwards drove to Bagneux where Wilde was buried. (The body was afterwards moved to Père la Chaise, where Epstein's memorial was erected.)

There were plenty of elegies and eulogies in the years to follow, and some of them, as we have seen, took the form of legends, kindly in their intention but ridiculous in their effect. Oscar Wilde will survive them all. But as what? A playwright? A conversationalist? A man condemned under an unjust law? A witty

man of letters? Perhaps an amalgam of all these—a creature of
contradictions, of self-pity and self-assurance, of laughing pain
and tearful comedy, of serious intent and flippant expression. He
was not a supremely important writer but he has a place in our
literature and in our history which no one else can fill, and far
greater writers than he are less sure of immortality.

Index

ment in dealing with the facts, and ought to discard everything which was not relevant to the issue before them, or did not assist their judgment. He did not desire to comment any more than he could help about Lord Alfred Douglas or the Marquis of Queensbury, but the whole of this lamentable inquiry arose through the defendant's association with Lord Alfred Douglas. He did not think that the action of the Marquis of Queensberry in leaving the card at the defendant's club, whatever motives he had, was that of a gentleman. The jury were entitled to consider that these alleged acts happened some years ago. They ought to be the best judges as to whether the testimony of the witnesses was worthy or not of belief. The letters written by the accused to Lord Alfred Douglas were undoubtedly open to suspicion, and they had an important bearing on Wood's evidence. There was no corroboration of Wood as to the visit to Tite-street, and if his story had been true he thought that some corroboration might have been obtained. Wood belonged to the vilest class of persons that society was pestered with, and the jury ought not to believe his story unless satisfactorily corroborated. Their decision must turn on the character of the first introduction of Wilde to Wood. Did they believe that Wilde was actuated by charitable motives or by improper motives?

The Jury and Lord Alfred Douglas.

The foreman of the jury, interposing, asked whether a warrant had been issued for the arrest of Lord Alfred Douglas, and if not whether it was contemplated that a warrant should be issued.—The judge said he could not tell, but he thought not. It was a matter that they could not discuss at that stage. The granting of a warrant depended not upon the inference to be drawn from the letters referred to in the case, but on the production of evidence of specific acts. There was a disadvantage of specu-

WILDE LIBEL ACTION.

MARQUIS OF QUEENSBERRY ON TRIAL.

EVIDENCE OF PROSECUTOR.

STRANGE LETTERS.

SENSATIONAL TERMINATION.

WILDE ARRESTED.

All the appearances of a sensational trial were presented at the Old Bailey on Wednesday, when the Marquis of Queensberry entered the dock to answer the charge of criminally libelling Mr. Oscar Wilde. The marquis was the first to appear, and was soon followed by Mr. Oscar Wilde, who took a seat at the solicitors' table. By the time Mr. Justice Collins took his seat on the bench the court was crowded. Sir E. Clarke, Mr. Mathews, and Mr. Humphreys appeared to prosecute; while Mr. Carson, Mr. Gill, and Mr. A. Gill represented the Marquis of Queensberry; Mr. Besley, with Mr. Monckton, watching the proceedings on behalf of Lord Douglas of Hawick, eldest son of the marquis.—The clerk read out the indictment to the effect that the marquis "did unlawfully and maliciously write and publish a false, malicious, and defamatory libel" concerning Mr. O. Wilde, in the form of a card directed to him.—The marquis said he pleaded not guilty, and that the libel was true, and that it was for

MARQUIS OF QUEENSBERRY.

the public benefit that it should be published.—Sir E. Clarke having opened the case for the prosecution, evidence was given by Sydney Wright, hall porter of the Albemarle Club, of the publication of the alleged libel.—Mr. Oscar Wilde was then called and examined. The latter entered the room, and, at my suggestion, Lord Alfred crossed the room and shook hands with his father. Lord Alfred had to go away early, and Lord Queensberry remained and chatted with me. Afterwards something was said about Torquay, and it was arranged that Lord Queensberry should call upon me there, but he did not come, it was in 1893 that I heard that some letters which I had written to Lord A. Douglas had come into possession of certain persons. I met a man named Wood, who said he had some letters which had been written by me, which he had found in a suit of clothes

OSCAR WILDE.

that Lord A. Douglas had given him. I said, "You certainly should have given them back to him." He took three or four letters from his pocket and said, "Here are the letters."